# Lean Auditing

# LEAN AUDITING

---

## Driving Added Value and Efficiency in Internal Audit

James C. Paterson

# WILEY

*Registered office*
John Wiley & Sons Ltd, The Atrium, Southern Gate, Chichester, West Sussex, PO19 8SQ,
United Kingdom

For details of our global editorial offices, for customer services and for information about how to apply
for permission to reuse the copyright material in this book please visit our website at www.wiley.com.

*Library of Congress Cataloging-in-Publication Data*

Paterson, James C., 1963-
  Lean auditing : driving added value and efficiency in internal audit / James C. Paterson. – First edition.
    pages cm
  Includes bibliographical references and index.
  ISBN 978-1-118-89688-4 (hardback)
  1. Auditing, Internal. I. Title.
  HF5668.25.P367 2015
  657'.458–dc23
                              2014031378

A catalogue record for this book is available from the British Library.

ISBN 978-1-118-89688-4 (hbk)          ISBN 978-1-118-89690-7 (ebk)
ISBN 978-1-118-89689-1 (ebk)          ISBN 978-1-119-01706-6 (ebk)

Cover Design: Wiley
Cover Image: ©iStockphoto.com/Rogotanie

Set in 11/13 Times LT Std by Aptara, New Delhi, India
Printed in Great Britain by TJ International Ltd, Padstow, Cornwall, UK

# DEDICATIONS

*This book is dedicated to:*

*Isabelle, my wife and companion – I love you:*

*And my children:*

*Tim, Will, Nick and Felicity.*

*I'm so proud of you all!*

*CAEs and others in governance, risk, compliance audit and assurance, who are working to bring about positive change against, sometimes, quite considerable opposition.*

*I hope that this book serves in some small way to acknowledge many of the challenges and dilemmas you face. I also hope it gives some comfort that you are not alone in facing these challenges.*

# WITH SINCERE THANKS

*To Lynda McGill – thank you for "reading every word" and for such patient, constructive and insightful input and for being so much more than just a conventional editor.*

*To all the Chief Audit Executives (CAEs), auditors and others, named and unnamed, who agreed to be interviewed: THANK YOU for your wisdom, practical good sense and for demonstrating just how useful the lean mindset can be.*

*To past colleagues in internal audit at AstraZeneca between 2002 and 2009 – we did work that was ahead of its time. Your efforts and achievements gave me the inspiration to go into consulting and training, and to write this book. Thank you.*

*To my clients and all who have participated in workshops with me across the globe. Thank you for your contributions, insights and enthusiasm – for learning and for sharing your war stories and practical insights. Your ongoing interest has kept me going over the nine months it took to research and write this book.*

# Table of Contents

# Foreword

*"Lean is a valuable concept, because it forces you to think about the bigger picture. It's a way of thinking; it's a mindset, with related tools and process behind it.*

*We start with identifying what are the valuable services and products that matter to your customer. And then thinking about what is necessary for you to deliver those in an acceptable level of quality and all the rest of it. Everything else is Muda (waste)."*

Norman Marks (GRC thought leader)

# Introduction

If you are reading these words, I imagine you have some interest in lean or in audit, or both, and may be wondering how these disciplines might be combined.

This is what I wondered in 2005 when I was Chief Audit Executive (CAE) for AstraZeneca PLC. Lean was suggested to me as something that could help the audit function step up its "added value" contribution, as well as improve its productivity.

I was uncertain at first about the applicability and usefulness of lean tools and techniques to internal auditing. But, as we learned about lean, and started to apply it, we were able to create a number of best practice ways of working and also achieved significant productivity gains (of around 20%).

This book outlines what lean can offer to internal auditing. It is based on over four years' experience applying these techniques as a CAE. Thereafter, I have been running my own company and lean auditing has been one of the core areas of my training and consulting work. I have been fortunate to travel to the US, across the UK and Europe, the Middle East, the Far East and Australia to share lean auditing principles and techniques. I have been heartened by the interest in what I have had to say, and in the results that have been achieved by applying these ways of working.

As I prepared to write this book, I was keen to ensure that the efforts of other CAEs and auditors who are working to improve the impact of internal audit should also be captured. I therefore interviewed a number of CAEs from a range of organizations in the UK, US and elsewhere and their views and insights are captured throughout the book. I have also been fortunate to receive insights from other leading figures in the internal audit world, including Richard Chambers, President & CEO of the Institute of Internal Auditors (IIA), Norman Marks (a well known thought leader in Governance, Risk and Compliance (GRC)), Sarah Blackburn and Nicola Rimmer (both former Presidents of the UK Chartered Institute of Internal Auditors (IIA UK)) and Chris Baker, Technical Manager of the IIA UK. Herein are also selected board members' observations about internal audit.

Consequently, this book represents not just the best of what I managed to achieve at AstraZeneca, and with my clients. It also captures a wider range of progressive practices in internal audit as well as related good practices in the GRC arena. You only need to reflect on the devastating impact of the financial crisis of 2007 and 2008, and countless other risk and governance surprises, to recognize there is considerable room for improvement in this field!

This book addresses many efficiency opportunities through lean ways of working. However, of equal or perhaps greater importance, this book offers a range of insights into what it means to add value, and through this, to reposition the role of internal audit as a key ingredient of organizational success.

As we will see, many of the CAEs I have interviewed for this book already have a "seat at the top table". Consequently, whilst a number of the principles, tools and techniques outlined in this book will be aspirational for some internal audit functions, they are successfully in operation for many others.

Whilst I will argue that the internal audit profession should play a more prominent, value-adding role, I do not believe that internal audit should take the lead in driving organizational performance and behavioural change. That is a role for the board and senior management. My belief is that internal audit should more clearly act in a *catalyst* role for organizational growth, continuous improvement and sustainability.

I hope to demonstrate that the use of lean principles and techniques can both inspire and support internal audit to take up such a role.

However, I also want to acknowledge that there can be significant barriers to achieving what I am proposing. Some of these barriers may be practical, but most come from the mindsets and preferences of board members, senior managers, and a range of others who prefer a traditional "compliance and control" role for internal audit.

In my opinion, the traditional "compliance and control" focus of audit acts like a heavy hand on the audit profession, limiting its ability to play a fuller role. The dominance of traditional ways of working partly stems from a legitimate need to gain assurance over the basics, but also from a significant inertia that has built up within the internal audit profession itself.

As this book proceeds I will try to outline how the lean audit mindset (and ways of working that flow from it) differs from the traditional internal audit mindset, and traditional ways of working. I hope to demonstrate that, if internal audit is prepared to relinquish some of its familiar work in compliance and control auditing, which may appear to offer a degree of security, it will in fact make the internal audit profession more secure in the long run. Indeed I would go so far as to say that by continuing to carry out a large portion of traditional controls and compliance work internal audit may *perpetuate a range of organizational and cultural problems with Governance, Risk, Compliance and Assurance.*

As a result, some of the principles and practices outlined in this book may be challenging for some of the more traditionally minded auditors, senior managers and board members. As far as possible, I will try to explain how progressive and traditional ways of working can work together side by side, but I think that truly operating with a lean frame of mind does challenge a number of long-held conventions about internal audit. To my mind being prepared to "rock the boat" is a necessity if we want to put internal audit on the right path to being properly acknowledged as a key ingredient for sustainable organizational success.

## THE VALUE YOU SHOULD RECEIVE FROM READING THIS BOOK

CAEs and internal auditors should be able to use this book as a resource to:

- Benchmark current audit plans, reports and ways of working;
- Identify practical ways to increase value adding activities, and minimize non value added activities within internal audit;
- Reposition the role that audit can play in the organization and understand the wider organizational benefits that will flow from that.

Board members and senior managers should be able to use this book to:

- Identify whether internal audit is truly playing a positive role in their organization;
- Identify traditional, stale practices in Governance, Risk, Compliance and Assurance, that are not really adding anything;
- See the benefits of embracing lean principles in the arena of Governance, Risk, Compliance and Assurance, more generally.

Academics and others with an interest in sustainable organizational growth should be able to use this book to:

- Deepen their understanding of the challenges that many audit professionals face on a day to day basis;
- Consider how lean principles might offer an interesting insight into debates about what makes effective Governance, Risk, Compliance and Assurance.

Those with an interest in lean should be able to use this book to:

- Understand how lean principles, tools and techniques have been applied successfully to the world of Governance, Risk, Compliance, Audit and Assurance;
- Consider other ways in which lean approaches might be applied in these fields.

I personally have several hopes for this book:

- That it will stimulate more granular "real world" discussions about the dilemmas and challenges that auditors face;
- That lean principles, tools and techniques will enjoy a more mainstream position in the audit profession, and that we will become much more rigorous when we talk about "adding value" and efficiency;
- To open up more reflection on a range of long established ways of working within internal auditing;
- To create a greater recognition that through the development of a *multi-disciplinary approach to internal audit* we will enhance the reputation of our profession, and properly emphasize the importance of leadership and softer skills *alongside* detailed technical skills.

## Overview of the Contents

This book is structured as follows:

### PART 1  LEAN AND LEAN AUDITING IN OVERVIEW

### 1  Lean Auditing at AstraZeneca

In which I briefly explain the origins of lean auditing when I was CAE at AstraZeneca and the results it delivered.

## 2 A Brief History of Lean, Notable Principles and the Approach Taken by this Book

In which I discuss the origins of lean, its key principles and how it has increasingly been recognized to deliver results in a range of fields. I also outline the different sorts of lean (e.g. Lean Six Sigma and lean systems thinking) and the approach this book takes to these.

## 3 Key Lean Tools & Techniques

In which I outline a selection of key lean tools and techniques that have proven their worth in terms of driving greater effectiveness and efficiency and also in an internal audit context.

## 4 The Development of Lean Auditing and its Benefits

In which I explain how I developed lean auditing with a range of audit functions, and the benefits that have been obtained, both for internal audit and key stakeholders.

## 5 The Hallmarks of Lean Auditing and the Organizational Culture this can Support

In which I discuss how some conventional and traditional audit ways of working can perpetuate problems with organizations' Governance, Risk, Compliance and Assurance practices. I then go on to explain how lean progressive ways of working will not just improve the impact of audit assignments but also play a role in improving the wider organizational GRC culture.

## PART 2 LOOKING AT INTERNAL AUDIT PLANNING AND ASSIGNMENT DELIVERY

## 6 Who are the Customers of Internal Audit?

In which I explore the question of the range of stakeholders who have an interest in audit and the benefits of having clarity about which of these stakeholders are key – if any.

## 7 What Really Adds Value – And What Doesn't

In which I use lean techniques to examine what we really mean by "adding value", and – just as important – to understand what doesn't add value.

This chapter also addresses the important topic of differences between stakeholder perspectives concerning what adds value (and what does not).

## 8 The Importance of Role Clarity in Assurance and the Insights Lean Can Offer

In which I highlight the vital importance of having clear roles and accountabilities in order to drive both effectiveness and efficiency; and some of the key tools that can be used to drive greater role clarity, both for key functions as well as internal audit.

## 9 The Audit Plan: Taking a Value Approach

In which I discuss the ways in which taking a lean, value-added approach to the audit plan can ensure that audit looks at the right areas, overcoming the common failing of having a disconnect between the audit plan and the key objectives and risks of the organizations they support.

## 10 Factoring in Risk Assurance in the Audit Plan

In which I discuss the crucial role of understanding the risk assurance picture before developing the internal audit plan. This approach challenges some common conventions in audit planning, including the way management is asked for their views on the areas that audit should look at.

## 11 Considering the Allocation of Resources to Optimize Value Add

In which I discuss how lean, progressive audit practices can encourage greater quality debates about the way audit resources are allocated across different risk areas in order to maximize the value derived from the plan. A number of the techniques outlined have been invaluable for a number of CAEs facing pressure on their budgets.

## 12 Assignments – Types, Scheduling and Resourcing

In which I highlight the need to move beyond standard assignment types and to resource and schedule assignments more flexibly, based on their value. Lean techniques help us to create a clearer flow of assignments during the year, reducing delays in starting to deliver the audit plan as well as the common problem of rushing to complete assignments towards the end of the year.

### 13 Using Assignment Scoping and Planning to Drive Added Value

In which I highlight the importance of properly scoping and planning assignments so that they can deliver the maximum value. This includes the important step of being clear about the key risks and controls that should be tested, and making the maximum use of intelligence so that the assignment does not simply repeat what is already known and has the maximum chance of delivering outcomes that matter.

### 14 Assignment Delivery – Managing What Really Goes On

Where I discuss the reality of what actually happens when audits start. I look at the many ways that time can be lost and offer a range of proven approaches to help drive audits forward in a purposeful way. In particular, I examine ways to think more carefully about what testing should be done and the challenge of knowing when to stop.

### 15 Using Communication and Quality Standards to Maximize the Added Value from Assignments

In which I discuss the ways in which assignments can get into difficulty in their latter stages. This can include difficulties and delays at audit closing meetings, finalizing audit reports (including agreeing actions) as well as meeting quality assurance standards. Lean, progressive ways of working help auditors drive assignments towards a value adding conclusion and overcome the many delays and distractions that are commonplace.

### 16 Assignment Follow-Up and Follow On

In which I show how lean principles encourage audit to take a fresh look at the process of tracking remediation of open actions and audit follow-ups. Lean ways of working can radically reduce the time and effort spent by audit doing follow up work, whilst driving greater reliance on management assurances.

### PART 3 LOOKING AT KEY UNDERPINNING CAPABILITIES, PROCESSES AND WAYS OF WORKING

### 17 Measuring Performance and Driving Improvements in Audit Ways of Working

In which I examine the way lean encourages us to take a fresh look at the metrics and key performance indicators collected and reported by audit. I also look at ways to enhance assignment methodologies, to strengthen quality control in a streamlined way and to drive value from External Quality Assessments (EQAs).

## 18 Using Lean Audit Principles to Underpin Cultural Change in the Wider Organization

In which I highlight in more detail the ways in which lean ways of working can help to improve the GRC and assurance culture of an organization. Areas that can be improved include streamlining the policy and compliance landscape, strengthening the role of risk and compliance functions, and improved assurance coordination.

## 19 Leading the Audit Function

In which I discuss the leadership characteristics and capabilities of Chief Audit Executives (CAEs) who lead lean, progressive, value-adding audit functions. In particular I share key messages from my own experience and from other CAEs about how they retain a sense of perspective in managing the many dilemmas that CAEs have to navigate.

## 20 The Audit Function: Selection, Training & Development and Ways of Working

In which I examine the way that lean, progressive, audit functions approach recruitment, staff development and leverage other skills, through guest auditors, guest advisors and/or co-source providers. This chapter raises some important questions concerning the optimal balance of skills within an audit function.

## PART 4 FINAL REFLECTIONS

## 21 Further Thoughts about Where and How to Start the Journey towards Lean Progressive Auditing

In which I examine choices around where and how to start or make further progress in relation to lean audit ways of working. A key message, based on my experience as a CAE and with clients, is that implementing lean auditing does not have to be time-consuming or expensive.

## 22 A Brief Look into the Future

In which I examine potential developments in audit and my hopes for the future. I also reflect further on the key dilemmas that internal auditors and CAEs face on a day-to-day basis and consider whether we can do more as a profession to support one another in this regard.

# PART 1
# Lean and Lean Auditing in Overview

# 1
# Lean Auditing at AstraZeneca

After 15 years working in a range of finance roles, I was appointed the CAE of AstraZeneca PLC in 2002. My appointment came a few months after the enactment of the US Sarbanes–Oxley Act, following the collapses of Enron and Worldcom.

If I needed a reminder that good financial control was important, this was it. I therefore spent the first two years in my role supporting and quality assuring the embedding of Sarbanes–Oxley disciplines, whilst also working on a range of other areas in GRC and assurance as well as developing the internal audit function.

By 2005 we had made progress on a number of fronts. However, it was clear that pressure on costs would increase, and as a result my audit management team and I decided that we should engage with the cost agenda in a proactive manner: "Better to work on our efficiency and effectiveness ourselves than have someone else do it for us."

At the suggestion of one of the Audit Directors, David Powell, we decided to work with colleagues in AstraZeneca's manufacturing function, who specialized in lean manufacturing techniques. We contacted John Earley (now Partner, Smart Chain International), who was working in manufacturing at the time, and after obtaining some key inputs from him, we developed a number of new ways of working within the audit function.

What impressed me at first was just how quickly and cheaply the lean techniques could be implemented and the scale of the efficiency gains achieved. In later years I also admired the way lean principles informed much of what we were doing to deliver added value: from audit planning to stakeholder engagement, from our approach to assignment delivery to the way we carried out testing, and from the way we reported our work to the performance metrics we used.

The lean auditing approach also offered a positive way of thinking about the role of internal audit and the value it could deliver that was appreciated by both senior managers, the board and audit staff. In addition, our approach to audit planning and the ways that we had changed our executive and board reporting gained recognition within the internal audit profession (within the IIA UK and also the Corporate Executive Board, Audit Director Roundtable).

Further details of the progressive practice we developed will follow in subsequent chapters. However, first it seems appropriate to say a bit more about lean.

### References and Other Related Material of Interest

Paterson, J. (2007) *Business partnership redefined*, Audit Director Roundtable. AstraZeneca case study

Paterson, J. (2008) *Internal audit for the 21st century*. IIA Scotland

Paterson, J. (2009) *Internal audit: the times they are a changing*. Chartered Institute of Management Accountants

Paterson, J. (2009) *Future developments in internal audit. IACON*

Paterson, J. (2012) *Giving assurance IIA UK*. Heads of Internal Audit Service

Paterson, J. (2012) *Developing an effective audit strategy*. IIA UK Head of Audit Service

# 2
# A Brief History of Lean, Notable Principles and the Approach Taken by this Book

Having explained that the application of lean made a significant difference to internal audit within AstraZeneca, this chapter sets out some background about lean: where it came from, its key principles and the benefits that are likely to result from putting it into practice.

## ORIGINS OF LEAN AND THE BENEFITS IT DELIVERS

Some argue that the story of lean can be traced back to boat construction in 16th Century Venice, but I suspect we could go back further to road building techniques and weapons manufacture in Roman times. However, the story of lean as a holistic set of principles, tools and techniques is widely understood to centre around Toyota's achievements after World War Two.

Influenced by developments in the US and elsewhere, for a period of over a decade Toyota developed various production line techniques into a complete management system, called the Toyota Production System (TPS). TPS comprised a range of product and process development techniques, supply chain management techniques, new approaches to problem solving (such as root cause analysis), improved approaches to customer service and new approaches to leadership and teamwork. In 1965 the Deming prize for quality was granted to Toyota for TPS.

As a result of TPS, Toyota became capable of making cars at a significantly lower cost than a number of major US motor manufacturers, despite their scale advantages. Toyota, alongside many other Japanese car companies (who were using similar approaches), therefore gained increasing success across the world.

The label "lean" for the techniques developed and applied by Toyota was first used in 1987 by John Krafcik, a student at that time of the Massachusetts Institute of Technology (MIT) International Motor Vehicle programme. Krafcik observed that Toyota's systems and processes:

- Required less investment for a given production capacity;
- Went from concept to delivery with less time and effort;
- Delivered products with fewer defects.

He observed: "It needs less of everything to create a given amount of value, so let's call it lean."

After this came a series of important books from key players in the MIT International Motor Vehicle programme:

- *The machine that changed the world* by Womak, Jones and Roos, that gave an account of the techniques employed by Toyota and other Japanese manufacturers and demonstrated the superior performance of this approach;
- *Lean Thinking* by Womak & Jones, which sets out the key principles of lean and also noted the successes of a number of other organizations in the US and Europe as a result of implementing lean techniques.

Typical benefits obtained from lean ways of working include:

- Reductions in: defects, lead times, cost, inventory and waste;
- Improvements in: customer satisfaction, productivity, capacity, responsiveness and quality.

Since then extensive research has been undertaken to deepen our understanding of the power of lean and numerous other lean books have been published. Lean techniques have been successfully applied in a range of sectors outside of motor manufacturing (e.g. in white goods and pharmaceuticals manufacturing) and, increasingly, in service sectors (e.g. airlines, healthcare). Lean has also been successfully applied in a range of support and service areas (including finance and administration).

## KEY LEAN PRINCIPLES, TOOLS AND TECHNIQUES

The overall philosophy underpinning lean is to maximize customer value whilst minimizing waste. The Lean Institute states that lean means: "creating more value for customers with fewer resources."

### The Five Key Principles of Lean

The five key principles of lean can be summarized as:

### Specify Value from the Point of View of the Customer

The aim is to have a deep and ongoing understanding of exactly what the customer is looking for and what they value. A common question in lean circles is "What is the 'Voice of the Customer' saying?" Lean asks us to be wary of giving the customer simply what is convenient for the producer, though it recognizes the place for offering new and innovative products/services (even if they were not requested), if they are going to be valued by the customer (e.g. the Apple iPod).

### Identify the Value Stream

Having understood what is valued, the goal is to understand, in detail, the sequence of processes and activities that deliver this value, all the way from raw materials (if applicable) to the final customer. Lean asks us to critically appraise the purpose of each of these steps: what value is added by each step (in the eyes of the customer) through the whole process, from end to end.

### Flow

Based originally on a production line mindset, but extended to a more general principle, lean encourages us to make value flow. Lean asks us to look out for waste in any form, such as rework, delays or other interruptions to delivering value. Other issues (such as overburdening or underutilization) should also be noted and addressed. This lean principle also requires close attention to the supporting or preparatory activities that underpin customer delivery.

## Pull

The lean goal is to deliver customer demand at the time it is needed – not too early (since that can be inefficient and wasteful) or too late (since that will normally not be what the customer wants), but "just in time."

## Seek Perfection in Ways of Working

Lean asks us to seek the ideal way – delivering exactly what the customer wants, when it is wanted, at a fair price and with minimum waste. This lean principle goes deeper than just being in line with competitors and what others are doing, (e.g. taking a benchmarking approach). Lean is a way of working that looks for maximum customer value with zero waste – at least as a goal. Linked to this principle is the "Kaizen" notion that one should strive for ongoing improvement, since few processes, if any, will achieve the goal of perfection.

The lean principles set out above should not be viewed as a linear step-by-step checklist, but rather as a set of underpinning principles informing all ways of working.

## Other Schools of Lean and the Neutral Approach of this Book

Associated with lean is the field of product quality and six sigma (which is used to drive a very low rate of deviation from required standards). This has led to Lean Six Sigma, which is useful for the manufacture of products that need to be made to a high product quality specification.

In addition, lean has been combined with systems thinking (which is concerned, amongst other things, with the ways different parts of an organization are interrelated), resulting in the lean systems approach.

Other approaches to lean also exist, but I take an open-minded approach to the various "flavours" of lean. I think each lean approach has something interesting to say, but I do not believe internal audit should be wedded to a specific lean approach. I have spoken to some CAEs who have been through a lean review (often as part of a wider organizational programme), but have found this has offered limited benefit. This can happen when those driving the lean review are mostly focused on looking for cost savings, or outsourcing opportunities, or do not have a deep understanding of the unique role of internal audit.

My experience suggests success in implementing a lean auditing approach is often about recognizing the context of specific organizations and adapting what should be done to deliver workable results, whilst staying true to the overall spirit of lean.

## Cost Reduction and Lean

It is worth writing a few words about lean in relation to cost reduction, since this is one of the key reasons lean attracts attention. Indeed, as mentioned earlier, when I was CAE of AstraZeneca cost management was one of the reasons I was interested in lean. However, lean ways of working should not simply be equated with cost cutting. John Earley (Partner, Smart Chain International) explains:

"Lean is not simply about cost reduction. Managing and reducing cost is a by-product of lean, it's not a driver for it.

Cost cutting measures may buy you time, but often they won't have transformed the business, and as a result the consequences of cost savings will pop up as costs somewhere else. They'll arise in customer complaints, or in other areas that might hit your reputation, or your bottom line. In other words, one part of the business might cost less, but the business as a whole suffers, and so often it becomes a negative spiral.

Lean takes a different approach looking at value as well as efficiency. Will lean reduce cost? Yes it will, but the idea behind lean is if you take care of the value the cost will take care of itself."

I think one of the reasons I enjoy working on lean auditing is that, whilst it supports productivity it does not do this in some bleak and heartless manner. To my mind, lean is as much about building added value and developing staff to do this, as it is about productivity and cost management.

### References and Other Related Material of Interest

Bicheno, J. & Holweg, M. (2008) *The Lean toolbox: the essential guide to Lean transformation.*

Lean Enterprise Institute (2009) *A Brief History of Lean.*
http://www.lean.org/WhatsLean/History.cfm

Lean Enterprise Institute (2009) *Principles of Lean.* http://www.lean.org/WhatsLean/Principles.cfm

Lean Systems Society (2014) http://leansystemssociety.org/

Morgan, J. & Brenig-Jones, M. (2009) *Lean Six Sigma for Dummies.* John Wiley & Sons, Chichester.

Womack, J. & Jones, D. (2003) *Lean Thinking (Revised & Updated).*

Womak, J., Jones, D. T. & Roos, D. (2007) *The Machine That Changed the World.* Simon & Schuster Ltd

# 3
# Key Lean Tools & Techniques

This chapter outlines the lean tools and techniques I have found to be most useful in an internal audit context. This list is small compared to the full range of lean tools and techniques, but – at this stage – I would rather give a flavour of what there is, rather than swamp the reader (since a full description of these tools could comfortably fill several books).

## UNDERSTANDING CUSTOMER NEEDS: THE KANO MODEL

The Kano model (created by Dr Noiaki Kano) is one of the most powerful lean tools for thinking about what customers do and do not value. It involves listening to the "Voice of the Customer" in relation to what is valued and mapping this out for ongoing reference. Of particular interest is the insight that there are different types of value related attributes. The three key types are summarized below:

- Basic requirements or dissatisfiers: This is an attribute or requirement a customer expects as part of a service or product and if it is not present the customer will be dissatisfied or unhappy (e.g. clean sheets in a hotel room, or food in a supermarket that is not mouldy). However, if the attribute is present it will not necessarily result in anything more than a neutral feeling. Although these attributes are basic, this does not mean they will be easy to achieve;

- Performance factors or satisfiers: These are requirements or attributes where the customer value perception will vary depending on the extent to which it is present: for example, "more is better and less is worse" or "easier to use is better and less easy to use is worse." This could include the ease of checking into a hotel, or the price of a car;
- Delighter or exciter factors: These are requirements or attributes that customers may not expect, but delight them when present (e.g. a complimentary breakfast at a hotel). These delighters need to be given at a sensible cost, but may make the difference between choosing one product or service over another – consider Apple products and the extent to which the look and the feel of these is valued by customers.

The Kano model can be set out in diagrammatic form as follows:

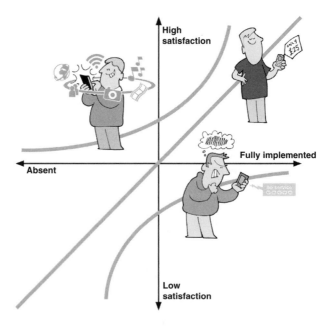

**Figure 3.1**   The Kano model, using a mobile phone as an example: delighter – added functionality; satisfier – price; dissatisfier – not working

The Kano model highlights an insight many will recognize: a given amount of time and effort may have a hugely different impact on customer satisfaction. In other words: *effort and added value are not always linked in a linear way*. Indeed, sometimes providing *less* can result in a more satisfied customer (e.g. a concise report compared to a longer one).

Thinking about what the customer wants through a Kano approach is central to lean auditing. The aim is to gain a deeper appreciation of what each of the different stakeholders of internal audit want and – just as importantly – what they do not want.

## GEMBA

"Gemba" is the Japanese word for the real place (e.g. the place where a news event takes place). In the context of lean it usually means the factory floor or workplace. A key lean technique is to "Go Look See" what is really going on (known as the Gemba Walk). This is the way any waste can be identified, and this is also the place where opportunities for improvement might be identified.

There are some similarities between the Gemba Walk and the western management notion of "management by walking about", with lean emphasizing the importance of:

• Engaging with what is actually going on when analysing issues or difficulties, with an emphasis on facts rather than opinions; and
• Ensuring that staff and managers pay close attention to what is going on, on a day-to-day basis, as a way of driving improvements in effectiveness and efficiency.

Shigeo Shingo, one of the leading lean practitioners from Toyota sums up the lean Gemba mindset:

"Get a grip on the status quo. The most magnificent improvement scheme would be worthless if your perception of the current situation is in error."

Gemba has a great affinity with internal audit, since it is all about looking at the reality of what is happening. The challenge for auditors is to apply this approach to their own ways of working. A good example of a Gemba approach would be to pay attention to the difference between how an audit manager or CAE would summarize the audit process (or how it is written in an audit manual), and *what it is actually like to carry out an audit assignment in practice*.

## Value Stream Mapping

In order to improve the way that activities and processes are carried out to deliver value, lean offers a range of tools and techniques to help visualize what is happening so that processes and activities can be improved. Specific approaches include:

- SIPOC mapping

    SIPOC refers to Supplier, Input, Process, Output, and Customer and is a framework that can be used to breakdown a process;
    In an internal audit context, a number of the key SIPOC elements are set out in Figure 3.2.

- Deployment flowcharts (or Swim Lane diagrams)

    Which can be used to illustrate, amongst other things, the roles of different functions in a process.

| Supplier | Inputs | Process | Outputs | Customers |
|---|---|---|---|---|
| Auditee | Objectives | Assignment scope | Insights | Auditee |
| Finance | Risk assessment | Assignment plan | Root Cause analysis | Client |
| Business Intelligence | Data | Staff allocation | Agreed actions | Senior Managers |
| Risk Management | Reports | Fieldwork/Meetings with management | Agreed report | Board |
| Compliance | | | | External customers and stakeholders |

**Figure 3.2**   The SIPOC model as applied to an audit assignment (simplified)

Process mapping is a technique familiar to many in internal audit. When applied to internal audit processes it can be a powerful way of drawing out a range of improvement opportunities in audit planning, assignment delivery and the process of drafting, editing and rewriting audit reports.

## IDENTIFYING WASTE (MUDA)

Lean principles regard waste (or Muda in Japanese) as being *anything a customer would not want to pay for.* No matter how normal difficulties, delays or waste seem, lean demands that we pursue waste free ways of working. However, Shigeo Shingo observed:

"The most dangerous kind of waste is the waste we do not recognize."

Indeed, much of my work with auditors starts with helping them to notice waste in audit activities that seems so normal it has become invisible.

Lean defines the normal waste items that so often get missed. Taichii Ohno of Toyota suggests seven key areas of waste in a production context:

- The waste of overproduction;
- The waste of waiting;
- The waste of unnecessary motions;
- The waste of transporting;
- The waste of over-processing, or inappropriate processing;
- The waste of unnecessary inventory;
- The waste of defects.

In a service context, other forms of waste include:

- The waste of making the wrong product;
- The waste of untapped human potential;
- Excessive information and communication;
- The waste of time;
- The waste of inappropriate systems;
- Wasted energy, resources and other natural resources;
- The waste of (excessive) variation;

- The waste of no follow-through;
- The waste of knowledge.

Other difficulties that can interrupt the flow of value to the customer include:

- Unevenness, or Mura in Japanese;
- Overburden, or Muri in Japanese.

To address the various types of waste that can arise, lean provides a range of tools and techniques, including:

## Heijunka

This technique aims to prevent issues arising by smoothing the flow of work. This includes techniques to standardize and sequence what is done.

## Jidoka – Also Known as Autonomation

This aims to prevent errors arising. The idea is to create machines, systems and processes that rapidly identify when poor quality occurs because of the impact on the customer as well as the resulting waste and rework that arises from poor quality.

## Just in Time

This is a widely known lean technique, and is about delivering the right quality product or service at the right time at an optimal cost.

## Andon – Visualization

Lean ways of working require ongoing monitoring of what is going on with clear, visible indicators or metrics. These allow staff and management to identify any issues or difficulties and act on them in a timely manner. In an audit context this is a particularly useful technique when tracking assignments.

## Root Cause Analysis (RCA)

RCA is a fundamental technique in lean, and one that should be familiar to internal auditors. Specific RCA methods include:

- The Five Whys: the approach encourages us to question why things are happening, so that the real reasons for difficulties are known, thus maximizing the chances of a proper solution;
- The Fishbone (Ishikawa) diagram: where effects/symptoms are traced back to their causes using a structured framework.

## A WORD OF CAUTION ABOUT LEAN TOOLS AND TECHNIQUES

In addition to my neutral stance on any specific brand of lean, I want to flag up an important message at the outset in relation to lean tools and techniques: these should be used to *enable and facilitate efficient and value adding internal audit work*, not become a thing in themselves.

John Earley (Partner, SmartChain International) explains:

"Which lean tools you apply and how you apply them is situation specific. There's nothing in the lean toolkit that is mandatory. This is where the difference between success and failure could be. You have to be very pragmatic how you apply lean.

To take an analogy: If you are going to hang a door, and you have got a toolbox full of tools, you don't use every tool in the box. You pick the tool that you need to do the job properly and you make sure they're in good shape and you know how to use them, and then you do the job, then you put the tools back in the box and wait for the next job.

When applying lean over a period of time, there's always a progression of things happening and the techniques that you use at one point in time may not be as important at another time. However, the constant factor that runs through that whole thing is the mindset and culture of customer value, efficiency and continuous improvement."

Norman Marks (GRC thought leader) offers similar advice:

"You don't have to necessarily go off to Japan and get a black belt in lean. You're not going to learn about lean internal auditing by going to Toyota and walking through their plant.

My advice is that this is mostly common sense. It's standing back and saying, I want to be of value to my customer, so what do they need? Not just what I want to give them, but what do they actually need for them to be effective.

Throw out the traditional and replace it with common sense. And just because everybody else is operating in a traditional way, doesn't mean it's best."

## References and Other Related Material of Interest

Kano, N. (1984) Attractive quality and must-be quality. *Journal of the Japanese society for quality control.*

# 4
# The Development of Lean Auditing and Its Benefits

It was originally intended that I would be the CAE at AstraZeneca for three or four years, but the work we did on lean auditing and the impact it was having encouraged me to stay longer (for seven years in all). Increasingly, I became interested in sharing the lean auditing ideas and practices that we had developed with other CAEs. In addition, I could see an opportunity to do more work in the field of leadership development and culture change (which I had done for two years prior to becoming CAE at AstraZeneca). As a result, at the beginning of 2010, I set up my own business specializing in lean auditing, Risk Assurance, CAE coaching and internal audit effectiveness (www.RiskAI.co.uk).

Whilst I have seen significant differences in the contexts and cultures that audit functions have to operate within, it is noteworthy that many of the challenges and dilemmas faced by audit functions across the globe are similar (albeit each with its own very specific flavour). Some common challenges and dilemmas facing the internal audit functions that I work with are:

- How to prioritize the differing needs of multiple stakeholders in the audit process: the board/audit committee, senior managers and those being audited;
- How to develop an audit plan that addresses the most important risk areas when there are often strong expectations that audit should focus on financial controls and compliance testing;

- How to get a place "at the top table", influencing senior management whilst retaining independence and objectivity;
- Managing requests to delay or cancel assignments, which can result in difficulties completing the audit plan each year;
- Getting information and data on a timely basis so that audit assignments can start without delay;
- Finding that many managers are not engaged with the audit process;
- Arguments over whether audit has enough evidence to demonstrate its findings, sometimes requiring additional testing;
- Disagreements concerning the wording of audit reports, the timescales that actions should be completed within, and the grading of reports.

The root causes for these areas of difficulty are various and may be linked to problems with communication and underlying systems. However, a number of the problems that arise are due to poor process disciplines in audit and, from my experience, questions about the role of audit, as well as the mindset of some managers and auditors.

As we will see during the course of this book, lean ways of working can help audit to navigate through many of these challenges and dilemmas, helping the internal audit function become more impactful, as well as providing a range of other benefits at an organizational level.

As I mentioned in the introduction to this book, my experience developing lean auditing techniques as the CAE of AstraZeneca provided a solid foundation to work with clients and workshop participants. However, other CAEs I have worked with have faced other areas of difficulty, which we addressed through new lean auditing approaches. In addition, other CAEs I know have developed their own good practices that further "raise the bar" on what value adding and efficient auditing can be like.

As a result, this book contains many internal audit best practices developed by, and with, other CAEs, alongside those developed during my time as the CAE of AstraZeneca.

## THE KEY BENEFITS OF ADOPTING A LEAN AUDITING APPROACH

The key benefits of adopting a lean audit approach to internal audit are:

- An audit function that is oriented towards engagement with key stakeholders, with a clear value add mindset;

- An audit plan that is more closely, and demonstrably, aligned with the key value drivers of the organization on an ongoing basis;
- An audit function that plays a key role in understanding the overall Risk Assurance landscape of the organization (encouraging "joining up the assurance jigsaw");
- An audit function that acts as a catalyst for positive change in the organization, delivered in a range of ways, not just audit assignments;
- Audit assignments that are appropriately resourced, and delivered to time and budget in the vast majority of instances;
- An overall audit plan that is scheduled and delivered with the minimum of delays or difficulties;
- Audit findings, reports and other forms of communication, that are short, insightful and recognize the wider context of the organization and the challenges it is facing;
- An audit function that is able to highlight appropriate efficiency opportunities, including instances where the streamlining of compliance and control policies and procedures would be beneficial;
- An audit function that can clearly demonstrate a positive return on its cost.

In addition, I will outline in this book how progressive, lean ways of working can act as a catalyst for driving improvements across a range of broader Governance, Risk, Compliance (GRC) and assurance activities.

## A FEW WORDS ON TERMINOLOGY IN THIS BOOK

At this point it is appropriate to offer several reflections on the terms "audit", "auditing", "internal auditing", "lean auditing", and "progressive auditing" that will be used during the course of the book. To start: many internal auditors use the term audit when referring to an internal audit. In addition, lean ways of working are often applicable to other types of auditing (e.g. quality auditing, efficiency auditing, health and safety auditing), not just internal auditing. As a result the terms audit and auditing will normally refer to internal audit and internal auditing, but may also relate to other types of audit functions and other types of auditing, depending on the context.

In relation to the term "lean auditing," I am referring to the practice of internal auditing as informed and enhanced by lean principles, tools and techniques. However, a number of progressive audit practices referred to in this book also focus on the themes of adding value and efficiency, which are central to lean ways of working. As a result, I will sometimes use the terms "lean auditing" or "lean progressive auditing" to refer to a "family" of audit practices that are judged to represent good audit practice in the eyes of leading audit practitioners, typically with a focus on delivering value and improving productivity.

My use of "progressive auditing" also reflects the fact that I am not overly concerned whether the term "lean auditing" gains strong currency within the internal audit profession. My prime interest is to stimulate some interest and offer practical insights in relation to the way the internal audit can push forward on a value adding agenda, and become recognized as an essential ingredient for organizational success. More than anything, I want to avoid the scenario in 10 years' time where internal audit has been consigned to an eternal prison of primarily working on regulatory compliance and control issues, with key operational and strategic risks largely regarded as "off limits."

# 5
# The Wider Benefits of a Lean Audit Approach – and How to Use This Book

As I mentioned in the introduction, lean auditing offers much more than simply a more efficient and effective way of carrying out internal audits. Given the unique role of internal audit it is possible to see a "cascade effect" in which new ways of working by audit have a wider impact on organizations. This effect will not simply derive from more impactful audit assignments, but also from the way that audit sees its role and leads organizational changes through its influence over key stakeholders.

To explain how this cascade works, I will outline the key hallmarks of a lean progressive approach to audit. I will then describe how this approach can impact other functions, such as compliance and risk (sometimes called the "second line of defence"), as well as management and staff (sometimes called the "first line of defence").

## Key Hallmarks of a Progressive Lean Audit Approach

In my experience, these include:

- A recognition of the unique role that audit can and should play in providing an independent and objective perspective on Governance, Risk, Compliance (GRC) and the delivery of organizational performance;
- An orientation towards adding value in everything that audit does;

- Having a clear focus on ways of working that visibly and demonstrably add value, that drive out non value adding activity, and eliminate other waste (Muda);
- Discharging the internal audit role in a pragmatic, but flexible way, with a clear strategy to act as a catalyst for organizational improvement and development;
- Having a role that encourages and supports the co-ordination of Risk Assurance across the organization, so that roles and responsibilities (including those of internal audit itself) are optimized to add value, and eliminate waste;
- A recognition that the role of audit is more than just carrying out audit assignments: it is about providing valuable advice and assurance that will improve an organization over the short, medium and longer-term;
- Measuring audit performance in a pragmatic, efficient but rigorous way, that drives value add and continuous improvement;
- Having clear requirements when selecting staff and developing them to ensure audit can deliver its full role and support the wider organization.

Many of these principles link to attributes and standards that have been developed by the Institute of Internal Auditors (IIA), the global professional body for the internal audit profession.

Particular IIA standards and attributes of note include statements that:

- The CAE should manage the internal audit activity to ensure it adds value to the organization;
- The CAE should share information and co-ordinate the work of other compliance and assurance providers with the work of internal audit;
- Internal audit should operate with an understanding that the "Three lines of defence" framework (with management, compliance functions and audit each in separate "lines of defence") is likely to be the most effective way to manage risks;
- Internal audit should act as an independent and objective function to assess, amongst other things, the effectiveness and efficiency of the organization's operations.

At face value, therefore, lean ways of working can appear to be a helpful "bolt on" to the current IIA standards, since they can support the delivery of a value adding and efficient audit service. However, as we will see later in this book, lean ways of working can question a number of commonly held perceptions about the role of internal audit, for example:

- That the role of audit should primarily be to deliver internal audits;
- That the audit plan should cover known risk areas of concern;
- That auditors should strictly adhere to predetermined assignment and test plans;
- That auditors should look for fraud in each and every assignment;
- That audit should proactively follow up the progress of management in remediating all open points;
- That audit should mostly be comprised of qualified finance and audit staff.

As we will see in later chapters of this book, I am not arguing that audit should ignore its role to look out for fraud, to follow up on open actions, or to have trained audit professionals, but unless care is taken there is a risk that:

- Internal audit ceases to be a key player in visibly improving Governance, Risk, Compliance and Assurance activities and processes;
- Internal audit is not seen to be a vital source of value add in organizations;
- Internal audit starts to become a *substitute* for processes and activities that should be carried out by management, or other functions.

## The Mindset of a Lean, Progressive, Auditing Approach

Underpinning a lean auditing approach is a mindset that some more traditionally minded internal auditors may find rather challenging, namely:

- A view that stakeholders should be regularly engaged in relation to what they value from audit;
- A view that stakeholders should also be challenged when necessary in relation to the role of audit, and the tasks it should perform;
- A view that audit should take a proactive interest in the Risk Assurance picture for the whole organization, and work to influence the roles of key functions if there are gaps or overlaps of concern;
- A view that audit should regard all risk areas equally in terms of their potential coverage and be careful not to favour traditional areas, such as financial controls or compliance;

- A view that the recruitment of staff into audit should be influenced by the value needs of the wider organization as much as the need for qualified audit staff;
- A view that audit should be just as interested in cultural and behavioural issues across the organization as straightforward audit findings;
- A view that management risk appetite judgments should be challenged when necessary.

Whilst this lean progressive audit mindset may seem radical to some, I am heartened to note that a recent review of the role of internal audit in the UK financial services sector has identified some of these areas (e.g. risk appetite and risk culture) as both legitimate and necessary areas for audit to include within its remit.

## The Wider Organizational Implications of a Lean Auditing Approach

Taking a lean progressive approach to audit can have a knock-on impact in relation to key policy and compliance functions, in the second line of defence, such as finance, legal, Health & Safety, HR and IT. Results can include:

- Driving much greater clarity about their oversight and assurance role;
- Enhancing the quality of risk identification and risk assessment processes;
- Strengthening the flow of information to these functions and onward reporting to senior management and the board;
- Providing more rigour in relation to the closure of open actions.

The typical shift in the role of policy and compliance functions is that they should take up a more robust role in both helping and challenging management to deliver and assure key compliance risks and processes on a day-to-day basis.

Taking a lean progressive approach to audit can also impact management and staff in the first line of defence. Results can include:

- A clear understanding that staff and management should rigorously manage and monitor key risks as well as the effectiveness of core compliance and control activities as a natural part of effective business oversight;

- An understanding that whilst judgement and trust have an important place, data and other information should be used on an ongoing basis to objectively assess risks and opportunities;
- A greater appreciation that difficulties, issues or "near misses" should be openly acknowledged, logged and constructively discussed, so that root causes can be addressed and a learning culture developed;
- A genuine openness towards appropriate challenge by audit and others in order to improve organizational performance.

In essence I am highlighting the important role that audit has to catalyze improvements in risk and control accountabilities, processes and culture, and not simply to feel constrained by shortcomings in this regard.

* * *

## HOW TO USE THIS BOOK

The following chapters describe lean, progressive, internal auditing in more detail.

The structure of the chapters in the next section is as follows:

- A brief summary of some common ways of working and some of the notable IIA standards;
- Some of the common challenges and dilemmas internal audit functions face;
- Some recommended lean ways of working that should drive improvements in added value and/or reductions in waste;
- A summary of key points for internal audit;
- A summary of points for senior managers and board members to consider.

Some CAEs or internal auditors may read the lean audit ways of working and find that they have much of this in place. One CAE remarked to me:

> "I would say that people could be doing lean auditing without really even having identified it or labelled it as such."

As mentioned in an earlier chapter, the use of the label "lean auditing" is not of great importance to me, compared to how the internal audit profession can better overcome areas of difficulty, and demonstrate its ability to deliver value and maximize its productivity by overcoming the things that may be holding it back.

If auditors or CAEs find they have implemented the ways of working described, this should provide a useful way of benchmarking how progressive and lean their internal audit function is (or is not). However, being a lean audit function means much more than just ticking the box around the practices in this book. It is about a culture and a capability within internal audit that is genuinely oriented towards both adding value and productivity on an ongoing basis. Chris Baker, Technical Manager of the UK Chartered Institute of Internal Auditors, explains:

> "I think that there could be issues around people's understanding of lean auditing. People can easily see it as just finding an efficient way of doing an audit. In other words, it is the methodology that is related to lean, not the focus of the audit and the outcome. They might think it's meant to relate to cutting out unnecessary administration and trying to avoid long drawn-out audit reports and taking ages to get your audit report produced. This probably comes from the layman's understanding of lean which is that it's about cutting things back to their bare bones.
>
> Of course lean has an element of this but it's not just about cutting out unnecessary activities, it's just as much about getting the focus of the audit right and using the time more wisely and more effectively."

As mentioned earlier, in order to ground this book in the "Gemba" of audit practice, I have interviewed a number of CAEs and internal audit thought leaders. From these interviews I have included a selection of "war stories" in relation to common audit challenges and dilemmas. And in order to make the spirit of lean ways of working come alive, I have also included their perspectives on more progressive ways of working, and where possible, the rationale for, or benefits that arise, from this.

Consequently, *I have not attempted to adopt a quantitative approach to each of the audit challenges and dilemmas described in this book along the lines of:* "A recent survey by X says that Y% of auditors encounter delays in gathering evidence before fieldwork." This is partly because survey results will depend on the sample of audit functions surveyed (which may vary between organization, sector and country), partly because the results will change from year to year, but mostly because whatever results are chosen, the actual position for a specific audit function will often be different, that is to say: some will experience the problem as described, some will not, and some will be somewhere in-between.

By adopting a qualitative approach, I hope that readers will get a grounded, unfiltered, sense of the challenges faced by auditors in line with the lean Gemba way of working. In addition, I hope that this approach will resonate with auditors' own experience, and represent something of a contrast to more high level, statistical accounts of audit practice, which I personally feel are all too common, and not always very helpful.

However, whilst this book wants to recognize the reality of the challenges and dilemmas facing auditors, it is fundamentally intended to bring to life how lean, progressive, ways of working are in place in internal audit functions across many countries and industry sectors. The perspectives offered are not intended to represent a complete picture of every good practice that is possible, but are provided in order to illustrate specific examples that represent the spirit of lean, progressive auditing, and the leadership and team ways of working needed to deliver this. As readers will discover, not everyone quoted sees things in a similar way. Nonetheless, I hope what comes through clearly is a mindset and ways of working that demonstrate:

- A clear orientation to understanding and managing stakeholders;
- A constant focus on adding value;
- A determination to drive productivity and eliminate waste;
- A desire to play a genuine leadership role in the organization.

## Advice on Reading the Following Chapters

The chapters that follow need not be read systematically in order. A reader with particular interest in a specific topic (for example, audit planning, assignment execution, or staff training and development) should be able to go directly to that chapter to consider the areas of challenge, as well as the best practice ways of addressing them.

However, I am not a believer that the only way to improve value add and productivity in internal audit is to follow each and every suggestion in this book. My advice is to consider which of the recommended practices are most likely to make a tangible difference, bearing in mind the specific context of each audit function, as well as barriers to implementing these practices.

In addition, despite the extensive research carried out to write this book, I have no doubt other progressive practices are in use, or being trialled, as I write this book. It is through the efforts and innovations of internal auditors all over the world, over the course of time, that will earn the audit profession increasing respect and recognition by senior managers, boards, other stakeholders and the general public. However, I hope that this book offers a useful distillation of a number of key principles and practical suggestions that can support this collective journey of moving the internal audit profession forward.

Some readers may feel, on reading this book, that a substantial project is needed to re-orientate internal audit towards lean, progressive ways of working. That may well be correct. However, CAEs and other stakeholders should be mindful that a large-scale change project within an audit function could sometimes impede either the delivery of the audit plan or the level of engagement between the audit function and management or both.

Personally, I have found that a step-by-step approach to implementing lean ways of working – addressing one area of difficulty, and then another – has worked quite successfully for many internal audit functions. Indeed for some functions, this has been the only practical way to move forward since they are often completely overwhelmed by their workload – which is one of the reasons they are interested in lean in the first place!

I will return to questions of where to start or continue to develop lean auditing ways of working in the penultimate chapter of this book.

# PART 2
# Looking at Internal Audit Planning and Assignment Delivery

# 6
# Who Are the Customers of Internal Audit?

Based on my experience of lean workshops and client assignments, it is quite possible that the title of this chapter may strike some readers as rather strange. The sources of disquiet might be either:

- Should an internal audit function have customers? Or;
- Surely it is obvious who internal audit's customers are!

I have sympathy for both of these perspectives. However, the application of lean principles to internal audit begins with a clear expectation that internal audit should deliver value add, with the minimum of waste, to the *external customers* of each organization they serve. As we will see, this mindset opens up some interesting and important perspectives that are worth exploring.

## COMMON PRACTICES AND IIA STANDARDS OF NOTE

As a starting point, it is worth noting that current IIA standards do not use the word "customer" explicitly. Instead, various stakeholders are referred to in relation to internal audit:

- The board – who should approve the charter of the internal audit function;
- The board and senior management – who should understand the IIA's standards;

- The board, senior management, other stakeholders and clients – whose expectations internal audit should understand.

Others mentioned in the IIA standards include:

- Internal and external providers of assurance services – in the context of assurance co-ordination;
- The external auditor – in the context of assurance over governance;
- Internal and external parties – in the context of the release of records.

The audit functions I have worked with have a range of specific governance and organizational arrangements that affect who their stakeholders and customers are. However, for the majority of audit functions, key stakeholder and customer groups are typically described using the following terms:

- The board or sub-committees of the board (e.g. the audit committee, the risk committee);
- The managers and staff of the functions that are audited (often referred to as "auditees");
- The managers of the managers whose functions are being audited (who may or may not be senior managers);
- Other assurance and compliance functions (including risk, health and safety, IT, security, etc.), as well as the legal function and/or company secretary;
- The external auditor;
- Regulatory bodies;
- Other external parties (e.g. auditors working on behalf of external customers or stakeholders) and I increasingly hear comments about auditors referring to the need to serve the needs of key external stakeholders.


## COMMON CHALLENGES & DILEMMAS

### Different Views within Internal Audit Concerning Which Stakeholders should Be a Priority

The challenge a number of CAEs and audit functions face is how to reconcile and prioritize between the different internal stakeholders that have an interest in the work of internal audit (see Figure 6.1). Over the

**Figure 6.1**  Internal Audit has many customers

course of several years I have heard a wide range of views about who internal audit should be working for.

In addition, even within an internal audit function there can be differences between the CAE's view of the key stakeholders and the views of their audit staff. These differences of perspective can also be seen over the course of a working career. One experienced CAE reflects:

> "When I first started out in audit, some 20 years ago, I was more interested in the value I added to the business managers I was auditing. One, it's an easier life, you keep people happy who you are dealing with 95% of the time, but over time I see it's a mistake to forget that you've got competing interests in terms of what other stakeholders might want."

Sarah Blackburn (Member of IIA Global Board and former AC Chair) offers a similar reflection:

> "When I started in audit I always thought that middle managers were the people we worked for, although I rapidly realized it should be top management and the board. That said we did do a lot of consulting work

for middle managers, where we were asked to look at processes, make recommendations on how things could be re-engineered."

Sarah's comments capture an important challenge for audit: the board and senior management are doubtless key customers and stakeholders, but audit is often asked to serve the needs of other managers.

My experience is that each audit function can have a different perspective concerning their key customers and stakeholders, and this can be influenced by a range of factors – historic, cultural, and organizational, as well as the specific preferences of influential stakeholders.

The difficulty in focusing primarily on the needs of "the auditee" was explained by one CAE:

"For a typical audit you deal with the details of processes, data and documentation. That's where the information lives and that's where the people who know the procedures and process operate. Of course these operational staff and managers are important, but if you want to specify the work that should be done you've got to factor in the perspective of the senior managers, since they are the ones charged with managing organizational risk.

In addition, if you want to tell a story, to add value, the basic factual results of your assignment are never as important as what it means to the organization.

The scope of an assignment can inherently limit what you do as an auditor and how you communicate findings. We've all done audits where you identify a finding around procurement, but that particular issue has implications far beyond this. If you don't assess the procurement risk properly, the risk you identify could also mean that you hire something or buy something that has a health, safety or environment (HSE) risk. In which case, the HSE function needs to know about it. So you need to be alert to this as you plan the assignment, taking into account senior stakeholder perspectives and – where necessary – being prepared to elevate what is found, so that everyone is aware of its implications and impact.

I think traditionally auditors have been hesitant to do that. It's so easy for audit to say 'the scope of the assignment is A, B, C' and not to go outside this, because then you drag extra people in and complicate matters and you just want to get the assignment done."

The desire to "get the assignment done" may have an appeal from an efficiency perspective, but it ignores the need to deliver value to key stakeholders and is therefore not particularly lean.

Helen Maneuf (CAE, Hertfordshire Shared Internal Audit Service (SIAS)) provides this perspective about differences between the "auditee" and the audit client:

> "The managers that you work with during an assignment are important but they are not the key clients of audit. The people that you have to ring up to get information for an assignment aren't really your customer. They are important but in reality they are part of the chain that gets you the product that senior stakeholders want to read."

Norman Marks (GRC thought leader) provides this perspective:

> "Focusing on who is the customer is an important question for Internal Audit. Maybe you will find differences from organization to organization, but if you don't address the needs of the Board, Audit Committee, or the CEO, but you're doing great things for the head of accounts payable, or manufacturing, you're not doing your job."

## Different Views Concerning the Primacy of the Board/Audit Committee or Senior Management

Whilst many experienced auditors are mindful of the need to prioritize the needs of senior stakeholders, the question of which senior stakeholders should be regarded as prime can pose something of a dilemma. Chris Baker, Technical Manager of the UK Chartered Institute of Internal Auditors provides one perspective:

> "For me, the prime customer is the audit committee. They have the job of giving an annual report or an annual statement for shareholders or stakeholders about the state of risk management and governance and control. Their prime source of assurance in relation to this is internal audit. For me, they should be top of the list in terms of audit focus."

My experience is that many CAEs share Chris's view – the prime stakeholder for audit should be the board and the audit committee. However, not all CAEs see things the same way. Rania Bejjani – Chief Internal Auditor (VP Group Internal Audit & Risk Management), Colt Technology Services Group Ltd – offers an alternative view, shared by many other CAEs:

"From my perspective the prime customer of internal audit is senior management.

I see the Audit Committee as my reporting line to whom I owe a duty of care and diligence but not as my customers. The audit committee is mostly a recipient of information; they think about it, they might make comments to management, things like that, but they are not going to act on the information, except in exceptional circumstances. They're not going to actually make the changes in the business. It is management and executives who will make the change and have the ability to drive the improvements, therefore they are my clients.

I see audit as a catalyst for change. And for us to be catalysts of change we need to be really impacting and influencing and pressing the right levers in the organization and that is the management of the business. They are the doers in the business."

## Stakeholders Disagreeing Who is Prime

Of course, whatever a CAE might think, different stakeholders can hold their own (and sometimes diverging) views about who internal audit should serve.

In some organizations, senior managers – such as the Chief Financial Officer (CFO) – believe that audit should primarily focus on their needs, carrying out, for example, extensive financial control testing and anti-fraud work. In other organizations, the board or audit committee will take the lead role, perhaps focusing the work of audit on policy and regulatory compliance work (especially when there is a demanding regulator).

At the extreme end, some senior managers even believe that the audit function should "go through the motions" of serving the board or audit committee. The result is that they offer little sympathy or support for assignments in areas they personally believe are not valuable. If this is combined with limited interest or backing from board members, the audit function can find it quite challenging to carry out a wider range of work in order to deliver maximum value to the whole organization.

Of course, board members have many risk and performance areas to oversee, so some CAEs might question whether it is appropriate to say that they are not getting enough interest or backing from board members (or senior mangers). In addition, CAEs may have reservations about saying they are not getting enough board support or senior managers, for fear of further disturbing these important relationships.

This sort of issue is rarely discussed in most internal audit literature and represents, to my mind, one of the fundamental ways that the model of "dual reporting lines" can break down. At present, in my experience, there are few places that a CAE can go when they have pressure from one key stakeholder and limited interest from the others.

## RECOMMENDED PRACTICES

From a lean perspective, the true customer is the external customer. Clearly, senior management and the board have an important voice when they are helping to communicate key customer needs to the organization. As a result, the key steps audit can take are outlined below:

### Define and Agree the Key Internal Customers and Stakeholders of the Internal Audit Function

Richard Chambers (President & CEO of the IIA):

> "My advice to any internal audit function is to start by defining the stakeholders. Knowing who the stakeholders are and knowing their expectations are key to crafting a strategic plan and helping define internal audit's value proposition."

Actions for Internal Audit to consider:

- Identify the key stakeholders of the audit function;
- Gather their needs and expectations (which will be discussed in more detail in subsequent chapters).

### Always Remember the Importance of the External Customer

The use of an external customer perspective may seem to be rather remote from the work of internal audit, but John Earley (Partner, Smart Chain International) highlights the importance of taking this approach:

> "Let's consider the internal audit function of a company, does the customer really care? Superficially, no, because they're still going to get a product or service tomorrow.

However, let's look a bit beyond the here and now and look further into the future and start thinking, well, if internal audit didn't exist maybe some of the controls and check points that actually end up ensuring that the organization does the right thing by its customers could be lost. There may not be a direct impact on what the customer sees as value, but the aim with lean is to look for an indirect one.

You may not be on the main through route delivering what the customer values, but the aim should be to be a contributing factor. So long as you can trace the link between what you are doing and what the external customer would value, you cease to be a backwater. You are a tributary, not a backwater or a lost lake."

The principle of using an external customer perspective to guide the work of internal audit was not particularly prominent when we first started implementing lean ways of working at AstraZeneca, since our prime concern was to better concentrate on the needs of senior managers and the board (which itself opened up a wide range of value adding opportunities). However, over the years, I have found that taking an external perspective has provided a powerful additional way to orientate the work of audit. For example, risks around the management of customer data (and other sensitive information), customer satisfaction or service levels, or how customer complaints are managed may not be highlighted on a risk register, or be of particular concern to senior managers and the board (especially if there are no obvious problems) but may in fact be vitally important areas to consider.

Taking an external customer perspective also throws an interesting light on CAEs who are inclined to align the work of their audit function more towards the needs of one internal stakeholder over the needs of another. This can happen when CAEs find they have a closer relationship with one stakeholder, who may be more sympathetic or engaged, than others. My advice is that CAEs and internal auditors should be wary of focusing too much towards the board, senior management or audit clients at the expense of others for any sustained period of time. In part this is because of the impact favouring one stakeholder group may have on the relationship with others (since no one likes to feel second class). However, mostly it is because of the fact that this might result in a distancing of audit's efforts towards the organization as a whole (and adding value to the external customer).

Actions for Internal Audit to consider:

- Have in mind what an external customer would think of the work the audit function is doing;
- Be wary of aligning the work of audit primarily to one internal stakeholder at the expense of the needs of other internal stakeholders, or external customer needs.

## Ensure the Whole Audit Function is Clear Who They Are Working For

To be oriented towards the delivery of added value all of the staff within an audit function need to be clear about key stakeholders, what they value and what they do not. One key area for consideration is to recognize the importance of communicating board and senior management needs, which may not be visible to most auditors on a day-to-day basis.

In practical terms, a CAE should ensure that the views of the board and senior management are communicated during the induction of new audit staff, as well as to all audit staff on an ongoing basis. A senior audit manager explains the practice in his audit function:

> "I don't think we sit audit staff down and say, the audit committee, they're the most important, but it comes across, I think, in the way that we talk about the audit committee. So every time I have meetings with different teams I'll provide the feedback on the audit committee meeting, and what they want. I believe everybody understands that the audit committee is important to us because of the way we talk about it within the team.
>
> I also believe everybody understands that senior business leaders are also really important, mostly because of the way we talk about what their requirements are and the respect to their needs and interests that we show when we talk about them."

Alongside clear communication of key stakeholders' needs, auditors should be encouraged to discuss the practical consequences of what to do when there are competing demands and resource limitations. One way to achieve this is to make clear the non-negotiable areas within the scope and the critical assurance questions that key stakeholders want to be addressed. Another approach is to agree with senior management a sponsor for each audit assignment, who can guide audit in relation to the work that will be of most value. In *progressive audit functions a sponsor will often not be the person being audited, but someone at least one level more senior than the manager of the area being audited.*

Actions for Internal Audit to consider:

- Clearly communicate the needs and expectations of senior management and the board;
- Discuss how to prioritize when there are competing needs or limitations on audit time;
- Where appropriate, nominate an assignment sponsor at least one management level above the manager being audited.

## CONCLUDING REMARKS

I am wary of suggesting there is a definitive answer to the question of who is the prime customer of an internal audit function. Indeed, the fact that there may be multiple customers, as well as professional obligations, represents one of many dilemmas that internal auditors face. However, lean does encourage us to regard this as a fundamental matter for close attention. My starting point is that an orientation towards meeting the needs of the board and senior management should always be in the auditor's mind, alongside a sponsor or client for each assignment. And behind this should be the "north star" lean mindset of being oriented towards what the external customer would want audit to do.

---

### SUMMARY OF KEY POINTS FOR INTERNAL AUDIT

- Consider ranking the importance of the stakeholders that have an interest in the work of the audit function;
- Ensure stakeholder expectations are clearly understood throughout the audit function;
- Always consider what key external customers (including regulators) would think of the work the internal audit function is doing;
- Consider a sponsor for each assignment who is at least one level more senior than the manager for the area of the assignment.

## RECOMMENDATIONS FOR SENIOR MANAGERS AND THE BOARD

- Are there any signs that either senior management or the audit committee is seen as a prime customer of the internal audit function?
- What expectations do you have in relation to internal audit's work and how does this link to what external customers would want?
- Are you satisfied that your expectations are being addressed and, if not, have you communicated this to your CAE?
- Are you satisfied that each audit assignment has sufficient senior management interest and engagement?

### References and Other Related Material of Interest

The Institute of Internal Auditors (IIA) (2012) *International professional practices framework*. https://na.theiia.org

The Institute of Internal Auditors (IIA) (2013) *International Standards for the Professional Practice of Internal Auditing (Standards)*. https://na.theiia.org/standards-guidance/mandatory-guidance/Pages/Standards.aspx

# 7
# What Really Adds Value – And What Doesn't

After exploring the question of who the prime customers of the internal audit function are, the next point to clarify is what *specifically* provides value to them. Furthermore, lean asks us to understand *how much* added value specific outputs deliver, and also asks us to pay close attention to what does not add value.

## COMMON PRACTICES AND IIA STANDARDS OF NOTE

IIA standards currently state that internal audit functions should be managed in order to ensure they add value to the organization. It is stated that "internal audit adds value when it delivers objective and relevant assurance," and also when it "contributes to the effectiveness and efficiency of governance, risk management and control processes."

## COMMON CHALLENGES & DILEMMAS

### A "Value Gap" between the Perceptions of Audit and Stakeholders

With such a clear emphasis on the importance of adding value in the IIA standards one might imagine that all audit functions would comfortably do this. However, my experience is that:

- Some auditors may not see adding value as a priority over and above other considerations;

- Some auditors may believe they are adding value, but key stakeholders may not always agree;
- Despite doing some value adding work, a portion of audit work may be regarded as non-value adding (for example, if it generates actions that are seen to be bureaucratic).

One of the reasons for a gap in the value internal audit is seen to provide may stem from a view that by simply following the IIA's high-level definition of adding value an internal audit function will be seen to be adding value in the eyes of key stakeholders. My experience is that whilst objective assurance might add value to the board and audit committee, it may not be particularly valued by senior or middle management. This is because they may be looking for help in addressing the current business issues they face, rather than receiving an assessment of the way certain processes were working three or six months ago. Over and above this, they may be sensitive to shortcomings for their area of responsibility being identified and then reported onwards to senior management and the board.

## The Importance of Paying Attention to Dissatisfiers

The following account by Richard Chambers (President & CEO of the IIA) emphasizes just how easy it can be for an audit function to lose contact with what stakeholders want, as well as the consequences of this:

> "There was an episode when I was in a leadership position for the U.S. Army internal review (internal audit) function. We were trying to figure out why so many of our audit departments were being downsized. In the wake of the fall of the Berlin Wall, the Army was downsizing but the internal audit function seemed to be getting smaller faster.
>
> I spent about six weeks talking to internal audit stakeholders, listening primarily to those who would be the equivalent of the CEO and CFO in the corporate sector. One commander explained how he made downsizing decisions. He said he needed the process to be collaborative in order for everyone to feel that they had been heard. His personal view was that internal audit was delivering value, but when he called in the directors of the different components, such as engineering and contracting, they were quite vocal about the lack of value that they were getting out of audits in their areas.
>
> This goes straight to the heart of the importance of adding value. A particular department may not be your primary focus but, at the end of the

day, they will be heard. Whether in a survey, in the executive boardroom, or on the golf course with the CEO, they will be heard. If they feel internal audit is not adding value, or is overbearing, or is not particularly user-friendly, they will be heard.

Another situation may not be as dramatic, but it can't help internal audit's reputation if these people have a sense that we're not adding value for them. It is very important to make sure that every recipient of internal audit's work has a strong appreciation for the value that they get – even if they're not the ones we work for directly."

Richard's remarks emphasize the need to balance the demands of a range of internal clients and stakeholders, as discussed in the last chapter. They also highlight that adding value is not simply about *what* internal audit does but *how* internal audit does it (i.e. the managers' dissatisfaction of internal audit being "overbearing" and "not particularly user-friendly").

Whilst it is important to take into account the needs of key internal stakeholders, a truly lean approach would encourage audit to distinguish between:

- Stakeholders who are speaking with their own functional or personal value preferences; and
- Stakeholders who are speaking from the perspective of the organization as a whole; and
- Stakeholders who are expressing value preferences on behalf of external customers and stakeholders.

Lean encourages an orientation towards the latter two perspectives where possible.

## RECOMMENDED PRACTICES

### Make a Commitment to Adding Value beyond Motherhood and Apple Pie

Being a lean, progressive, internal audit function starts with making a clear commitment to adding value, as well as driving out waste. Making this commitment often comes from recognizing that an internal audit function needs to demonstrate its value in order to thrive in the long run.

Ivan Butler (CAE, Denbighshire County Council) explains how he started his lean auditing journey:

> "A few years ago, as part of a council-wide efficiency review, each department had to go before our corporate executive team to explain how they delivered their service, what value this added and whether this could be done more efficiently.
>
> We were a service in our own right, when we went before the executive team one of the executives said: "What would happen if you weren't here? What is the point of internal audit?" I responded with the usual stuff, talking about giving assurance, preventing fraud and helping managers. We were doing some good things, but it made me think a lot afterwards. In particular, I realized that if they said: 'We just want you to do your core assurance work' we could probably do that with a much smaller team.
>
> So, from that point on, we have been on a journey thinking about the ways lean principles can help us deliver more, and over the years it has opened my eyes to different ways of thinking, and realizing there is a lot of stuff in audit that we can do differently."

The principle that internal audit should see its role beyond just getting through the audit plan and delivering reports is central to thinking about adding value. In fact, I would argue that a focus on delivering audits can sometimes get in the way of an audit function delivering value. Nicola Rimmer (former President of the IIA UK) provides this perspective:

> "With the corporate failures over the last few years, you can't just say providing an audit is adding value. You've got to have the insight and business intelligence to know where to audit and also to be able to help management move things forward, provide them with a bit of direction, provide them with information about best practice, as well as challenge when appropriate. That's where the added value comes in, it's not just providing audit reports."

In practical terms, therefore, a lean audit approach encourages an audit function to consider its remit, strategy, audit methodology and other ways of working, and to consider the extent to which adding value and productivity is highlighted as a clear priority.

However, lean, progressive auditing is not just about "bolting on" phrases concerning adding value and waste elimination, although that is an important step to take. It is about re-orienting all aspects of the audit function's activities towards these goals, as will be discussed in later chapters.

Actions for Internal Audit to consider:

- Revisit the audit remit, strategy and methodology and consider how explicitly these address the need to provide added value, and the need to drive out waste;
- Consider how the audit function would be resourced if it was cut to a minimum "bare bones" level;
- Start a process of thinking how to articulate the value that audit provides from activities over and above the bare minimum.

## Strive to Clarify What Adds Value and What Does Not

The lean mindset is simple: to become a valued part of the organization, it is essential to properly engage with key customers about what they actually value. One CAE offered the following advice:

> "The first thing you've got to do, before you can say whether you are adding value, is get a definition of what added value means to your key stakeholders."

At the outset it should be noted that different senior managers and different board members often have their own views about how audit can add value, based on their experience and a range of other factors. In my experience a number of common themes emerge. These common themes are summarized in Table 7.1 with reference to three key stakeholder groups, the board, senior managers and other middle managers.

Other common themes are provided in Appendix A.

Understanding stakeholder needs through Kano analysis allows an audit function to be clear about specific ways of operating that may affect how it is valued. It is tempting to regard some of these perceptions of what adds value as rather irrational (e.g. if they do not appreciate the outcome of a specific assurance assignment); however, Richard Chambers (President & CEO of the IIA) supports the need for auditors to engage stakeholders on questions of what adds value:

> "We should never lose sight of the fact that we do not define value. It's our stakeholders who define what value is. You must start with the stakeholders as you work through this process."

Where there are areas of alignment between key stakeholders, internal audit has at face value a clear mandate to deliver to those requirements.

**Table 7.1**   Common Themes

| Characteristic/Output | Board | Senior Managers | Other Managers |
|---|---|---|---|
| Advisory work | Some appreciate this but most want assurance | Some appreciate this (i.e. a satisfier and sometimes delighter) | Some appreciate this (i.e. a satisfier and sometimes delighter) |
| Assurance work | Creates satisfaction | Sometimes depends on the outcome | Sometimes depends on the outcome |
| Cost of audit | For some not a major concern if the quality is there | Would prefer lower cost (i.e. dissatsfier) | Would prefer lower cost (i.e. dissatsfier) |
| Cost savings identified | For many not a major driver | Many value this (i.e. satisfier or delighter) | Depends whether the savings benefit them or not |
| Report length | Require sufficient detail to be useful | Prefer shorter (i.e. dissatisfaction if too long) | Dissatisfaction if not balanced |

For example, if all key stakeholders want shorter audit reports, then making reports shorter will deliver added value and at the same time probably take less time and resource! Thus, *being lean does not mean that everything should be cut equally.* Some areas could be reduced significantly, or cut out completely, with no loss of added value (they may even elicit a positive reaction), whilst other areas may need greater audit attention to deliver untapped value.

However, alignment between key stakeholders (such as senior management and the board) in relation to what they want should not always be regarded as a clear sign that audit is adding value. For example, senior management and the board may want a lot of detailed compliance checking to be done by the audit function, but that might not always be the most value-adding thing to do when an external customer perspective is factored in, because, for example, another area of greater concern to them may not be working as well as it could be.

Actions for Internal Audit to consider:

- Map out what, precisely, stakeholders value and do not value;
- Take into account how things are done, not just what is done;
- Consider what an external customer would want from the audit function, and also what they would be prepared to pay for;

- Consider how the audit function is aligned to deliver these added value expectations (see later chapters).

## Identify Different Perceptions of Value and Develop a Plan to Address the Most Problematic Areas

As discussed earlier, stakeholders may have different views about what adds value and what does not. A key difference is often a management preference for advisory assignments, compared to a board preference for more assurance assignments.

It is very tempting and understandable to want to downplay the importance of these differences for fear of upsetting stakeholders, but lean principles demand clarity and alignment around adding value; for example, being clear during the audit planning process about the balance between advisory and assurance assignments.

This importance of paying attention to differences between stakeholders, rather than ignoring them, is endorsed by Richard Chambers (President & CEO of the IIA):

> "If your audit committee says, 'We want you focused on assurance over financial controls,' and executive management says, 'We really would like for you to give us more insight and advice on key operating controls,' then you have a dilemma.
>
> As a CAE, you have a responsibility to serve both management and the board. If the board is telling you one thing and management is telling you another, it's a slippery slope. You can't just say, 'Well, management, I'm sorry but the board wants this,' because, ultimately, management allocates internal audit's resources.
>
> My advice, when there are differences between key internal stakeholders, is to get a reconciliation of expectations. Pull management and the board into a conversation, and make sure everybody understands: 'Look, we're here to serve all of you, and we want to make sure that we do so in an open and transparent way, so all stakeholders' expectations are known.'"

Some CAEs successfully manage stakeholders in this manner. However, in my CAE coaching work, I find some CAEs having to rethink the way they relate to their stakeholders, since for them a significant dynamic in their relationship has been simply to deliver what the stakeholders want without any serious challenge!

Maintaining relationships with key stakeholders whilst being able to challenge them is one of the delicate balancing acts that a CAE must achieve in order to be effective. Perspectives on how this can be done are contained in the next chapter, which discusses the relationship between lean and the attributes of independence and objectivity.

Actions for Internal Audit to consider:

- Pay attention to key differences in stakeholder views on what adds value and what does not;
- Recognize that just doing what stakeholders ask does not mean that an audit function will be lean;
- Manage different value perspectives proactively between key stakeholders and also if these are not clearly aligned with external customer needs.

## DELIVER VALUE TO MULTIPLE STAKEHOLDERS – BUT MANAGE BOUNDARIES

As outlined earlier, lean does not favour any specific internal stakeholders in relation to the delivery of added value, since the ultimate aim is to add value to the external customer. However, it does explain why the board and senior management will often take precedence over line management (since in terms of materiality and impact their needs may be of greater benefit to external customers).

However, ignoring the needs of line managers can result in difficulties, partly because they may give negative feedback, but also because their needs may sometimes align more closely with those of the external customer (for example, line manager concerns about the functionality or reliability of a new system that will be customer facing or the way processes are impacting customer service levels).

Andy Weintraub, (experienced internal audit leader), and a former colleague of mine, outlines his solution to delivering added value to multiple stakeholders:

> "How do you prioritize between stakeholders? I try to make all of the managers I work with feel important. Fortunately in many instances their requirements have different timescales to those of the board or senior management, so you can factor that in and meet most of what each wants. If we're in an assignment, the senior manager that's responsible for that area is my priority, but I can also be bearing in mind that there is an audit committee question that needs addressing as well – but that won't need to be reported on until the next quarter."

Progressive, value-adding auditing centres around an awareness of multiple stakeholder needs, alongside a recognition that audit has only limited resources and therefore boundaries need to be placed on requests of lesser importance. The best functions aim to manage these multiple demands with a degree of empathy, often giving something to management (even if it is just pointing them towards some guidance or best practice) whilst offering a clear explanation of why there are limitations on what audit can do.

Actions for Internal Audit to consider:

- Be clear that many stakeholders will have a range of needs and expectations for internal audit;
- Prioritize and manage these needs and expectations based on value add criteria;
- Manage any gaps between stakeholder expectations and what can be delivered and be creative in offering alternative ideas to maintain relationships.

## The Delivery of Value should Always Take into Account Cost

Some CAEs tell me that their board members value long and detailed reports. This is fine, but lean encourages us to consider both value and cost. Consequently, if the board member knew that the long report was taking four days to write, they might be content, but often they might prefer a shorter report taking one or two days. Thus a lean approach encourages greater clarity of choices being made and their impact on customer value: should audit use the time saved from a longer report to do two days more auditing (perhaps looking at root causes), or two days auditing elsewhere, or as a way of lowering costs?

Consequently the response to the question: "Does audit have enough resources?" should not be a simple "yes" or "no", but rather "Well it all depends what you want from internal audit." A good case study of how to get a better, richer, engagement with key internal stakeholders in relation to resources is provided by Richard Young, (CAE of the Universities Internal Audit Consortium (UNIAC)):

> "We work with a large number of different audit committees and senior management teams, so there is a degree of change every year. As things change we organize time together, for example, a half-day away day.

We say: do you want to treat audit as an investment or an expense? We work together to help these stakeholders see audit as an investment. And if you want to invest in something you want the best possible return. And if you want to get the best possible return that's about investing time on an ongoing basis where we can sit round the table and explore what we are planning to do for you and why. As a result we can see these stakeholders valuing more audit work in relation to business projects and other strategic issues, rather than just core compliance and financial control areas.

I think it's fundamental that we continue to get the debate going on investment versus cost in relation to audit. That's where lean comes in. Concentrating on the right areas first, then once this is clear cutting out the waste, the things that we've done because of tradition rather than because they are really important."

Actions for Internal Audit to consider:

- What is the attitude of key stakeholders to internal audit: do they see audit as an investment rather than an expense?
- Appropriately engage key stakeholders to link audit activities with added value.

## Delivering Delighters is Often Simpler than You Think

I sometimes ask auditors to consider specific occasions when they have delighted stakeholders. Often there is a pause and silence, with some auditors explaining that it should not be expected that internal audit should "delight" stakeholders.

However, some auditors are able to cite examples when they have delighted senior management, and when they do this, it is often notable that this may not have taken a lot of time and effort on their part. For example, one CAE explained to me that her relationship with a CEO had been transformed by doing two relatively short assignments directly for him that were time critical but highly sensitive, and handling these in a way that built trust between them. She explained:

"I was relatively new to my role and wanted to start things off in a good way with the CEO. I volunteered to take the lead looking at a couple of specific issues in the first few months, delegating other work, and taking great care to communicate with discretion. Some difficult issues emerged, but it shifted the CEO's perspective of what I could do and the value internal audit was capable of delivering."

Sometimes a simple output (e.g. a diagram in an audit report) or a minor innovation can add lots of value – the trick is to create a culture within internal audit that is on the look out for these new ideas, trying things out and getting feedback as to whether they are working.

Another senior auditor offered the following reflection:

"I think the profession needs to be prepared to do some things differently. I think we get stuck sometimes because something has never been done before. We're not that adventurous as a profession.

Whilst being innovative might feel risky to some audit functions, if this innovation is informed by insights based on what stakeholders like and do not like, then the risk is going to be quite low, especially if new approaches are positioned as pilots. Indeed I would argue that the greater risk to audit in the long run is that it does not change with the times, and becomes stale."

Actions for Internal Audit to consider:

- Reflect on instances when "delighters" have been delivered and showcase these within the audit function;
- Examine the amount of innovation within the audit function, how often are new approaches tried?
- Look to pilot new approaches to increase audit's delivery of added value.

## Listen, and Respond, to the "Voice of the Customer"

As discussed in an earlier chapter, understanding the "Voice of the Customer" is fundamental to being a lean, value adding audit function. Thus, getting feedback after each assignment is essential. Of course, many audit functions do this through a questionnaire approach but often it is the "auditee" who has just been audited that is asked for feedback. However, the "auditee" may not always be the key customer. On a number of occasions, clients and workshop participants have recognized that feedback should be obtained from other stakeholders, not just "auditees," on a more regular and disciplined basis.

I also hear auditors explain that response rates to questionnaires can be quite low, and the quality of responses can be disappointing (e.g. "they ticked the boxes and didn't make any comments"). Auditors tell me this is to be expected given the workloads and other priorities of managers. However, delivery without feedback does not reflect a lean way of working. The spirit, the essence, of lean is to be passionate about understanding what customers think. After all, a low response rate may not be a neutral sign; instead it may be a sign of apathy towards what audit is doing. Likewise a pattern of long delays before managers give their feedback, or where audit regularly has to chase management for responses, should be regarded as a warning sign of potential disconnect from adding value to the organization, and not just accepted.

Looked at another way, an organizational culture in which poor or late responses to audit questionnaires is normal, is a culture that can and should be improved by lean ways of working.

Audit functions that strive to add value, try alternative approaches to getting feedback, rather than just sending a questionnaire. Successful approaches include (short) face to face debrief sessions (even immediately after an audit assignment), or through stakeholder meetings at intervals in which the performance of audit and the value of recent assignments is discussed. One CAE explained their approach to feedback:

> "I'm an advocate of a qualitative approach. It takes time going round to see key players at intervals, but it's a good discipline. What did you want from recent assignments? What did you get? How did you find the team? How quickly did we respond? Did our work make a difference? That kind of thing."

In a recent External Quality Assessment (EQA) for an audit function, I noted that whilst there was a feedback process after each assignment, the audit management team only received updates of the overall feedback scores on a quarterly basis, with just a few qualitative comments included in summary form. My advice was that having a feedback process was good, and it was also encouraging that most managers responded, but there were signs that the feedback process was becoming something of an administrative exercise. Going forward, the CAE agreed that key strengths and weaknesses from assignment feedback should be "fast tracked" to him as soon as they were received, so that he and the audit management team could escalate and respond to any serious issues quickly if needed.

Andy Weintraub (experienced internal audit leader) sums up the mindset of progressive auditing, determined to add value:

> "Recognize things won't always go well in audit. There are bound to be times when you are going to stumble, when there are going to be issues. My personal approach is to ensure these don't fester. My advice is not to let things wait, to take care of them right away, most especially if they are things that could impact the reputation of the internal audit function."

Actions for Internal Audit to consider:

- Obtain feedback on a timely basis from stakeholders above and beyond the "auditee";
- Ensure low response rates from management are understood. This should be a warning sign of potential disengagement by management, not just regarded as "one of those things";
- Ensure that qualitative responses are fast tracked within the audit function and key concerns properly understood (in terms of their root cause within audit) and addressed on a timely basis.

## CONCLUDING REMARKS

The dilemma facing many audit functions seems to be the need to reconcile professional obligations to deliver independent and objective assurance and advice, alongside the delivery of a range of other customer wants and needs, not all of which are in alignment.

I hope auditors reading this chapter will have noted the rigour of the lean approach to understanding what adds value (somewhat akin to applying an analytical audit mindset to this often quite subjective area). Furthermore, lean ways of working demand an ongoing engagement with the need to add value, and reduce non-value-adding work, as a key engine for driving effectiveness and efficiency.

---

**SUMMARY OF KEY POINTS FOR INTERNAL AUDIT**

- Make a clear and unambiguous commitment that the audit function should be oriented towards adding value;
- Obtain feedback from stakeholders to understand satisfiers, dissatisfiers and delighters;
- Consider the external customer perspective of value;
- Create a priority action plan to manage dissatisfiers and increase instances of delighters;
- Consider key differences in stakeholder views about value add/ non-value add, as well as instances where this may not be aligned with external customer needs. Identify which are the most important and develop a plan to manage those of most concern;
- Look again at the process of obtaining audit client and stakeholder feedback – is it up to date and complete? Are responses of a good quality? How quickly is feedback acted upon?

---

**RECOMMENDATIONS FOR SENIOR MANAGERS AND THE BOARD**

- Consider what delights, satisfies and dissatisfies you about internal audit and engage audit about this;
- How does this align with what the external customer would want, or other stakeholders?;
- If audit reports are lengthy, clarify the time and effort being taken to write these reports and explore whether this is a good use of audit's time;
- Clarify who is asked to give feedback on the performance of audit and establish what the feedback has been and what has been done about it.

---

### References and Other Related Material of Interest

Steffee, S. (2014) Losing Value. *Internal Auditor Magazine* (USA), June issue, pp. 13–4.

van Wyk, A. (2014) Mind the Gap. *Internal Auditor Magazine* (USA), August issue, pp. 40–5.

# 8
# The Importance of Role Clarity in Assurance and the Insights Lean Can Offer

In the previous chapter I discussed some of the dilemmas that auditors face because they have multiple stakeholders who may have different views about the value and purpose of internal audit. In addition, auditors face the dilemma of often needing to deliver difficult messages, whilst maintaining good working relationships.

To help me manage these dilemmas when I was a CAE I used coaching support from time to time. From this I gained two key insights in relation to disagreements with management:

- Some disagreements arise because of disputes about roles and responsibilities. For example, a manager saying: "I didn't check that because I thought you (the auditor) were going to do that" or "I didn't think I had to keep documentation of who had been trained, that's the job of the HR function, not me";
- Other disagreements are the inevitable outcome of two legitimate roles having a different perspective. For example: "Our audit work suggests there is a greater risk in this area than you seem to think."

Thinking about roles was helpful to me as a CAE, since it helped me to recognize that bringing up certain issues would inevitably be difficult, but a necessary task if I wanted to do my job properly. On other occasions, it helped me think ahead about potential misunderstandings about respective roles and responsibilities so these could be constructively discussed at an early stage.

In my consulting and CAE coaching work the importance of thinking about roles and responsibilities has been a regular area of focus; this chapter seeks to illustrate just how important the perspective of roles and responsibilities is as a tool to drive the efficiency and effectiveness of the internal audit function.

## AN IIA PERSPECTIVE ON THE UNIQUE ROLE OF INTERNAL AUDIT

The role of internal audit is unique in most organizations. It is normally determined by both senior management and the board and will often have the following characteristics:

- Reporting to both executive management and a non executive board member (consider how unusual this is for most functions);
- A remit to deliver independent and objective advice and assurance on GRC etc. matters (whilst adding value);
- A function that should ideally not assume any management responsibility (again, consider how rare this is).

For over a decade the framework of the "Three lines of defence" has been used by some internal auditors to explain, amongst other things, how the role of internal audit can be understood in simple terms (see Figure 8.1). The idea is that:

In the first line of defence: management and staff should manage risks and opportunities on a day-to-day basis, in line with policies, processes and standards as required;

In the second line of defence: other compliance, policy and oversight functions, such as finance, legal and purchasing, should help create the policies, processes and standards that inform management and staff as to what is expected, and should be available to support them with answers to questions, etc.;

In the third line of defence: internal audit (or other independent assurance and advisory roles) should advise and assure whether the other two lines of defence are working properly.

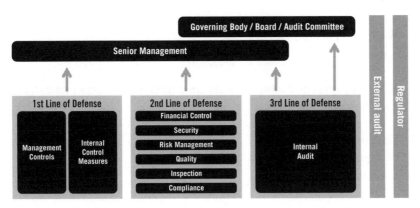

Adapted from ECIIA/FERMA *Guidance on the 8th EU Company Law Directive, article 41*

**Figure 8.1**  The three lines of defence model

The status of the three lines of defence framework has been somewhat unclear until recently, and even in 2014 I have found as many as 30–40% of auditors attending my workshops are not aware of it. I have found instances where an even greater proportion of board members and senior managers are not familiar with this framework. Even if they are, a number are not convinced that this framework should be adopted (partly because of a view it will require additional resources, but also because of questions that were raised about its effectiveness in various financial institutions after the 2007–2008 financial crisis).

Fortunately, the IIA has made an important step forward in relation to the three lines of defence, issuing a position paper "The three lines of defence in effective risk management and control" in January 2013. The position that the paper takes is that for effective risk management it is important to consider carefully the different roles that should be in place in an organization. The paper explains that, whilst there should be "effective co-ordination between these lines of defence", "lines of defence should not be combined or coordinated in a manner that compromises their effectiveness". Lean principles would strongly support both recommendations; if different parts of an organization do not have clear roles we will inevitably see ineffectiveness or inefficiency.

Interestingly, the notion of three lines of defence can be found in a medical context. For example, to protect the human body we have:

- The skin;
- White blood cells;
- Antibodies.

The three lines of defence can also be found in a military context. For example, in relation to a castle, there are:

- The walls of the castle;
- The guards that defend the walls;
- The king/queen's guard.

My belief is that if "three lines of defence" has proved its worth in a medical context, as well as in warfare, it probably has some merit if an organization has an interest in its long-term health and success.

## COMMON CHALLENGES & DILEMMAS

### Thinking Audit is a Compliance and Controls Monitoring Function

There is a significant legacy of custom and practice that has placed a number of audit functions in a monitoring and checking role (e.g. checking for compliance issues or duplicate payments). Whilst there can be a role for audit to carry out some basic monitoring and checking, if the boundary of this role is not managed, it can lead to a range of difficulties.

One case in point concerns the UK's National Health Service (NHS). Between 2007 and 2009, there were some serious incidents in relation to patient care in some locations of the NHS. Various reviews took place to identify key lessons. The UK Audit Commission (which has now been dissolved, for reasons unrelated to this discussion) was asked to examine how the patient care issues could arise when there had been a range of assurance statements signed off by managers and auditors during the years in which the issues arose. The results are contained in a very interesting report "Taking it on Trust," issued in April 2009. Numerous causes for the shortcomings were uncovered, including fundamental points about what assurance was being provided in a range of areas (including clinical audit and data assurance). The report also included learning points concerning the role and focus of internal audit, with various observations relevant to the current discussion about the role of internal audit:

One key point was the observation that:

> "Greater attention needed to be paid to compliance mechanisms, and these needed to be more clearly distinguished from internal audit, which should review the effectiveness of the compliance framework, not be a substitute for it."

Thus, when audit becomes a "free resource" and starts substituting for second line activities, it no longer becomes able to act as a safety net if these tasks are not being carried out. As a result, if internal audit then becomes too stretched to carry out compliance monitoring a failing may occur.

Another key point was the observation that:

> "Use of internal audit could be improved, with greater emphasis given to the quality of assurance derived from it rather than cost minimization. Its use should be placed in a wider framework of review, as there are alternatives to internal audit in many cases."

Here we see the danger of audit being valued primarily in terms of being low cost, without thinking more broadly about the key areas where value is at risk and what assurance is being provided over them. In addition, the comment about alternatives to internal audit highlights the key role front line staff, managers and other functions can and should play in ensuring that things are being well managed.

## Believing the First and Second Lines have only a Limited Assurance Role

I regularly have a laugh with workshop participants about the old adage: "When it's all going well – everyone wants to take the credit, but when things go badly – it is always someone else's fault" (see Figures 8.2 and 8.3)

Thus, during audits it is not unusual for auditors to encounter difficulties pinning down who is responsible for managing a specific risk or process. This can result in wasted time "chasing around" for the right people to interview; it can also cause difficulties finding someone to take responsibility for an audit action point.

**Figure 8.2**     Accountability – when it goes well we all want to take
the credit

**Figure 8.3**     Accountability – when it goes badly it was someone
else's fault

Another common area of concern from auditors is the poor oversight provided by second line functions (e.g. HR, IT, Purchasing, etc.). The in-joke in audit circles is "Some policy owners and managers seem to think that because a policy has been issued on an intranet site, everyone will now be in compliance." Unfortunately staff and line management (in the first line of defence) often blame the poor guidance from policy functions as one reason they were not in compliance ("There was no training for this" or "The guidance was unclear"). Partly this may be a way of avoiding their accountabilities, but sometimes I have sympathy with managers and staff. The underlying issues here are a lack of clarity of roles and *a lack of specificity in terms of what it means to effectively "roll out a policy."*

## Thinking Audit Needs to Check Remediation

Another area that comes up during my work with audit functions is the question of who should be accountable to verify that audit recommendations have been remediated. Whilst IIA standards state that audit "must establish a follow-up process to monitor and ensure that actions have been effectively implemented", it is common to find that the onus for verifying actions have been implemented falls on internal audit, rather than management.

When the responsibility for issue closure is placed on internal audit's shoulders, a portion of audit time can be spent chasing up progress on actions and verifying whether audit action points have been remediated. At face value this time spent on verification might seem a fair use of audit's time, since audit may seem the best qualified to carry out this role; however, from a long-term value perspective the problems can be:

- A lack of ownership of issue closure by staff and management, leading to slower progress in remediation;
- A view that audit, not management, should be criticized for a lack of progress on remediation;
- A culture in which risk and control are seen to be owned by audit, not management, which is likely to increase the chances of new issues arising in the future.

## Stakeholder Misunderstandings about the Assurance that Audit Can Deliver

In my experience a number of CAEs find that senior managers and the board have a rather imprecise understanding of the assurance role of internal audit. Here are the observations of one CAE:

"It is quite surprising to find people often struggle to tell you what adding value means, other than in cliché high level terms 'I want you to provide assurance on X and Y, and tell me everything is all right'.

And – in my view – the best audit response should often be: 'Well if that's what you want you can't get that level of assurance from internal audit because I'm not looking at everything and I couldn't possibly look at everything anyway. Hopefully I'm looking at the key risks, and we can give you some assurance around those, but we can only do so much.'"

Thus, the misunderstanding that can arise is a view that the role of the auditor is to check *all* of the risks and *all* of the controls for an area, rather than just the *key risks* and *key controls*. This gap in understanding reveals itself if a problem arises in an area that was previously audited, and rated satisfactory; where some stakeholders might say: "Why didn't the auditors find this issue the last time they did an audit?" One response I hear is that the auditor can only provide "reasonable and not absolute assurance", but this is often not so clearly defined, sometimes leaving doubts in the minds of key stakeholders about audit's assurance role, and whether its assurances can be relied upon.

## Lean Insights

Lean disciplines demand clarity of roles in order to optimize the smooth flow of value. As mentioned earlier, the use of a "swim lane diagram" is one tool to understand how different roles and functions deliver a process or objective.

Another powerful tool is the McKinsey RACI accountability framework. McKinsey developed this framework in order to support the effective implementation of business strategies. It has now become one of the most widely used accountability frameworks. Whilst not developed directly through lean ways of working, the RACI approach is often used when working on lean improvement activities. In my experience it has proved to be very helpful when implementing lean auditing and is also invaluable when developing Risk Assurance frameworks and Risk Assurance maps.

The RACI framework is useful for mapping out responsibilities in a process or activity and describes the following roles:

- Responsible (R) persons (often the doers);
- Accountable (A) persons (those who have their neck on the block);
- Persons who are to be Consulted (C): two-way communication expected;
- Persons to be Informed (I): one-way communication needed.

Other variations to RACI exist, RACI–VS (Verify and Signatory) and RASCI (including a supporting role – S). I personally use a variation: RASCI–O, which includes Oversight (O) roles, which can be helpful in relation to cross-functional risks, processes or other activities.

The key point is that role clarity should be seen as an important foundation for ensuring organizational efficiency and effectiveness. It can also be very helpful in an auditing and assurance context, since many risk control breakdowns can be attributed to problems with roles and responsibilities. Indeed, in my experience, a number of organizations have underlying cultural problems with accountabilities. Fortunately, progressive, value-adding auditing can play an important role in naming this sort of cultural issue, as discussed below.

## RECOMMENDED PRACTICES

### Engage Stakeholders on the Importance of Role Clarity and the Power of the Three Lines of Defence Model

Phil Gerrard (CAE, Rolls-Royce):

> "The audit committee tends to focus on the third line. Often because they get very little information about the second or first line, so it's pretty well invisible. One of the approaches to adopt is to say, 'We've got very limited resources. But there are others who manage these areas, so how can we get more comfort from the work that's being done in the business and make this more transparent to you?'

> Then explain the three lines of defence model and emphasize that internal audit is the backstop. Surely everything else has gone horribly wrong if we are the people that find out there's a problem. There should be various tiers of management who should be uncovering and escalating

issues and not forgetting other functions such as finance, purchasing, health and safety."

Actions for Internal Audit to consider:

- Ensure key stakeholders understand the three lines of defence model;
- Take some examples of control failings and explain these in terms of failings in the three lines of defence and highlight how the three lines are not "excessive" but essential;
- Highlight that for some risks (e.g. fraud) first and second line monitoring controls are much more likely to deliver what is needed than the third line of defence;
- For key risks or processes of concern, map out accountabilities in the first, second and third lines of defence and carry out a gap analysis.

### Ensure the Role of Internal Audit is Understood in Wider Terms Than Just Financial Control and Compliance Auditing

It is to be expected that most internal audit functions will do some auditing of financial controls and compliance. However, it is important that the difference between carrying out basic monitoring (on behalf of management) and assurance (to ascertain that management checks are already in place) is understood.

Sometimes this will involve explaining the wider role of audit to key stakeholders. One CAE explains their approach:

> "We provide training sessions for new Audit Committee members on a range of topics such as risk, governance, and best practices in internal audit.
>
> They get an overview on best practices and our perspective on an optimal value-adding role for audit early on. I think it is often quite an eye-opener. You might have someone who sees auditors as the ones who do monitoring, re-inspecting or prevent fraud. However, I explain that this will not add as much value as the other roles we have started to take on.
>
> I also emphasize that the whole organization has a role to play to manage risks effectively, it can't all come down to me and my team."

Chris Baker (Technical Manager, IIA UK) provides this overview reflection:

> "There is a lack of understanding of what the three lines of defence is about. It can arise when internal audit has a reporting line to a finance director who thinks the role of audit is to do finance checks and hasn't recognized that internal audit has a much wider role.
>
> Through my External Quality Assessment (EQA) role, I'm seeing more and more organizations embracing improved co-ordination of roles, which is enabling internal audit to move outside of a narrow finance focus.
>
> However, there are pockets where internal audit has a traditional role due to stakeholder preferences."

In the chapter on audit planning, we will look at other ways to highlight audit's wider assurance role.

Actions for Internal Audit to consider:

- Use benchmarking to highlight the increasingly broader role of internal audit functions beyond just focusing on financial controls and compliance;
- Look at the audit role and examine areas where it could add value beyond financial controls and compliance.

## Promote Greater Clarity in Relation to Roles and Responsibilities in the First and Second Lines of Defence

The McKinsey RACI approach, or some other accountability mapping approach (e.g. swim lane mapping), can help clarify roles and accountabilities in the first, second and third lines of defence.

RACI accountability mapping techniques can be very fruitful when applied to key policy compliance activities. These activities are contained within the useful "Seven elements of an effective compliance programme", extensively in use in the US. It highlights key activity areas in relation to effective policy compliance, including:

- Drafting policies with appropriate understanding of legislative requirements and organizational adaptations;
- Agreeing detailed procedures and associated risk assessments;

- Preparing and delivering training and ensuring key staff have been trained and understand what is required;
- Agreeing which day to day activities will be monitored/supervised and by whom;
- Agreeing how any queries or exceptions should be managed and any associated onward reporting;
- Agreeing how any issues of concern will be investigated and any disciplinary issues managed;
- Agreeing who should carry out audits.

Using these activity areas (modified to fit the context) key stakeholders can be consulted to agree their respective roles, mapping this to a RACI (or RASCI–O) format (see Figure 8.4). Once this has been done accountability gaps and overlaps can be identified and resolved, after which it will then be possible to translate this into relevant job descriptions and targets.

In relation to strategic risks, there is often a nominated senior manager for each key risk. However, in practice, below this top line clarity there can often be uncertainties about roles and accountabilities at an operational management level. Once again, a RASCI mapping exercise can help to pin down who should be doing what in relation to key risks. This is especially useful when cross-functional processes are involved. After the first line accountabilities have been mapped and agreed, second and third line accountabilities can then be addressed.

Actions for Internal Audit to consider:

- Seek to drive clarity in relation to who is accountable for doing what in relation to compliance activities in the first, second and third lines of defence;
- Take a selection of key objectives or key risks and establish whether accountabilities have been clearly established at an operational level;
- In relation to key risk areas and key roles, establish whether key task requirements have been translated into job descriptions and personal targets.

### Audit should be Flexible on Occasions, but be Mindful of Becoming a Substitute

Whilst role clarity is a key ingredient of being an effective and efficient organization, it is important that internal audit does not adopt an overly

| Compliance accountability framework | 1st Line of Defence Business Area Management | | | 2nd Line of Defence Compliance & Policy Functions | | | 3rd Line of Defence Assurance Providers | | |
|---|---|---|---|---|---|---|---|---|---|
| | Unit Management team members | Unit General Manager | Regional / Divisional Management | Specialist Compliance Functions | Policy functions | Corporate functions | Internal Audit | Other Independent assurance | External audit |
| **Ethical Culture (Control Environment)** | | | | | | | | | |
| 1. Establish Roles & Responsibilities | | | | | | | | | |
| 2. Determine key Policies | | | | | | | | | |
| 3. Communicate key Policies | | | | | | | | | |
| **Delivery of procedures, training and action** | | | | | | | | | |
| 4. Maintenance of detailed standards and processes | | | | | | | | | |
| 5. Training – Development and delivery | | | | | | | | | |
| **Monitoring business as usual & Reporting issues upwards** | | | | | | | | | |
| 6. Monitoring of activities | | | | | | | | | |
| 7. Reporting issues, incidents or risks | | | | | | | | | |
| **Improvement actions and investigations** | | | | | | | | | |
| 8. Management of issues & corrective Actions | | | | | | | | | |
| 9. Investigations & Disciplinary Action | | | | | | | | | |
| **Audit & Assurance** | | | | | | | | | |
| 10. Independent assurance / audit | | | | | | | | | |

**Key:**
R Responsible
A Accountable
S Support
C Consulted
O Overview
I Informed

**Figure 8.4** Accountability mapping framework

rigid approach in terms of how it approaches its role, inhibiting its ability to help when needed. As one CAE said to me:

> "If there is a fire, you need to help put it out first."

Nicola Rimmer (former President of the IIA UK) provides the following observations on how audit might think about its role, in the context of the three lines of defence model:

> "Audit should not hide behind the three lines of defence model.
>
> If monitoring in the first and second lines is not happening you need to be saying it's not there at present and that's why we are going to do some work. You need to say to management 'We'll do this now, but you need to be building that capability and if that capability is not built quickly enough that will become a control issue.'
>
> This point is even more pertinent for UK financial services after the new IIA Financial Conduct Authority code for internal audit in UK financial services. The new code requires internal audit function to comment on the adequacy of the second line of defence."

In summary, auditors have the dilemma of doing supportive, monitoring work that stakeholders will value, but over the longer term the risk is that audit repeatedly takes on work that belongs to management, impairing its ability to deliver across a wider range of value-adding areas.

Actions for Internal Audit to consider:

- Don't rigidly adhere to the three lines of defence, be pragmatic when you can see an opportunity to help;
- Keep track of the amount of time audit is spending doing monitoring or other second line of defence work;
- Engage stakeholders to manage the amount of audit time spent on this work and to embed these tasks in other roles wherever possible.

## Ensure Stakeholders have a Realistic Understanding of Audit's Assurance Role

The good news for internal audit is that many stakeholders recognize that audit is an important – and often rare – source of reliable information about what is really going on in an organization.

However, the downside of this is that stakeholders can develop a dependence on what audit is saying to the point that they may have an over-optimistic impression of the amount of assurance they are getting. For example, stakeholders might think that 20 days of audit effort on a particular assignment gives them a much greater coverage of all of the associated risk areas than is actually the case.

It is vital that CAEs ensure that stakeholders have a proper appreciation of the amount of assurance they are giving, because otherwise:

- When things go wrong in an area that has been reviewed by audit it is much more difficult to understand why audit did not find the problem;
- It is much easier for stakeholders to imagine that audit is adequately resourced, when in fact it is often only auditing a portion of all of the risks in a given area.

At the most basic level, a conversation about the depth and breadth of assurance audit is able to give can start with a simple explanation along the lines of: "You do realize that in a 20-day assignment, three days are spent planning, five drafting the audit report, agreeing actions and then finalizing the reporting. As a result only 12 days, or 60% of each audit, is actually spent doing fieldwork. When you add on top of that the fact that there are over 500 transactions each month in the process under review, you should appreciate that our audit will have to focus on just the most important risk areas."

Actions for Internal Audit to consider:

- Identify whether there might be the possibility of stakeholders misunderstanding the depth and breadth of assignments that audit carries out (see Figure 8.5);
- Communicate clearly about depth and breadth in scoping and reporting so that misunderstandings cannot arise;
- Use the practical limitations of depth and breadth to emphasize the need for other lines of defence to manage risk and controls on a day-to-day basis.

## CONCLUDING REMARKS

The key dilemma facing audit functions is the need to operate in line with a defined and approved role and remit, whilst at the same time being appreciated for being flexible and pragmatic.

| Breadth<br><br>Depth | Narrow<br>(e.g. Selected risk) | Medium<br>(e.g. Selected risk areas) | Wide<br>(e.g. All risk areas) |
|---|---|---|---|
| **Low**<br>(e.g. Key control design) | Limited scope review | Key risks review | Comprehensive review |
| **Medium**<br>(e.g. Key control design & operation) | Limited scope audit | Key risks audit | Comprehensive audit |
| **High**<br>(e.g. Controls Operation in detail) | Focused investigation | Key risks investigation | Comprehensive investigation |

**Figure 8.5**    Assignment depth and breadth – options for audit

Some senior managers and board members are of a very firm view that audit is a service function and that it should not hide behind the three lines of defence model. The logic is that if there is an issue that needs to be addressed and resources are constrained, audit should step in. I agree that a rigid adherence to the three lines of defence model is not a value-adding thing to do – lean ways of working would say that being flexible and pragmatic may be what the external customer would expect, when this is needed.

However, taking an external customer perspective (as lean would encourage us to do), I think it is safe to say that they would expect most things in an organization to be done "right first time" and would question why audit should be routinely double-checking activities, very often some time after the event. I suspect they would think that having internal audit as a permanent substitute for "right first time" does not reflect an organizational culture that is committed to delivering value and reducing waste.

From this perspective, the three lines of defence model can be regarded as a framework that *downplays* the role of internal audit. It highlights what most people think on a day-to-day basis: that it is management and staff who run an organization, supported by specialist functions. If they do their job properly, the external customer would expect just the right amount of third line of defence assurance and advice to stop things going wrong, but no more than that. Furthermore, I think most external customers would expect a third line of defence to be free ranging, not locked into any specific tasks, so that it can turn to any important area before issues arise.

However, for internal audit to take up a more free-ranging, autonomous role, it may sometimes:

- Challenge the capability of internal audit management and staff to deliver advice and assurance across a range of (sometimes unfamiliar) areas; and
- Challenge the preconceptions of stakeholders who believe audit should have a more traditional role.

As a result, a shift in the role of internal audit function may require both a change in the mindset of some CAEs and senior audit managers, as well as a broader range of capabilities in the audit function. In addition, since there may be political sensitivities if internal audit takes up a more autonomous role, influencing key stakeholders and managing organizational politics becomes a key skill for CAEs who want to lead a progressive audit function, as will be discussed in Chapter 19.

---

## SUMMARY OF KEY POINTS FOR INTERNAL AUDIT

- Share the IIA publication "The three lines of defence in effective risk management and control" with senior management and the board;
- Establish whether there is clarity about accountabilities for compliance processes and key risks, *at an operational level below senior management*;
- Ensure the balance of audit time between compliance and financial controls is made transparent to stakeholders and engage in a debate about other value adding areas for audit to review;
- Keep track of the time audit spends on monitoring and agree ways of working so that audit does not become a substitute for this work for any length of time;
- Ensure senior managers and the board have a solid understanding of the depth and breadth of the assurances they are getting from audit.

RECOMMENDATIONS FOR SENIOR MANAGERS AND
THE BOARD

- Read the IIA publication: "The three lines of defence in effective risk management and control";
- Consider what you expect from line management and other policy functions in terms of their role in risk management and whether you are expecting audit to carry out monitoring on behalf of others, or assure it is being done by others;
- Clarify what accountability mapping has been carried out for key policy compliance and the management of key risks. This mapping should involve having more than just a top level name, but have been translated into operational terms;
- Understand the balance between audit's work in financial controls and compliance areas and other risk areas and weigh up what this means in terms of the value contribution audit can make;
- Ensure you are clear about the depth and breadth of assurances audit is able to give.

### References and Other Related Material of Interest

Audit Commission (2009) *Taking it on trust.* http://archive.audit-commission. gov.uk/auditcommission/subwebs/publications/studies/studyPDF/3523.pdf

Department of Health and Human Services, US Office of the Inspector General (2003) *OIG Compliance Program Guidance for Pharmaceutical Manufacturers.* http://oig.hhs.gov/authorities/docs/03/050503FRCPGPharmac.pdf

House of Lords, House of Commons (2013) *Changing banking for good: Report of the Parliamentary Commission on Banking Standards.* http://www.parliament. uk/documents/banking-commission/Banking-final-report-volume-i.pdf

Raisel, E. (1999) *The McKinsey Way: Using the techniques of the world's top strategic consultants to help you and your business.* New York: McGraw-Hill.

The Institute of Internal Auditors (IIA) (2013) IIA Position Paper: *The Three Lines of Defence in Effective Risk Management and Control* https://na.theiia. org/standards-guidance/Public_Documents/PP_The_Three_Lines_of_ Defense_in_Effective_Risk_Management_and_Control.pdf

# 9
# The Audit Plan: Taking a Value Approach

Since becoming a CAE in 2002, I have found internal audit planning to be an increasingly interesting and important topic. It is the process by which audit resources are allocated for the years or months ahead. It is also one of the key ways in which the budget for the audit function is decided. Over the course of my career as a CAE my approach to audit planning has evolved significantly, not least because of lean ways of working. When I began consulting and training I started running workshops looking at audit planning with CAEs and senior audit managers. Over nearly five years we examined issues such as:

- How should managers and stakeholders be engaged in the audit planning process?
- What is a good audit planning process, and how much time and effort should it take?
- How to determine whether the audit plan is a good one?

From a lean perspective these questions can be translated into:

- Who should be the suppliers and customers of the audit plan?
- What is a streamlined, waste free, audit-planning process?
- Is this the most value adding audit plan?

In relation to the last point, it is important to note that, from a lean perspective, the test is not simply "Is this a valuable audit plan?" – which is probably true of many audit plans – but rather: "Is this *the most value adding audit plan*, with an appropriate allocation of resources?"

This question links back to the discussion about the role of internal audit in the last chapter: Is the role of audit to provide assurance over a narrow range of control and compliance areas, or is the role of audit to provide assurance over the most important, most valuable areas? The lean perspective is clear: internal audit should focus its efforts on the most valuable areas, subject to the provisos that audit does not inappropriately duplicate other monitoring and assurance efforts and is able to offer something of value.

## COMMON PRACTICES AND IIA STANDARDS OF NOTE

Internal auditing standards require that the CAE must establish a risk-based plan consistent with the organization's goals as well as the risk appetite levels set by management and the board. These standards go on to say that if there are shortcomings in management's risk identification, the CAE must use their own judgment about key risk areas, taking into account input from senior management and the board. The standards also set out the need to review and adjust the audit plan in response to changes.

A common approach to developing the audit plan is therefore to develop an audit universe of key areas that could be audited and then to rank this universe on the basis of a range of criteria: such as risk, management interest, the time since the last audit and an assessment of the control environment as well as whether the work is required for regulatory compliance purposes. After this the draft audit plan will be submitted to senior management and the board for comment and approval.

## COMMON CHALLENGES & DILEMMAS

### Audit Planning Shortcomings Often Arise in EQA Reviews

With the common practice of ranking the areas within the audit universe using a range of detailed "risk based" criteria it might seem straightforward to meet the IIA standards. However, Chris Baker, (Technical

Manager, IIA UK) makes an important observation about audit plans that adopt this approach:

> "Although the institute is looking for a risk based approach to audit planning, I still see too many audit plans that have a tenuous link to the organizations' risks and I think this is one of the areas where internal auditors still aren't very good in demonstrating that they are looking at things that really matter."

The key point here is that *a risk ranking of a series of processes, locations and systems within an audit universe is not necessarily the same as being truly aligned to an organization's key value drivers and risks.*

Sarah Blackburn (Member of IIA Global Board and former AC Chair) provides additional insight from her experience of EQAs:

> "I've just been doing an EQA in an organization where the audit plan is split up into lots of pieces of work. I can see that the Audit Committee are very unhappy, and I am too, looking at it. Because they've got too little depth on things that are important, and even where they are looking at processes it appears that they are focusing on the stuff that's tickable.

> Every member of the audit committee that I've spoken to so far has basically said, well the audit reports don't really tell us anything. They're generally saying everything's all right because they are looking at the stuff that's easy to audit and they are not asking more fundamental questions in relation to the risk areas that are much more significant."

## What is the Problem with an Audit Universe?

Over the course of my career, my views on the importance of an audit universe have varied. The lean test is: "Does the audit universe deliver value to the external customer, or key internal stakeholders?" I think an audit universe can deliver real value, *provided* the time and effort spent on the audit universe is justified, in terms of the way it helps to focus the work of internal audit on the right areas.

When I explore the question of the balance between effort and payback, some auditors tell me that their audit universe and associated risk scoring is so complex only one or two members of the audit function know how to use it. In addition, several CAEs have confided to me that if they end up with a proposed plan using the audit universe and a risk scoring approach that does not accord with their expectations, they will adjust the risk weighting factors until they get the plan they were looking for!

My current assessment is that an audit universe can be a useful way of tracking what work has been done by audit and other functions, and can be a good way of considering potential future areas to look at (as long as it provides a complete and up to date picture of the risk assurance universe). However, my experience is that it is very easy to find risk weighting factors being applied to the audit universe that can be overly complex and time-consuming for the benefit obtained. Additionally, when I am told about the risk weighting factors that should be used there is no clear consensus what factors should be used and what weighting to apply to each factor.

## Should the Plan be Based on Gross or Net Risk?

Another key question is whether gross or net risks should be used as a basis for the audit plan. The use of net risks will normally take into account the things that are being done to manage risks, allowing the audit plan to focus on the things that management judge are not being managed so well.

However, an alternative view is that the use of net risk information can mislead audit, and that gross risks should be considered. The argument is that the use of net risk information may result in audit being steered away from certain areas "because management is confident that area is under control" when – in fact – this is not the case.

Another angle on the gross vs. net debate derives from the still quite common audit practice of asking management: "What do you think we should audit?"

At face value asking management for their views about which risks are of concern appears to be customer oriented (at least in terms of internal stakeholders), but the danger is that internal audit simply addresses known or suspected issues that may or may not deliver additional value or be key from an external customer perspective. In addition, auditing known areas of concern can:

- Result in audit largely confirming what management already know;
- Reinforce the notion that audit is a second line of defence function that should do checking for management, which may also dilute management's accountability for managing the risk;
- Limit the ability of internal audit to cover other areas.

This topic will be explored further in the next chapter on risk assurance, but it is worth noting that when I talk to CAEs about the gross vs. net dilemma there appears to be no clear consensus on the best approach to follow.

## A Focus on Cost Rather than Value

I have worked with audit functions in the UK public sector for several years and have a huge admiration for many colleagues working there. However, following the financial crisis, UK public spending is being severely reduced, leading to a significant amount of downsizing and consolidation across a range of functions, including internal audit. Such an environment can be a catalyst for adopting lean ways of working, and many of my early clients in lean auditing were from the UK public sector.

However, I have realized, from discussions with CAEs I have worked with, that an expectation of a number of stakeholders has simply been to reduce costs. The result has been, as one CAE described it, "a race to the bottom" to look for the bare minimum assurance, with the lowest cost staff.

Looked at from one perspective, members of the UK public might not want the luxury of expensive internal auditing that is doing nice-to-have work. However, the danger is that short-term savings are being achieved at the expense of more damaging and expensive issues arising later, particularly when staff cuts take hold, with a risk of a less effective safety net to catch things before they go wrong.

The risk of stripping audit back to the bare bones applies across all sectors when there are profit and cost pressures. However, it highlights an important choice: *when an organization is downsizing, should audit be the first function to be downsized because it is an overhead function, or the last, because it can act as the safety net to catch issues before they cause material damage*? I know my preference, so long as the audit function is looking at the right things!

## Staff Capability may be a Factor as Well

An additional area of challenge for some audit functions is the extent to which the audit plan may be affected by the skills of internal audit staff. Chris Baker (Technical Manager, IIA UK) offers the following perspective:

> "Sadly you'll find audit functions who are reluctant to tackle the most important areas, because they can be challenging to execute, and they feel as though they don't have the confidence or the ability to look at them."

There can therefore be a tendency to preserve the status quo. This can also be reinforced by keeping the audit universe relatively "tame", mostly focusing on processes, locations and systems, which are easier to audit and therefore do not highlight staff capability shortcomings. However, auditing less important areas reinforces the notion that audit is essentially a lower grade checking function, which makes it less easy to attract, and to justify paying for, higher quality staff.

All the while big value issues and key emerging risks may be unfolding above (or below) the assurance radar screen, which may result in audit failing to deliver the value adding contribution it could.

A concern I hear from audit staff is that working on key risks will be a stretch for their skills, so those assignments may not be very effective or efficient. I personally think these difficulties can be managed, but recognize that this shift towards true risk based assurance can be challenging.

## RECOMMENDED PRACTICES

The lean perspective on audit planning aligns very closely with key IIA requirements. In particular, to be confident of a flow of value from the audit planning process, the audit service must engage with senior management and the board in relation to the key value drivers of the organization and the risks that might impact their delivery. Engagement by audit should encourage a clear prioritization of stakeholder needs, factoring in the likely perspective of external customers as well, where possible.

Any audit universe should strictly be a means to an end. It may add value to key internal stakeholders or external customers if it:

- Keeps track of past work (internal audit's own work and others);
- Ensures there are no important blind spots;
- Supports senior management and board engagement (by showing all the areas to be considered);
- Is not overly costly in terms of time or effort for the benefits gained.

Most of all, lean disciplines would be concerned if any audit universe was simply concerned with systems, processes and locations. Lean would demand, in addition, that it was also closely aligned to:

- An up-to-date assessment of value drivers, and key initiatives;
- Material regulatory requirements and obligations;
- External customer imperatives (such as product and service quality and timeliness).

To meet these requirements it is important that there is a timely and reliable flow of information to the audit function, so all key issues can be explicitly borne in mind when developing the audit plan.

Actions for internal audit to consider:

- Is the time and effort spent on any audit universe scoring clearly worth it?
- Is it possible to *clearly see* value drivers, key risks, initiatives and customer imperatives etc. within the audit universe?

## Prioritize the Audit Plan, and Focus on Value

Chris Baker (Technical Manager, IIA UK) provides an important insight:

"When I do an EQA I always look at audit planning, to begin with, to try to get a feel for where the internal audit function sits. If I can see the audit team getting involved with senior stakeholders and what's on their agenda, and looking at how well risk management has been designed, and whether risk management processes are being applied and are working, and building an audit plan from this that has a clear linkage to key risks, then it is highly likely the rest of the EQA is going to be positive.

If there is a disconnect from senior management, or the risk management process, or key organizational priorities and risks, there is likelihood that other shortcomings will follow."

Here is advice from Norman Marks (GRC thought leader):

"Consider what is on the agenda of the Board. And ask: are you addressing all the issues that arise from, or contribute to, the success of the Board in managing these agenda items?

What are you doing that's not on their agenda and if it's not on the agenda why the devil are you doing it?

Of course it's also sensible to look at any issues that should be on their agenda but are not, but you need to be clear that they are of importance."

Jonathan Kidd (Chief Audit Executive for the UK Met Office) explains what his function is doing:

"Increasingly we are moving towards the more strategic view where the senior managers and the audit committee appreciate the limited resource we have and the opportunity cost of not positioning the audit function to support the delivery of strategic priorities.

Everything that we do, the whole way we present what we do is now aligned with what the organization is trying to achieve."

Actions for Internal Audit to consider:

- Create a planning process that clearly is intended to deliver the maximum value add;
- Establish a clear, transparent link between key value and risk areas and the audit plan.

## Create a Streamlined Planning Process

I well recall that when we looked at the audit planning process when I was CAE, we had a number of auditors engaged in the audit planning process. This gave us a lot of insight into what we could look at, but risked taking up a lot of time and resource (within audit as well as management). We clarified and streamlined this process, which also helped us ensure we did not disappoint middle managers who might make suggestions for audit work, which we could not deliver due to having only finite resources.

Greg Coleman (Corporate Assurance Director, ITG) explains his approach to engaging internal clients and stakeholders in a focused and efficient way:

"We have a reasonably structured audit planning approach where we start with the strategic plan from the organization and look at what that means in terms of new initiatives and related risks over the next year or two.

We then hold one on one meetings with senior management to talk about key risk areas and consider what other functions provide assurance. But then to save time, and maximize stakeholder insights we hold a couple of workshops to prioritize key risks and validate assurances. This is done with members of the audit team combined with other colleagues from key functions, such as legal, finance, health & safety, IT and corporate affairs. After doing this we obtain sign off of the plan from senior management and the audit committee."

Actions for Internal Audit to consider:

- Ensure there is a simple process map of the audit planning process and ensure the audit function and key stakeholders understand how it works;
- Look out for a planning process that consumes a lot of audit resource and sets unhelpful expectations within management;
- In addition to one-to-one meetings, consider workshops with key contacts as a way of validating risks and assurances.

## Take a Gross Risk Perspective (at Least at the Start)

Here is advice from Phil Gerrard (CAE, Rolls-Royce):

"You need to understand what are the big gross risks because if they are not featuring on the key, or top risks, the inference is that they are being managed down to a relatively low likelihood or a more acceptable impact. That may be valid, but the impact could be still significant if mismanaged. So whilst they no longer look like top priorities, there are lots of assumptions underpinning that.

The role of audit has to be to challenge the quality of the mitigation that's gone into that risk assessment."

Sarah Blackburn (Member, IIA Global Board) endorses this view:

"I believe risks should be addressed by internal audit at the inherent level. My logic is as follows: Whilst I'm glad to hear the organization thinks it has got good controls over some areas, I still want someone to take a look that this is indeed true from time to time."

Wee Hock Kee (former President of the IIA Malaysia and a former colleague of mine at AstraZeneca) comments:

"I think we have a duty to move up the value chain, not only looking at issues from a control perspective, but increasingly trying to tie things back to the risk management and the governance framework."

Actions for Internal Audit to consider:

- Pay close attention to the way the planning process weights gross vs. net risks; ensure gross risks are not inadvertently downplayed;
- Pay close attention to "black swan" risks that have a high impact and a low likelihood; these are often discounted in audit planning processes.

## Upgrade the Audit Universe, but Don't Necessarily Let it Drive the Plan

As discussed earlier, all too often an audit universe does not really align with key organizational risks and value drivers. My advice is to look at how it can be expanded to better capture all of the key priorities, major projects and key risk areas that matter. Greg Coleman (CAE, ITG) explains the outcome of work on the audit planning process that incorporates lean principles:

> "We now have a more advanced audit universe, that includes not just the locations but the key processes within the locations, as well as key third parties we trade with, a range of IT risk areas as well as key projects and other risk areas. It is significantly bigger than it was in the past and better captures the total risk assurance dimensions of the group.
>
> However, we actually drive the audit plan by focusing on organizational priorities and key risks and use the audit universe to complement this rather than to drive it."

The power of having a good audit universe is that it can help inform a discussion with senior management and the board about the amount of coverage that internal audit is able to provide against key areas. In addition, if the audit function is required to deliver an opinion on the overall effectiveness of GRC activities in an organization, a robust risk assurance universe or audit universe can be a very helpful tool to ensure no material gaps in coverage – by either audit or other assurance providers.

Norman Marks (GRC thought leader) explains:

> "It's about stepping back and asking what are the key risks that we should be considering, if not actually addressing. I call these the risks that matter.
>
> I believe that top executives and board should have confidence that through internal audit assurance over the management of key risks, they

can assume that everything is working right in terms of managing their more significant risks, unless they're told otherwise."

Actions for Internal Audit to consider:

- Does the current audit universe solely concentrate on processes, systems and locations? If so, look at ways to upgrade this to better reflect what the key risk assurance areas should be (e.g. latest objectives and projects);
- Use an expanded audit universe to better understand the completeness of the overall risk assurance picture and coverage by audit.

## Gather a Picture of Current Performance as well as Issues, Incidents, "Near Misses" and External Intelligence

A vitally important part of having a value add focus is to look at the performance management information and progress against key value drivers, as well as:

- Other performance metrics (e.g. customer satisfaction levels);
- Incidents (e.g. product defects or recalls);
- Near misses (e.g. a systems interruption);
- Other external data of interest (e.g. developments in a significant market or recent regulatory fines or other issues of note externally).

Gathering a range of information about key value related issues in a disciplined manner can provide huge insights into risk assessments and can also be invaluable when considering potential areas for audit attention.

Nancy Haig (Chief Audit Executive for a global consulting firm) explains the approach of her audit team:

> "We also are continuously monitoring the external environment. We're doing a lot of research – paying attention to what's going on outside, what might have gone wrong elsewhere, so we can bring that to the table ourselves, and we can present those ideas back, both for management attention, and for consideration in our plan."

Some organizations, especially in financial services, make considerable use of data analytics as a means of guiding the work of audit.

For others, the first step is simply to pull together the basics around all key issues and incidents (over and above past internal audit findings and open internal audit issues), since these can provide warning signs of potential value destruction.

Actions for Internal Audit to consider:

• Consider how performance information, incidents and near misses (as well as other audit and regulatory reviews) can give insights to areas of actual or potential value creation and value destruction;
• Consider how this information should be factored into the audit planning process (and by extension the risk management process);
• Determine whether there is a disciplined approach to gathering relevant external intelligence (e.g. regulatory developments, fines or other news stories) that may shed light on organizational risks.

### Examine Carefully Which Issues will Really Impact Value and the External Customer

There has been some excellent research over a number of years in relation to how value is created and also the key reasons that value is destroyed.

Obviously the reasons for value destruction are numerous and include failings in the management of "traditional" risk areas, such as financial, regulatory and operational. However, according to a range of studies (including research by Booz & Company in 2013), the largest source of value destruction is often cited to be the mismanagement of strategic risks, such as the failure to adjust to changing customer demands, the failure to effectively integrate a new acquisition, or the mismanagement of reputational risk.

Taking the perspective of adding value, or protecting value from being destroyed, if the mismanagement of strategic risks results in, say, 60-80% of the major instances of value destruction, why wouldn't audit resource be allocated to ensure these risks are assured in a similar proportion?

Actions for Internal Audit to consider:

• Examine/research the main reasons for value destruction or reputational damage of relevance to your organization (see Figure 9.1);
• Consider the allocation of audit resource across key risk areas and the reasons for any disconnect between these proportions and actual audit coverage in the audit plan.

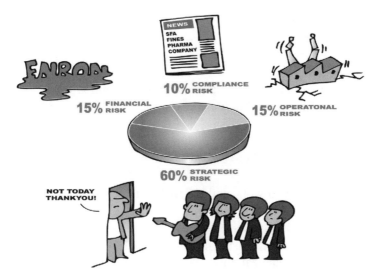

**Figure 9.1**    Key sources of value destruction (illustrative)

## Gain Inspiration from the Committee on Internal Audit Guidance for Financial Services in the UK

Another excellent source of inspiration for a more value added approach to audit planning has come from the "Committee on Internal Audit Guidance in Financial services." It was set up to consider the lessons for UK internal audit functions in the aftermath of the financial crisis of 2007–2008. Recommendations were issued in final form in July 2013, and have been supported by the UK Financial Conduct Authority, representing a new benchmark for internal audit functions in the financial services sector in the UK.

Although the recommendations focus on financial services, they are actually very interesting for internal audit in other sectors. In particular, the recommendations get to the heart of a number of big issues around value. Of particular relevance are the recommendations which say that internal audit functions should consider within their scope:

- The design and effectiveness of governance structures and processes;
- The strategic and management information presented to the board;
- Risk appetite and control culture;

- Key corporate events;
- Risks of poor customer outcomes.

These recommendations closely align with the key value considerations for many organizations (note the explicit mention of the external customer!). Also consider how many conventional audit universe models will miss these areas.

Actions for Internal Audit to consider:

- Whether or not you work within UK Financial Services, familiarize yourself with the recommendations of the UK Committee for Internal Audit guidance in Financial Services;
- Consider how the areas listed in that guidance could impact the value issues for your organization;
- Address any key gaps in the audit universe and audit plan (or assurance from other sources).

### Use Audit Planning to Drive Additional Value Add Beyond the Audit Plan

One of the key things I learned as a CAE was *how much value can be obtained from the audit planning process* over and above the creation of the audit plan itself. For example, a good planning process can also deliver:

- A deeper and more up-to-date understanding of senior management and board perspectives in relation to key and emerging risks;
- An understanding about perceptions around risk appetite and the need for assurances, including differences in perceptions on risk appetite between key stakeholders and questions about assurance roles and responsibilities;
- An opportunity to reflect on themes in relation to past audit findings, alongside other issues, to consider whether cultural issues may be causing problems.

Consequently, it can be beneficial to use the audit planning process to:

- Properly engage all key senior managers and relevant board members in the audit plan, and demonstrate "spin off" benefits in the process itself;

- Gain perspectives in relation to the risk register and risk management process (e.g. "A number of key stakeholders are all worried about a particular risk, or an aspect of a key risk, but the risk they highlight doesn't really feature in the latest risk assessment");
- Facilitate deeper discussions about risk appetite and/or current assurances;
- Build closer relations with key stakeholders.

Actions for Internal Audit to consider:

- Consider the added value that the planning process itself is delivering over and above the audit plan;
- Make appropriate adjustments to the audit planning process paying particular attention to the engagement of key stakeholders;
- Be sure to feedback to stakeholders to ensure that the audit planning process is seen to add value in its own right.

## CONCLUDING REMARKS

The dilemma facing most audit functions is the need to develop a systematic and disciplined framework within which to make judgments about what should be audited over the course of one or several years, whilst at the same time staying in contact with the latest challenges in the organization.

Taking a lean perspective, I do not think there is one "best" process for progressive, value adding audit planning. This can be for a whole host of different reasons; past history, stakeholder interests, the complexity of the risk context, the process and systems environment and the complexity of the organization and assurance provision.

However, the clear focus for any lean, value-adding approach to the audit plan is *that it should aim to deliver the maximum value*. As a result, whatever planning approach is adopted, lean encourages us to seek, as much as possible, a strong, logical and highly transparent link between key risks and value drivers and the plan (in that order), so that assumptions can be challenged or varied easily. Anything that comes across as a "black art" (with many data entries and weighting factors) runs the risk of losing that connection, as well as being both time consuming and prone to error, or override, when it gives the "wrong answer!"

---

**SUMMARY OF KEY POINTS FOR INTERNAL AUDIT**

- Discuss as an audit function whether the audit plan is delivering the maximum added value. If not, which areas add the most value and which the least?
- Map out the current planning process – is the connection with risk and value add direct enough? – and consider streamlining the steps (through the use of workshops, etc.);
- Consider what the external customer would want audit to look at and also look at the report by the Committee for Internal Audit guidance in Financial services;
- Consider whether business intelligence, key performance and key risk indicators feature strongly enough in the planning process;
- Clarify the current role of the audit universe, is it aligned closely enough to the risk assurance universe and key value priorities of the organization?
- Discuss whether senior management and board level engagement is adequate and whether "spin off" benefits in relation to the risk and assurance processes are identified and shared.

---

**RECOMMENDATIONS FOR SENIOR MANAGERS AND THE BOARD**

- Ask the CAE to explain the audit planning process and whether it has been reviewed independently;
- Ask the CAE to confirm how complete their audit universe is and how it relates to the business strategy, key objectives and key risks;
- Read the report by the Committee on Internal Audit Guidance in Financial services in the UK, there are some very interesting areas to consider, whether or not an organization is in UK Financial Services;
- Clarify what research has been done on the sources of value add/ value destruction of relevance to the organization;
- Ask the CAE to advise what their consultations with board members and senior managers suggest in terms of:
  - Different perceptions of risk and risk appetite;
  - The quality of the risk management process;
  - Views in relation to the role of internal audit.

## References and Other Related Material of Interest

Booz & Co. (2012) *The root causes of value destruction – how strategic resiliency can help.* http://www.strategyand.pwc.com/media/file/Strategyand_The-Root-Causes-of-Value-Destruction.pdf

PricewaterhouseCoopers (2008) *An opportunity for transformation: How internal audit helps contribute to shareholder value.* https://www.pwc.com/en_US/us/internal-audit/assets/internal_audit_shareholder_value.pdf

# 10
# Factoring in Risk Assurance in the Audit Plan

Having oriented the audit plan clearly towards adding value, a fundamental question is how to ensure that the audit plan takes into account the assurance activity that is already, or should be, taking place in order to avoid waste (Muda).

## COMMON PRACTICES AND IIA STANDARDS OF NOTE

IIA standard 2050 discusses the need for audit to coordinate its activities with others to ensure proper coverage and minimize the duplication of efforts. This ties very closely to lean principles. The IIA practice advisory on Assurance Mapping goes on to explain that "assurance from line management is fundamental" – which confirms and reinforces the point about the importance of having three lines of defence operating effectively in order to properly manage risks.

## COMMON CHALLENGES & DILEMMAS

### Auditing Known or Suspected Issues

In the last two chapters I have explored issues around the role of internal audit and also the risk factors that should be considered when developing the audit plan (and specifically whether to focus on gross or net risks). In addition, there is an assurance perspective to consider. Here are the reflections of an experienced senior audit manager:

> "If it's transparent that the right people are making the right decisions on a problem area and there's an action plan with a clear target date, what value are you going to add by doing an audit? They know it's a problem!"

One CAE commented:

> "If everybody acknowledges there are issues, and these are being worked on, what's the point of going to do an audit? It would be borrowing their watch to tell them the time, to confirm what they already know and are addressing, with zero added value."

I recall a conversation with a regional finance director about the possibility of auditing an overseas unit where there were some questions over what was going on. It was a location that was borderline for audit attention and there was no hard evidence of a problem (in fact there was no problem as far as we can tell several years on).

Wanting to be helpful, but being mindful of resources, I suggested that audit do some work jointly with a member of his finance team, leveraging their knowledge and reducing the resource from audit, and providing an assurance message together. However, the regional finance director's response was not as appreciative as I had hoped. In fact, he said: "No, let's leave it, it's not important enough for me to allocate one of my staff members to look at it, they are too busy on business issues!"

This was a wake up call for me, raising the question: how often is audit doing work because it is seen to be a free resource, rather than because what it does is felt to be really valuable?!

## Uncertainty about Risk Assurance Roles

In my experience many audit plans *implicitly* take into account the fact that there may be other compliance or assurance functions covering key risks when they are doing their audit planning. Thus, if there is a health and safety function, many internal audit functions will not cover this area in their audit plan. This may be a sensible judgment; however, a relatively informal approach to taking other assurances into account runs the risk of making assumptions about coverage by other functions that could lead to gaps or overlaps.

## Considering the Motivations behind Assurance Requests

One CAE shared the following story with me:

> "A few years ago we were asked to carry out a learning review of a big systems project. Several functions were involved, the business, IT and a third party outsource provider. The request came from a senior business manager who was responsible for the business end of the project. We knew he was not happy with what had happened, cost overruns and the like, which he felt was due to failings by the IT function and the third party provider.
>
> So we did the learning review and we found that whilst there were lessons to be taken on board on the IT side of the project, there were just as many lessons for business management, including the way they had not made their expectations known, as well as the way they had not delivered what was needed to IT on time. Our report set this out, highlighting lessons for all sides, in a very measured and balanced way – we thought.
>
> And then in the audit closing meeting and subsequent feedback process we got terrible feedback from the business manager, which I then followed up. I said: 'What's the problem? You wanted this review!', and the response was: 'Yes, I requested the review, but I was expecting you to focus on the weaknesses of the IT function, not my department!'
>
> It struck me that we knew that there was a political angle to this assignment, using audit to 'hit' another department. This was the value the manager was really looking for. However, we had naively assumed that doing a balanced review, in accordance with the IIA standards, would be sufficient to make him happy."

On hearing this story at a lean auditing workshop in Europe, one CAE confided to me that they suspected that many of the audit assignments they had recently been given by their new Chief Executive were, effectively, assignments targeted at senior leaders the Chief Executive did not rate, to see if there was anything that could be found to hasten their departure!

Again we have a dilemma for audit – at face value meeting the needs and expectations of stakeholders might be seen to add value, but if these needs and expectations are grounded on a political agenda, or some other irrational view of added value, audit will find itself in difficulty.

## RECOMMENDED PRACTICES

Taking the perspective of the external customer, lean ways of working demand disciplined co-ordination and communication between all functions, including management, risk, compliance and other assurance functions (including internal audit), since there is likely to be waste if one function looks at an area that has been recently checked by another. Indeed, taking an external customer view would go beyond that, looking to understand how much assurance has been provided, and what were the results of that work, in order to judge what additonal work (if any) should now be done.

In addition, lean also reminds us that simply carrying out assignments because some senior stakeholders want an area to be looked at may not always be in line with what the external customer would value (especially if we do not properly understand the motivations behind the request).

### Have a Clear Process for Working through What to Do in Relation to Known or Suspected Issues

One CAE explains:

> "If there is a known issue, it is better to require that management should put mitigating plans in place first, and then audit the area when the remediation is supposed to have been implemented."

A fundamental mindset in progressive, value-adding auditing is to be interested in management concerns and issues, but not to volunteer an assignment without being clear what value, specifically, is going to be added.

Rania Bejjani (CAE, Colt Group) explains:

> "I aim for conversation and dialogue with the business about their needs. I want to know why do they want audit to do an assignment? How come this is so important for them? How does this link to the strategic objectives and key risks of the business? What are their concerns? What is already being done? What can they do themselves? What is the impact to the business? How will this assignment add value to them and to the business as a whole?

> The aim is to really understand what is going on, the linkage to the bigger picture and what is needed. As you have these conversations you can uncover the wider context and interdependencies, a root cause or

explanation or rationale for either doing or not doing an assignment. You might even uncover an alternative course of action.

When you adopt this sort of approach you avoid assignments that don't really matter or serve the business. In addition, the assignments you do take on should come up with some very interesting findings. Unless we are able to add value, there is no point in doing the work."

Thus, *if there is a known issue*, audit can ask: "Given you know there is an issue, what should we really do? If you are unsure about what remediation is needed, perhaps we can offer some advice about what should be done, but we won't audit the issue, because you know it's a problem already."

Of course, sometimes audit can add value by looking into known issues, perhaps by looking into root causes, the possibility of other spin off issues, or the quality of action plans underway. However audit should always be asking why management cannot do this for themselves, and be very clear what the purpose of audit's involvement actually is.

*If management suspect something might be a problem*, but are not certain, then a joint audit approach can be a good option since it makes the most of management expertise and also reduces the resource audit needs to commit. Another argument for this approach was given to me by a CAE who said: "Sometimes you need to ask management to put some 'skin in the game' to make sure you are not being given unimportant work to do."

If there is a general belief from management that internal audit should audit known issues, or investigate suspected issues, the CAE should consider what this signifies in cultural terms. One perspective I hear from some auditors is: "Management value us getting involved in things," but lean encourages us to probe what sort of value this is delivering. If it is about getting a free resource, or doing their job for them, that may not increase the value add from audit in the eyes of the external customer. In addition, the greatest risk is that internal audit involvement in these sorts of issues perpetuates a culture in which internal audit takes over the monitoring role to check controls and propose improvement actions, not management.

To illustrate the importance of thinking from an assurance perspective when developing the audit plan, here is another story. One of my clients was being asked to carry out a lot of anti-fraud work in their audit plan. As we discussed this, the CAE realized that underlying this interest in lots of anti-fraud work by audit was a senior management mindset that regarded the audit function as having the prime responsibility for fraud prevention. I offered some support around the three lines of defence model and the CAE then carried out an exercise in accountability mapping for fraud, and thereafter a series of education workshops for managers.

A year later a major fraud arose and the CAE remarked to me that he was very pleased we had done what we had done the year before:

> "If we hadn't done anything to re-educate management around what it really takes to prevent frauds, I am sure that we would have got the blame for what went wrong. As it was, there was a much better debate about processes in finance and purchasing, and the lessons for them. The realization was that it has to be these first and second line functions with the prime fraud prevention role. After all, they are the ones who are most likely to be able to stop a fraudulent or duplicate payment being made, not internal audit."

I have also heard CAEs explain that senior management or the board sometimes want them to look at an issue because: "they don't think the manager is capable of checking this thoroughly" (either because of resource constraints or capability shortcomings) or "they don't trust the manager of that area". However, if any of these points is true, it reveals a much deeper problem in the overall control environment than the specific issue that was of original concern!

I hope that these stories illustrate the power of approaching the audit plan with a lean perspective, namely:

- The need to deliver value to the customer;
- Having a clear and appropriate audit role;
- Avoiding waste.

Adopting a value add, assurance mindset when developing the audit plan may rapidly result in audit having a range of challenging conversations with stakeholders. However, these conversations need to take place if audit is to start to change old-fashioned stakeholder mindsets about the role of audit. In my experience step-by-step change may be all that is possible from year to year. But by clearly communicating a desire to add value and eliminate waste, alongside an understanding of key stakeholder concerns and needs, a shift in the mindset of senior stakeholders can be achieved over a period of time, and in turn a reappraisal of the optimal role for audit.

Actions for Internal Audit to consider:

- When discussing potential assignments always explore the question of the value that audit's work will provide;
- Seek to ensure that the root causes for assignment requests are clear and address any misunderstandings about the role of audit;
- Pay close attention to clues about motivations and deeper political and cultural issues that may be driving requests for audit to carry out particular assignments.

## Explicitly Address Risk Assurance in the Audit Plan

I first started working on risk assurance mapping as a CAE at AstraZeneca in 2003, so by the time we started working on lean auditing in 2005–6, we were already very mindful of the power of these techniques and integrated them into our ways of working.

In both the lean auditing and assurance mapping workshops that I run, I emphasize the benefits that can be obtained by adopting a risk assurance approach to audit planning. Indeed, this is one of the reasons my company has the name "Risk & Assurance Insights." In 2012 the book *Combined Assurance* by Gerrit Sarens et al. makes the suggestion that "Combined assurance should drive the audit plan." I fully agree with their analysis and, fortunately, there is already a growing body of practice in this field. Here are some of the advocates.

Leigh Flanigan, (CAE, CSIRO, Australia):

"I always emphasize to management that internal audit is not the only provider of assurance; there are many other parts of the organization and possible sources of assurance. I highlight that to them, but also work with management to help them better understand their role in providing assurance."

Ivan Butler (CAE, Denbighshire County Council):

"In the past we developed a plan using the audit universe. Now our assurance framework is the number one ingredient."

Nancy Haig (CAE, global consulting firm):

"If we are talking about lean and adding value, make sure that you're looking at things holistically. Where are the key risks? Are they IT? Are they compliance? Are they financial? Are they environmental or health and safety?

Then consider who's covering these risks. We may find, for example, that assurance over stock levels has been covered by external auditors. Or the IT department or tax department are performing monitoring functions. So it's always a matter of looking at where risks are and determining if somebody else is already validating that those controls are working and if so, moving to the risks where there is no or limited coverage from elsewhere.

A big part of being lean is making sure you don't do repetitive or redundant work without being clear as to why."

(See Figure 10.1).

The "Taking it on trust" report by the UK Audit Commission has some excellent guidance on the attributes of robust assurance, so that over-optimistic assurances are not assumed. A case study based

**Figure 10.1**   A vital ingredient for audit success: joining up the assurance jigsaw

on work by the Plymouth Hospitals NHS Trust considers factors such as:

• The reporting lines of any reviewer;
• The frequency and timeliness of reviews;
• The scope of any reviews (considering depth and breadth);
• The skills of reviewers;
• The robustness of action plans and whether remediation is tracked.

Other attributes of importance in my experience include the quality of planning assurance assignments, the need to focus assignments on a risk basis, the robustness of onward reporting and issue escalation and the extent of coverage compared to the relevant risk universe.

Actions for Internal Audit to consider:

• Read the IIA practice guidance 2050–2 on assurance mapping;
• Always be explicit about other assurances when developing the internal audit plan;
• Read "Taking it on trust", alongside the case studies featured so that a balanced assessment of the *amount of assurance* that is being provided by others can be considered.

## Recognize the Power of Direct Assurance or Other Sources of Independent Assurance

Bringing together the earlier discussions about roles alongside assurance mapping, two other progressive practices are worthy of note: direct assurance or other independent assurance.

Thus, if cloud computing is raised as an issue that could be audited, a more traditional approach is simply to carry out an audit assignment to look into this area. However, a more progressive, assurance-based way of addressing the question could be to agree that the Chief Information Officer (CIO), or equivalent, should update senior management and the board on what is being done in relation to cloud computing. This can be achieved by requesting a report from the CIO, or by agreeing that the CIO should make a presentation to senior stakeholders about what is being done. Internal audit could even offer to help the CIO consider the likely risk areas and assurance questions that are likely to be of most concern to key stakeholders.

The benefits of the direct assurance approach are:

• Senior stakeholders obtain direct assurance from the person accountable for the risk on a timely basis;
• The person accountable for the risk recognizes this is an important
  area because of the senior management and/or board interest;
• Any improvements needed may be identified and put in place very
  quickly, sometimes even during the process of preparing for the senior management and board update;
• Limited audit resource is needed;
• Any follow-up or follow-on work required to be done by audit in
  that area has a much better chance of being focused on areas of most
  importance, taking into account what has been presented, as well as
  the risk appetite of key stakeholders.

Other direct assurance alternatives include getting direct input from
purchasing in relation to the screening of third party suppliers, or direct
input from compliance functions in industries such as utilities, financial
services and pharmaceuticals.

I have also seen third parties being brought in to provide an assurance
perspective on technical and emerging risk areas where audit would
have limited skill capability to look at the area.

Nancy Haig (CAE, global consulting firm) sums up the approach I
am advocating:

> "I think that internal audit can be the catalyst for ensuring that the appro-
> priate amount of assurance work is being done by different functions."

Actions for Internal Audit to consider:

• During the audit planning process consider instances where direct assurance might be a preferable first step, rather than just an audit assignment;
• Be prepared to help the person accountable for providing the direct
  assurance with advice on the key areas that must be addressed;
• Consider follow-up or follow-on assignments by audit to test key
  areas of concern after any direct assurance inputs.

## CONCLUDING REMARKS

The dilemma facing many audit functions during audit planning is to make
the choice between looking at known issues – which have management

and stakeholder support – and looking at other areas – which challenges stakeholders' current understanding of risks. Alongside this is the need to maintain relationships and also keep the audit team busy!

It is understandable, therefore, that audit should be sympathetic about looking at areas management are concerned about; auditors need to be pragmatic and flexible about the needs of internal stakeholders. However, a lean audit mindset challenges any cosy status quo in which audit is guaranteed work by doing essentially management's routine monitoring or checking. The danger is this approach does not really offer that much value add to the organization overall, and also prevents audit from looking at the most important value issues in the organization.

Fortunately, I am seeing increasing signs that the old ways are starting to change, supported by an increasing awareness of the IIA guidance on the three lines of defence and the latest guidance for UK financial services internal auditing. Of course, there is a place for looking at traditional areas, such as financial controls and compliance. However, thinking about assurance roles and responsibilities encourages others to take up their roles in routine monitoring and, hopefully, to increasingly be seen to be providing reliable assurance. The result of a greater assurance role from management and other functions is that internal audit is able to work across a range of non-standard risk areas, making a greater contribution to the larger risk assurance picture where much more value is at stake. Phil Gerrard (CAE, Rolls-Royce) offers this final reflection:

> "Risk assurance based planning is key in allocating your resources. It's key as a CAE to understand your positioning in the three lines of defence model, and to challenge and debate this with the respective management teams.

> To allocate resources where assurance is limited and risk is highest."

---

### SUMMARY OF KEY POINTS FOR INTERNAL AUDIT

- Clarify the value (or not) of auditing known or suspected issues;
- Encourage the use of getting direct assurance by management and other functions to reinforce their accountability for risk and control;
- Consider carrying out joint assurance assignments with management and other functions to ensure they have some "skin in the game";
- Be explicit in the audit plan about the assurance role of management and other functions.

---

**RECOMMENDATIONS FOR SENIOR MANAGERS AND THE BOARD**

• Clarify the portion of the audit plan that is spent on auditing issues that are already known or suspected;
• Encourage proper ownership of risks and controls by other functions, seeking up-to-date reports and direct assurances from them;
• Understand how much work audit does in collaboration with other functions;
• Request an assurance map as part of the planning process, but recognize this may take time to develop.

---

### References and Other Related Material of Interest

Audit Commission (2009) *Taking it on trust.* http://archive.audit-commission. gov.uk/auditcommission/subwebs/publications/studies/studyPDF/3523.pdf

Sarens, G., Decaux, L. & Lenz, R. (2012) *Combined Assurance: Case Studies on a Holistic Approach to Organizational Governance* (ebook). The IIA Research Foundation.

The Institute of Internal Auditors (IIA) UK Chartered Institute of Internal Auditors (2009) *Practice advisory 2050–2: Assurance Maps.* https://global. theiia.org/standards-guidance/recommended-guidance/pages/practice-advisories.aspx

# 11
# Considering the Allocation of Resources to Optimize Value Add

In the past two chapters on audit planning I have explained:

- The importance of taking a value approach to the audit plan; and
- The importance of thinking about risk assurance (to avoid waste).

However, as mentioned earlier, lean ways of working do not simply encourage audit to have a value-adding plan, but push audit to consider *the most value-adding plan in relation to an optimal amount of resources.*

Consequently, this chapter explores in further detail the ways to look at the allocation of resources in the audit plan in order to consider what is the best possible plan. This leads on to another important topic: how to present the audit plan to key stakeholders so that:

- Key choices in relation to the allocation of resources are understood (e.g. between activity areas, key objectives and key risks);
- Key stakeholders understand how any different needs and interests have been addressed in the plan (e.g. the balance between advice and assurance within the plan);
- The impact of resourcing constraints is crystal clear.

## COMMON PRACTICES AND IIA STANDARDS OF NOTE

The IIA sets out (in IIA standard 2010 C1) that an internal audit function can consider consulting assignments based on their potential to improve risk management, add value and improve the organization. The standards explain that agreed consulting assignments should be included in the audit plan.

IIA standards also explain that the CAE should communicate the plan and resource requirements and obtain sign off from the board and senior management, including any interim changes needed.

## COMMON CHALLENGES & DILEMMAS

### Getting the Right Balance between Assurance and Advisory Assignments

At many of the workshops I run I carry out a poll concerning the portion of audit time that is allocated to advisory assignments. On rare occasions no advisory work is done (for example, when the audit service is outsourced, or a large portion of mandated assignments dominates the plan). However, more generally – and I have polled many hundreds of auditors – the portion of audit resource spent on advisory assignments typically ranges between 5% and 25%. The reasons for the differences in the proportion of audit resources spent between assurance and advice seems to be linked to a range of factors: historic, cultural, the business context and stakeholder preferences.

However, a common thing I hear is that board members are keen to get the maximum amount of assurance from audit, and as a result CAEs feel they have limited scope to do much advisory work. So, some CAEs do not explicitly state what the balance is between assurance and advisory work in their plan. Moreover, other CAEs do not even explicitly budget for advisory work and instead "squeeze it in" when there is time in between assurance assignments. The reasons for limiting the amount of time spent on advisory work, and not highlighting this can be due to the way some audit functions are expected to charge for their time, or because some CAEs can feel somewhat guilty about the amount of advisory work they are doing (often due to a belief that the board would not be happy to hear about advisory work).

I recall a CAE at one workshop explaining that she spent 50% of her available resource on advisory assignments. The other CAEs at the workshop were visibly stunned by the amount of time being spent on advisory assignments. However, the CAE justified it on the basis that her organization was going through a tremendous amount of change and she felt it was better that audit should be proactively advising on these issues, rather than sitting back and finding fault later on. Of particular note, later on in this workshop, we learned that this CAE was one of only a few who had been able to increase the size of her audit function, with the majority of others having to reduce their resources!

Nicola Rimmer (former President of the IIA UK) offers the following perspective:

> "In relation to the provision of advice, I think a lot of audit functions can sometimes be perceived as sitting on the fence and say they don't want to get involved for reasons of independence. Independence can get used as a shield."

A further theme from the influencing workshops I run for CAEs is that limitations on the amount of advisory work delivered can lead to a distancing between the audit function and the rest of the organization. This distancing has adverse consequences in two respects:

- The audit function has poorer networks in the organization, being seen as an internal policeman, with less "money in the bank" in terms of goodwill when an audit assignment gets into difficulty; and
- The audit function obtains less intelligence about what is going on in the organization, both in terms of information being forwarded on, as well as fewer informal (coffee room) conversations about what is going on.

However, there is a balance to be struck, as Chris Baker (Technical Manager, IIA UK) notes:

> "The worst-case scenario is that organizations don't get any assurance or get very little assurance from audit because consultancy work is dominating their work. And the opposite can apply with organizations failing to benefit from the auditor's experience to help them head off an issue."

A further dimension concerning the provision of advisory support is to recognize that very often requests for advice can come from middle management rather than senior management. Lean principles support advice to both groups if there is going to be a connection with external customer value add. However, limited input from audit to the most senior levels of management, and spending the majority of advisory time on middle management requests may mean audit is not making a value adding contribution to some of the major value related challenges facing the organization.

## Core Assurance Work on Compliance and Control Takes Over

I have already discussed some of the problems with audit plans being dominated by work on core assurance areas, such as financial controls and compliance.

One CAE offers an interesting perspective why this is such a common challenge:

> "If you've got Audit Committee members concerned about compliance and basic controls there might actually be quite a lot of activity going on to manage these risks, but sometimes this work doesn't always reach them in a clear way.
>
> As a result it's tempting for them to latch on to audit as the most visible assurance provider."

## Challenges to Rationalize the Plan Against Key Value Related Areas

In the audit planning workshops that I run, we benchmark audit plans, in terms of both content and presentation formats. A common presentation approach is to list out the range of audits planned, with the number of days allocated to each proposed assignment. In some instances, this is supplemented by details of coverage across risk areas (IT, finance and compliance), by business area and also geographical regions.

However, a key question is how does this information help to ensure that the plan is addressing the most important value related areas and the key risks of the organization?

In a number of instances I have heard CAEs confessing that they "retrofit" their audit plan (developed via an audit universe and/or management consultation) to the objectives and key risks of the organization. When this occurs, the danger is that connections between key value issues and the audit plan are not actually that strong, resulting in a disconnect between the plan and what is of most value. This approach is often one of the reasons for a disconnect between the audit plan and key risks, that can be revealed during an EQA (as discussed in Chapter 9).

## The Impact of Resources Constraints is Not Always Clear

Another pressure that CAEs can feel is the need to "make do" with the budget and staff headcount they have, since audit is not a front line function. One fairly common practice I have seen to explain the impact of resource limitations is for the audit plan to list the assignments that "nearly made it onto the plan." I have heard mixed reports about whether listing these assignments is successful in getting the right sort of conversation about the resources that should be allocated to audit. From my discussions with CAEs often all that happens is that the CAE is encouraged to "do their best to squeeze in additional assignments" if they can.

An even more difficult issue for CAEs to raise is the extent to which the skills and capabilities within the audit function have impacted the plan. The most obvious impact is where an assignment is considered for inclusion on the audit plan, but then removed because "that's an area that can't be audited." However, a more insidious problem is that risks are excluded from thought automatically (c.f. the earlier discussion about common shortcomings in most audit universes), so that these limits on audit coverage are not transparent. Imagine an external customer's perspective to such an approach: "You ignored key areas because they were too difficult for you? But how does this serve my needs?!"

## RECOMMENDED PRACTICES

The starting point for a progressive audit plan is to deliver the maximum value as efficiently as possible. Therefore, whether assignments should be oriented towards advisory rather than assurance will depend on a range of considerations, e.g.:

- If an advisory assignment enables audit to be engaged with important value drivers (e.g. new product launches, etc.) that are not yet ready to be audited; and/or
- If this enables assignments to be completed, and actions taken, quickly with minimal delay (e.g. without waiting for an audit report to be drafted, checked and negotiated over).

In terms of overall resources for the audit function, lean, progressive ways of working encourage a transparent and conscious trade-off between resource and adding value. There is no such thing as a correct amount of audit resource; rather those accountable for managing the organization should understand the interaction between cost and value add and make the appropriate decisions to maximize added value (in their eyes and ideally the eyes of the external customer), recognizing there will, of course, be competing claims on limited resources.

## Understand Value Opportunities from Advisory Assignments

Here are some reflections from a senior audit manager in the UK:

> "With advisory assignments I always like to make sure it's not pre-empting an audit. If we're not planning to audit in that area and it's important, then it's a good area to offer advice. But if we were six months away from doing an audit and a manager wants a piece of advisory help, I'm more careful about our role.
>
> The other thing is, people not actually knowing what they want from the advisory work. Let's bring the auditor in, with an ill-defined concept of what success would look like. In this situation you have a lot of opportunity for upsetting people and disappointing people and actually undermining the role of audit rather than reinforcing it. So when you get a piece of advisory work, have a clear scope, have a clear objective, understand what it is you are trying to achieve."

Fortunately, there are indications that the value to be gained by doing advisory work is being increasingly recognized. Nancy Haig (CAE, global consulting firm) reflects:

> "I think that people are starting to understand that there's real efficiency and value in internal audit as being there up front as opposed to the back end, when it can sometimes be too late."

Chris Baker (Technical Manager, IIA UK):

> "I'm absolutely certain that advice is fundamental and part of what it means to add value. Not simply because it's included in the IIA standards but I see it when I do EQAs: stakeholders of internal audit expect it.
>
> I think there's a higher degree of expectation these days, given the financial climate and constraints that are around. Internal audit needs to make a contribution to how the organization achieves its objectives.
>
> I recommend to CAEs that they should be clear about the amount of advisory work they are doing. For various reasons many CAEs feel a bit apologetic about this. They don't create this separate section in their audit plan and spell it out."

An additional benefit from being transparent about the balance between advice and assurance is that it can bring out different stakeholder views about how audit should spend its time, and be a trigger for working through stakeholder differences. Resolving these differences can often require a deeper level of dialogue between the board and senior management, for example revealing that if senior management were more open and honest about issues, the board would be less inclined to want independent assurance!

Actions for Internal Audit to consider:

- Assess the amount of time spent by audit on assurance assignments compared to advisory assignments;
- When developing the audit plan consider whether there are occasions when advisory assignments would offer an opportunity to more quickly deliver added value;
- Make audit time on advisory assignments (past and planned) transparent to stakeholders.

## Being Transparent about the Use of Audit Time Across Different Risk Areas

Other key choices in the audit plan that are often implicit can benefit hugely from a more explicit, transparent approach. Clearly setting out the proposed allocation of audit resource in the plan between risk categories can be very powerful.

**Table 11.1**   Audit time allocation across risk areas

| Risk Area | Contribution to Value Add/Loss % | Past Coverage by Audit % | Proposed Coverage by Audit this Year % |
|---|---|---|---|
| Financial | 15 | 30 | 25 |
| Compliance | 15 | 25 | 25 |
| Operational | 25 | 25 | 25 |
| Strategic | 45 | 20 | 25 |
| Total | 100 | 100 | 100 |

Table 11.1 illustrates that even though audit is allocating its time equally across key risk areas, this does not align to the actual importance of each area in terms of its contribution to value add and potential value destruction.

Of course, judgements will need to be made about the extent to which each area impacts the value add/loss of the organization, and the extent to which audit coverage should be orientated around these proportions. However, this sort of analysis can prompt a good discussion about why audit may be allocating a relatively small portion of its resource to strategic risks, but more to financial controls and compliance where i) there may be less risk, and ii) there are a range of other compliance and assurance functions that already look at these areas!

Such an analysis can also be accompanied by providing details of the "effective audit coverage". This measure considers the extent to which the risk areas concerned will be "fully assured" over the course of a number of years. Of course, "fully assured" would need to be defined, based on the relevant risks and controls. However, when this is done, key stakeholders can often find that some areas are being assured considerably more often than others. Table 11.2 builds on the last example:

**Table 11.2**  Analysis of audit plan coverage

| Risk Area | Contribution to Value Add/Loss % | Proposed Coverage by Audit % | Number of Years Auditing to Cover All Relevant Risks |
|---|---|---|---|
| Financial | 15 | 25 | 3 |
| Compliance | 15 | 25 | 4 |
| Operational | 25 | 25 | 5 |
| Strategic | 45 | 25 | 10 |
| Total | 100 | 100 | N/A |

Table 11.2 highlights:

- Spending 25% of audit resource on financial control risks means that audit covers the relevant processes and controls every three years;
- Likewise, 25% of audit resource on compliance means that audit covers the relevant processes and controls every four years;
- By contrast, because of the greater scale of operational risks, spending 25% of audit resources on these areas means audit will only cover these every five years;
- Finally, this analysis shows that full coverage of strategic risks is around every 10 years, which in practical terms means that there are some strategic risks that audit will never audit (because they will have come and gone within that period of time).

One CAE explains their approach, based on this way of thinking:

"Whilst we use a risk assurance based approach to developing the audit plan, it is important to explain the limitations in audit's coverage.

To manage expectations we created a risk assurance universe that we use to complement the plan. This is then categorized into three key tiers, based on their respective importance in risk and value terms.

Then when we develop the audit plan, we make sure that we communicate the audit coverage of the three different risk tiers."

In order to be clear about the trade-off between value and cost, the aim should be to ensure that senior management and the audit committee have no illusions about the amount of auditing that is being done by the audit function against the different levels of risk. As Figure 11.3 illustrates, audit coverage of key units (Tier 1) will typically be greater that coverage of less important locations (Tiers 2 and 3).

**Figure 11.3**   Audit plan coverage – by tier (illustrative)

Actions for Internal Audit to consider:

- During the audit planning process regularly carry out sanity checks to ensure that the planned allocation of audit resources:
  - matches the key value issues for the organization,
  - covers key risk areas with appropriate frequency;
- Ensure these choices are transparent to stakeholders when presenting the audit plan.

## Make the Impact of Resource Limitations Crystal Clear

Implicit with the approach just described is the fact that the audit plan will not address some risk areas. Phil Gerrard (CAE, Rolls-Royce) explains:

"I think it's important to present the plan showing not only what we are looking at, but what we are not looking at. The aim is to get across the reality of a risk focus, and a better understanding of what effectively amounts to the Audit Committee's risk appetite."

One very effective method I have found, which transparently communicates the connection between the proposed audit plan and its value add, is to map out the proposed coverage of key risks and priorities alongside i) other assurances, ii) past audit coverage and iii) stakeholder interest. The aim is to make crystal clear which areas are being fully assured, which will have some assurance, and which are not being assured at all.

Such an analysis typically highlights that some areas receive considerable assurance year in and year out and others have not been independently assured at all.

Some stakeholders may not be entirely happy with a transparent mapping of key areas and assurance or audit coverage, since it may raise questions in relation to limitations of audit resources, and disrupt long established preferences about the areas audit looks at (and does not look at). However, it is important that CAEs lead the way in making assurance and audit coverage transparent, since this is a key way to drive discussions about the effectiveness of the overall assurance picture, whether audit coverage is being optimized towards the areas that matter the most, and whether audit is being appropriately resourced.

Actions for Internal Audit to consider:

- Ensure it is crystal clear in audit planning papers which risks and objectives are and are not being assured or audited;
- Be cautious of saying audit has enough resource without putting it into context;
- Be prepared for some pushback from certain stakeholders who may not want to make audit and assurance coverage so transparent.

### Core Assurance Is to be Expected and will Add Value if done in the Right Way

Lean principles encourage a strong focus on value adding advice and assurance in relation to key value issues. However, this does not mean that assurance over "core" financial controls and compliance should not be a part of the internal audit plan. Typically lean progressive auditing focuses core assurance work to look at the areas that matter the most and ensures other control and compliance functions are discharging their roles effectively.

Stephen Foster (Senior Vice President Corporate Audit Services, and CAE, Cargotec AB):

> "My main learning point over the past few years has been that you can't have modern auditing without an element, a fundamental element, of traditional auditing. You have to have that as a base. That's your foundation.
>
> I come from a CFO background and in that environment your position of power is that you know what's going on, you have the facts.
>
> It's the same with the modern audit function. They will not maintain or gain that credibility if they don't have the foundations and the facts. I don't see the two as being mutually exclusive. I just see it being as an evolution. And if you lose sight of the traditional then you will fail, but you do need to balance it increasingly with services that add value to the business."

In my experience, key stakeholders often want "core assurance" over and above the strict amount that it contributes to key value issues. However, the trick is to put this work within the context of other compliance and assurance activities, to closely manage the amount of time spent on this work and to optimize the focus of audit's work in these areas.

Actions for Internal Audit to consider:

- Recognize that despite the fact that "core assurance" may not strictly be as important to key value issues as other work, some work will normally be expected;
- When core assurance work is done, ensure that audit's work is correctly focused and pay close attention to the effectiveness of compliance monitoring and checking by management and other functions.

## The Audit Plan Should Address Capability Issues within the Audit Function

Whilst IIA standards demand that audit must have the skills to do its work, the danger is that this is interpreted as grounds for not auditing some areas, rather than being used as a trigger for getting additional capabilities into audit. For example, it can be tempting to ignore certain risk and value areas in the planning process on the basis that: i) audit does not have the capability to audit these and ii) additional resources are not going to be made available. However, though it may be tempting to "short-circuit" the correct logic, it can create a self-fulfilling prophecy of keeping resources static, because staffing shortcomings are not identified.

A progressive approach to auditing is to transparently spell out the need for either additional internal resources or co-source resources in order to provide assurance over areas of value, or to make it clear that capability constraints are limiting what can be covered. Norman Marks (GRC thought leader) offers the following encouragement in relation to audit capability gaps:

> "A long time ago internal auditors said we can't audit procurement or human resources because we're accountants. We don't say that any more, do we? So why should we use that kind of excuse for new risk areas nowadays?"

Actions for Internal Audit to consider:

- Ensure risks are not excluded from consideration in the planning process because of audit capability limitations;
- Ensure there is a clear statement about any capability gaps in the audit plan that are limiting coverage;
- Is there a clear enough discussion in the plan about the opportunities or barriers to getting additional internal resources or external co-source support?

## Think Through How the Plan will Deliver any Overall Opinions Required

Phil Gerrard (CAE Rolls-Royce) offers the following observation:

> "Too many internal auditors look at the micro end of the audit plan, rather than how the whole programme fits together, and how that will help them form an opinion and help the audit committee with their annual governance statement. I would like to see more CAEs think about that."

For several years now I have run sessions with CAEs and audit committee members entitled "How assured am I?" in which we examine whether the audit plan, alongside other assurances, provides enough assurance to deliver a robust overall assessment of the GRC and assurance framework of the organization. In a number of instances our discussions have highlighted that assumptions are being made about the breadth of assurance coverage, the quality of the assurances provided, and the rigour of remediation tracking.

As a result, many audit functions find they need to recommend strengthening the assurances that are being obtained from management and compliance functions in relation to certain areas, as well as stepping up audit coverage of key risk areas. Once a better assurance framework is in place, internal audit can then more confidently engage in additional value adding assignments. Nancy Haig (CAE, global consulting firm) explains her approach:

> "If we have come up with a good plan where people are comfortable with the amount of assurance work we're doing, and recognize the work of others, then most of the time I've found key internal stakeholders will be happy with whatever extra work that we take on. And normally they see that it's adding real value for us to be involved in the design of a new process, or to provide input in due diligence work."

Actions for Internal Audit to consider:

- Be explicit in the audit plan how the assurance coverage contributes towards any overall governance and risk opinions;
- If there are gaps consider recommending strengthening assurances from management or other compliance functions, not just doing additional audits;
- Ask for audit planning to be explicitly probed in relation to the link with overall assurance messages during an External Quality Assessment (EQA).

## CONCLUDING REMARKS

The dilemma facing most audit functions is how to approach the audit plan afresh when there is likely to be a considerable amount of inertia in past ways of thinking about the role of audit and what constitutes a sensible plan. A lean audit approach provides constructive way of overcoming this inertia by asking: How do we achieve the most value adding audit plan possible, and validate whether the allocation of resources is optimal?

Lean, progressive ways of working encourage audit to be transparent about key value drivers, risks, the overall assurance picture and the choices and constraints that affect what should be done.

Of course, CAEs should take a clear lead in proposing what they believe is the right audit plan, based on value, but no matter how confident they are about the proposed audit plan, CAEs should be a role model for transparency about what is being proposed and why. My CAE coaching work suggests that whilst some stakeholders find this transparency challenging (since it may reveal resource and capability shortcomings) it normally stimulates important debates about the most value adding role for audit and the importance of strengthening the overall assurance framework.

---

### SUMMARY OF KEY POINTS FOR INTERNAL AUDIT

- Look at the balance of time spent by the audit function between assurance and advice and consider whether the balance is right.
- Map out key value drivers and risks and consider why these are not being addressed, being wary of making assumptions about the quality of other assurances or a view that certain areas cannot be audited.
- If audit is spending lots of time auditing mandatory areas (e.g. compliance or financial controls), explore the scope for increased coverage by management, compliance or other functions.
- Is the impact of resource and capability constraints on the plan transparent? Can stakeholders clearly see what is not being covered or only covered infrequently?
- Use an EQA to examine the robustness of the link between the audit plan, other assurances and any overall opinions that are required. This can often be a useful way to "shake" the organization from complacency in this arena.

---

### RECOMMENDATIONS FOR SENIOR MANAGERS AND BOARD MEMBERS

- How transparent are the key choices underpinning the audit plan, for example, the balance between advice and assurance, and key risk areas?
- Is it clear which risk areas are not being looked at by audit?
- Clarify how resource or capability constraints are impacting the audit plan.
- Ask the CAE whether this is the most value-adding plan that is possible.
- How clear is the link between the audit plan, other assurance activities and any overall opinions that might need to be made about the overall effectiveness of GRC and assurance frameworks?

# 12
# Assignments – Types, Scheduling and Resourcing

In the last three chapters I have outlined some of the key principles and practices required to create a risk and assurance based audit plan that aims to deliver the maximum value. However, before considering how to plan specific audit assignments, there is an important interim step to consider: how to schedule and resource the audit plan in a way that maximizes added value and minimizes waste. Key points to manage include:

- What sort of assignment is required;
- How much resource to devote to each assignment;
- When assignments should be scheduled;
- How much flexibility to build into the plan to deal with new and ad hoc assignments.

## COMMON PRACTICES AND IIA STANDARDS OF NOTE

Common practice is to determine the amount of resource that will be needed to deliver each assignment. This is often based on a standard assignment resourcing allocation (often within a particular range for each individual audit function, which can be anywhere from 5, 10, 20, 40 or even 80+ days).

The current IIA standard (IIAS) 2010 states that the "CAEs must review and adjust the plan, as necessary, in response to changes in the organization's business, risks, operations, programmes, systems, and controls." In my experience, CAEs deal with this requirement differently, some filling their plan with assignments up to the resource limit they have, and then notifying stakeholders when changes are needed, whilst others leave a resource buffer so that new and ad hoc assignments can be automatically accommodated.

IIAS 1220 also requires internal auditors to weigh up the costs of assurance and advisory assignments in relation to potential benefits – very much in line with lean principles.

## COMMON CHALLENGES & DILEMMAS

From numerous workshops and consulting assignments, the main challenges and dilemmas in relation to scheduling the audit plan appear to be:

### Plan Flexibility Is Impacted by a Number of Standard Assignments

When discussing flexibility within the audit plan, some CAEs explain that they have very little, since their plan is dominated by a number of standard "required" assignments, each of which is supposed to follow a standard approach with a set amount of resource expected. For example: each year six key financial systems must be reviewed, comprising 40 days each, amounting to 240 days each year. As a result, some CAEs explain there is only limited capacity to take on board new assignments.

### Large Assignments Can Easily Deliver a Poor Return for the Resource Expended

Inevitably, some audit assignments require a greater resource allocation than others, particularly when the assignment is new or is looking at a common theme across a number of different parts of the organization. However, some CAEs have explained to me that these larger assignments (often 40, 60 or 80 days, sometimes more), can be something of a "black hole", which are hard to track, and that may deliver comparatively poor value for the resource allocated to them.

## Challenges in Scheduling the Plan, at the Start, During the Year and at the End of the Year

For some audit functions, developing the audit plan can take a number of months and will usually require formal sign-off by senior management and the board. Since these meetings are relatively infrequent, it is not unusual to find that the audit plan is not formally approved until just before, or even just after, the audit year starts. Some CAEs explain to me that they would like the audit plan to get off to a quicker start, but their team is often busy around the end of the audit year finishing off assignments that need to be completed for the previous year's plan. The peak in the number of assignments that need to be completed arises for a range of reasons, including "slippage" of assignment delivery (which will be discussed in a later chapter) or because of the postponement of assignments earlier in the year (e.g. managers saying: "We are very busy right now, can you come back to do your audit later on?").

The pattern of delays in starting the plan, rescheduling assignments during the year and a peak towards the end of the year has a degree of circularity about it, because a delay in starting assignments at the beginning of the year, can delay what gets done, resulting in the same rush to catch up later on in the year!

This pattern is normally not good for the morale of the audit function, since the working day can be extended and training and holidays can be cancelled towards the end of each year. It can also adversely impact audit quality, since the priority is often to "get the report issued", over and above the delivery of a valuable and insightful report.

## Ad Hoc Requests and Investigations Can Adversely Affect the Delivery of the Plan

Some CAEs explain that over the course of the year they receive a number of ad hoc and special requests, which can include working on fraud investigations or looking into other pressing matters. If the resource required for special requests or investigations exceeds the resource budgeted, delivery of the rest of the audit plan can be affected.

## RECOMMENDED PRACTICES

I have already noted the link between lean and the IIA requirement to weigh up the cost/benefit of audit and advisory assignments. In addition, the challenges outlined above are good examples of the kinds of waste that lean is concerned about:

- Muda waste – as a result of waiting or rescheduling;
- Mura waste – as a result of unevenness in the work schedule;
- Muri waste – that arises because of overburdened resources.

Specific principles and practices that reflect a progressive way of working, incorporating lean techniques, are summarized below.

## Orientate Resource Allocation and Timing towards Adding Value

The first key point to make is that the resource allocated to any assignment should be proportionate, as far as possible, to the value that will be gained from the work. As a result, the notion that the resource allocated to audit assignments should be determined by custom and practice, or the amount of time taken in the past, is something that a lean audit approach would challenge.

As a starting point, it can be useful to calculate how much assignments cost, not just in terms of travel and co-source support, but in terms of audit staff and supervision time, and then the time of all of the managers and other staff in the organization who must support and respond to auditor demands. Often it is possible to see that 10 days of auditing field work requires another five days of preparation, five days for reporting and another 10 days of time from management and staff, amounting to 30 man days in total. With this sort of analysis it rapidly becomes clear that focusing on minor issues in the assignment could result in a net loss of value.

Jonathan Kidd (CAE, UK Met Office) describes the changes he saw on moving into a lean auditing mindset:

> "In relation to scheduling the audit plan, the number of days we scheduled for an assignment has changed a lot. It used to be done through a range of standard types, for example a 15 day audit, 25 day audit, 35 day audit and so on.
>
> As we adopted lean ways of working it became more dynamic so, where before it would have been 20 days, now it's going to be 16 or 17.
>
> As a result the number of audits that were able to be done went up quite dramatically. So dramatic that I had questions from management. I had

a senior manager saying to me 'Are you driving your team too hard?' However, they were working the same hours, nobody was doing overtime, they were able to do more audits. The stuff that was not worthwhile and taking up time was not being done any more."

Karen Dignan (CAE, Group Head Office, OMG) explains the progressive "fit for purpose" approach to assignment resourcing and scoping:

"We are being more flexible but also more challenging on the amount of time we spend on assignments. We will accept a more diverse range of how much time we will spend, the aim being to more closely match assignment lengths to the likely value add."

Richard Young, (Director, UNIAC) explains the approach of his audit function:

"If we've completed reviews on creditor payments for the last five years and found very little, why don't we just approach it differently? If we have to do a review, then let's do it in less days, but be more concentrated."

In addition to having a strong sense of the cost of assignments and the need to resource these proportionately to added value, it is important to recognize that the timing of when an assignment should be delivered can impact its value. Norman Marks (GRC thought leader) provides an important insight:

"I talk about providing assurance at the speed of the business. It really comes back down to, what is it we need to deliver and when? It's not just the assurance that is valuable, but how quickly that assurance is delivered and how it is packaged."

Karen Dignan (CAE, Group Head Office, OMG) has put this way of working into practice:

"Some of the big things we're doing relate to strategic changes. If you're going through a big outsourcing or an acquisition or disposal there would be little value approaching these assignments in a conventional way. Instead we work out – quite quickly – what time frame we need to operate within and therefore how we should best use that time efficiently and effectively to look at the key things and then slick ways of reporting onwards without delay."

Actions for Internal Audit to consider:

- Develop a culture in which the full cost of assignments is more explicitly considered when deciding the length and focus of an assignment;
- Consider the case for widening the range of assignment resourcing options so that each is "fit for purpose";
- Ensure there is clarity about the way in which the timeliness of work will provide value.

## Consider What Type of Assignment is Required

At AstraZeneca one of the changes we implemented when we adopted lean principles was to recognize more clearly that there should not be just one type of assignment. Two key choices we considered included:

- Advisory or assurance assignment;
- The depth or breadth of the assignment (which could include whether an investigation might be needed).

Beyond this there were other choices such as:

- Whether the assignment would look at the design of controls or their operation as well;
- The extent to which IS and IT controls should be included;
- Whether an "in flight" project review was needed, or a project learning review, or a benefits review after the project has been completed;
- Even if an "in flight" project review is required, what stage of the project should be considered and what risk areas should be considered?

These choices should be driven by the value that the assignment is intended to deliver.

Even if an assignment of a particular type has been decided, lean principles demand that we consider carefully how it is best organized to deliver value efficiently. In AstraZeneca we began to split up some assignments into two stages. The first stage might be a "risk framework review" or "high level review" that would examine management's understanding of the key risk areas and how these were being controlled (often from a design perspective).

Then, depending on what was found, there might be a follow-on assignment three or six months later probing specific key risks and controls from an operational perspective. This approach reduced the number of longer assignments that sometimes had a less favourable cost/benefit balance. In addition, this approach delivered the added benefits of: i) being able to stop work after the first high level review, if that provided sufficient assurance, and: ii) enabling much more focused follow-on assignments, based on insights gained from the first assignment.

This approach can also be used to examine issues in selected locations or departments, but not necessarily all, sharing the key themes with all areas, and then doing selected follow-up assignments.

Richard Young (Director, UNIAC) pursues this way of working further:

"In some instances, the best scenario may be three short assignments in a year. Your first piece of work is understanding key risks, controls and accountabilities. The next piece of work examines in more detail the quality of management monitoring routines and their disciplines around following up anomalies and issues. Finally, you can drill down into the detail of controls and the data if you have concerns about that. It's a staggered approach that takes management along the way and is much leaner with its use of time.

Of course there are logistical challenges, but the problem with blasting through assignments is that audit clients aren't always getting the value from audit that they could be."

Actions for Internal Audit to consider:

- Create a range of assignment types (e.g. Design Review, Operational Review, Focused Audit, Comprehensive Audit, Investigation) and consider carefully what sort of assignment type is required;
- Pay particular attention to the rationale for the longest, most resource intensive, assignments;
- Try splitting larger assignments into "high level reviews", followed by a "follow on audit" some months later if required.

## Obtain Buy-In to the Overall Phasing of the Plan at the Time of the Audit Plan, Not Later in the Year

In order to generate a smooth flow of assignments throughout the year, the audit planning process needs to be mindful of the scheduling of assignments. Key points and areas for consideration are outlined in the following actions for internal audit to consider:

- Set out the proposed high level timing of the plan as it is being prepared: and get senior management views to timing requirements or sensitivities.
- Agree with stakeholders which assignments the audit function can "just get on with" in the first quarter. These should be assignments that are clearly of value, where a quick result is wanted, and which are uncontroversial in terms of board and senior management support;
- Ensure that management has a collective responsibility for getting assurance delivered on schedule. The fundamental cultural point is that it should not just be an accountability of audit to deliver the audit plan. Once senior management has input to the high level phasing of the plan, this should be communicated to the managers affected as early as possible, seeking to resolve any difficulties early on, rather than encountering them later. If changes need to be made to assignment timing senior managers should be engaged on what work can be substituted for this, rather than leaving audit alone to negotiate this.

### Update the Plan on an Ongoing Basis and Maintain Some Contingency

There seems to be a range of practice in relation to how much of the total available resource of the internal audit function should be planned. One senior audit manager in the UK explained:

> "Somewhere between 70–80% of our originally planned audit plan usually gets delivered. Lesser assignments will roll off and something else will roll on, not because of any weakness in our planning process, but simply because things can change. However, if the business is going through more changes we are prepared to be more flexible so that we can address the new issues that really matter. We then just explain the changes we have had to make at intervals."

The process of "roll-on/roll-off" is something I see quite a lot, especially where a greater portion of the total audit resource is budgeted. Progressive ways of working try to identify these assignments up front and recognize that the assignments with a likely lower added value should not normally be completed in the first three or six months of the year, so that they can "roll off" the plan later in the audit year if needed.

Phil Gerrard (CAE, Rolls-Royce) highlights the importance of having some flexibility in the audit plan:

> "To me delivery of 100% of the audit plan I put to the audit committee earlier in the year would be a dire indictment of my function.
>
> Stand back and think what you are saying. 100% completion of an audit plan means that the risk environment has changed not one iota in the last 12 months. It's nuts. Yet there are people putting this down as a good KPI."

Given that the audit plan rarely goes to plan it is important to find an efficient way of rescheduling assignments. Jonathan Kidd (CAE, UK Met Office) outlines how he manages the plan on a quarterly basis, detailing a practice which an increasing number of audit functions adopt:

> "We follow a very tailored project management approach. We have the overall requirements for each quarter and then as a team we draw out the assignments on a whiteboard, taking a Gantt chart perspective. We factor in holidays, training days, business events and the timing sensitivities of the assignments.
>
> We then map out staff time and key milestones for each assignment. These include not just fieldwork milestones, but when the closing meeting is planned for, when we will issue a draft report, when we expect final comments on the report and when we plan to issue the report with agreed actions.
>
> Of course it changes, but it's a very good way to start each quarter, with everybody having a responsibility to manage their own portfolio. They all know that I expect those audits to be done by the end of the quarter, but there are tolerances and if there is an issue then I expect them to come and speak to me and we'll work through how we might do that."

This just-in-time approach to scheduling assignments exemplifies lean in action.

Another practical way to manage the impact of ad hoc work is to consider specifically how to resource fraud and other ad hoc investigations (e.g. as a result of whistleblowing calls). In some organizations, stakeholders agree that whistleblowing investigations should be investigated by finance or legal or compliance (or HR for employee related matters). The argument is that this is a second line of defence activity and should be dealt with by second line functions. As a result, audit provides a small amount of advice and oversight (in its third line of defence role) if needed. Other audit functions sometimes take the lead role in investigations, but to avoid investigations derailing the delivery of the plan, they will agree a limit of the resource they will use, expecting management to provide support over and above that which was budgeted, or obtaining funds for additional co-source support as needed.

Actions for Internal Audit to consider:

- Explicitly consider the extent to which a degree of resource buffer should be built into the audit plan for (important) ad hoc assignments;
- Agree which audits may roll-off the plan and be careful about delivering them too early in the year;
- Ensure there is a systematic process for updating the audit plan;
- Agree how ad hoc work or investigations should be managed in terms of their impact on the rest of the audit plan.

## CONCLUDING REMARKS

Again, the dilemma facing many audit functions is how to balance between tried and tested assignment types, using standard ways of working compared to a more tailored approach based on a more tailored cost benefit assessment.

Lean auditing also recognizes that a value adding plan is not just about the content of the assignments proposed, but it is also about delivering these in the form and at the time that the key stakeholders will value. As a result, some audit functions do not plan ahead for the next 12 months, but simply plan on a rolling three- or six-month basis. Lean ways of working may support this approach, but the risk is that stakeholders and audit get locked into a pattern of what is urgent, rather than what is important. As a result I personally prefer a 12-month plan that is updated routinely every three or six months and then by exception as needed.

Lean auditing encourages audit functions to have a relatively smooth schedule of assignments, phased in a way that avoids excessive bunching, and ensuring the plan gets off to a good start and does not rush at the end. Needless to say, in lean progressive audit functions, the vast majority of auditors should have a reasonably clear view what work they have coming up over the next month or so, so they can make use of any spare time to get going with assignment preparations.

However, even if an audit plan is scheduled appropriately, this does not guarantee that the execution of each assignment will deliver the maximum added value. The next chapters explain how to drive added value in each audit assignment, so that the potential value adding contribution of each assignment identified at the planning stage is actually delivered in practice.

---

## SUMMARY OF KEY POINTS FOR INTERNAL AUDIT

- Revisit current standard time and resource allocations for assignments and create a culture in which a greater variety of assignment types and lengths is expected based on the value add being sought;
- Challenge assignments with a significant resource allocation – can these be split into two or even three parts?
- Start phasing the plan during the audit planning process so that timing requirements are clear;
- Always have a clear understanding what the first quarter's plan will look like, whether or not the plan has been formally approved;
- Obtain senior management commitment to the overall scheduling of the plan during the year and communicate this to relevant managers as soon as possible;
- Ensure that delivery of the plan as scheduled is seen to be as much a responsibility of relevant management, not just audit;
- Agree ways of working in relation to additions to, and removals from, the plan so this is straightforward;
- Agree roles and resource allocations for investigations and other ad hoc assignments, so these do not derail the delivery of the rest of the audit plan.

**RECOMMENDATIONS FOR SENIOR MANAGERS AND BOARD MEMBERS**

- Ask the CAE what different types of assignments the audit function delivers: good practice encourages a range of approaches;
- Ask the CAE to advise whether there are any delays or difficulties in delivering assignments evenly over the course of the year;
- Clarify the accountability on management, not just audit, to ensure audit assignments are delivered on time;
- Understand and agree how potential new assignments should "roll-on" and any less important assignments should "roll-off" and what needs to be explicitly approved or reviewed;
- Understand and agree how investigations should be resourced so that the audit plan, and any overall assurance requirements, can be delivered without disruption.

# 13
# Using Assignment Scoping and Planning to Drive Added Value

If an audit plan is to comprise assignments that add value, there should be a reasonable understanding between stakeholders and internal audit of the specific value each assignment should deliver. In order to achieve this, there should be a flow of information from the audit planning process into the assignment scoping and planning process. This often requires keeping track of why an assignment was put on the audit plan. Many CAEs find this question is one that they or their management team are best placed to answer, since they are often those who best understand the reasons why an assignment was selected.

However, there may be occasions when assignments have been placed on the plan without particular clarity about the value being sought from the assignment. If this is the case, perhaps because the audit plan was not developed with a strong orientation towards adding value, it is still quite possible to achieve a significant step-up in the value add and efficiency of each and every assignment through a strong assignment planning process.

The starting point for achieving a step up in the value add from assignments comes from thinking carefully about the objectives, scope and plan of each and every proposed assignment from a lean perspective.

## COMMON PRACTICES AND IIA STANDARDS OF NOTE

It is common practice (and expected in the IIA's standards) that internal auditors should develop a plan for each assignment, covering its objectives, the planned scope, timing and resources. It is expected that auditors should consider the objectives and significant risks of the area under review and relevant governance, risk management and control activities and processes. There will normally be a "sanity check" that the assignment resources are suitable and that any deadlines are achievable. IIA standards also emphasize that there should be adequate criteria to enable internal audit to evaluate the areas within scope.

## COMMON CHALLENGES & DILEMMAS

### Impatience to Get Going Can Result in Difficulties and a Lack of Value Focus

I have every sympathy for CAEs and auditors who are under pressure to deliver the audit plan and who feel that they must "get on with" starting each assignment. There is no doubt that some audit functions can spend too long on research and thinking about what they should do, which is neither efficient nor value adding.

However, I know of a number of audit functions that have had a culture of principally using prior assignment scopes and plans, making a bare minimum number of changes and issuing these without significant management engagement. However, a number of functions that do this face subsequent problems, such as:

- Delays and inefficiencies later on in the assignment; and/or
- Disappointing feedback from stakeholders about the value from these assignments.

### Not Fully Thinking Through Assignment Resourcing

An associated problem with starting assignments quickly is that the amount of resource and time allocated to an assignment is predetermined by what was done in the past, rather than the correct cost/benefit balance on this occasion.

One CAE explained to me:

"When I first started in auditing, if you got 25 days for an assignment, you used 25 days.

You might think 'I can probably do that assignment in 15 days', but there was limited incentive to free up the time. So with a spare 10 days of time it used to encourage me to do things that were not particularly essential, but of personal interest, or to tidy up my files, or go home early!"

## Disagreements or Changes in Relation to the Assignment's Purpose and Scope

With my clients and at audit workshops we discuss the reality (Gemba) of assignment scoping. Many different issues emerge:

- Not being able to get any real engagement from management in relation to the scope of the assignment;
- Encountering the opposite problem: where management have very strong preferences about what the assignment should (and should not) cover;
- Encountering questions and disagreements about who is accountable for managing the risks in relation to a particular scope area;
- Finding out later in the assignment that the assignment scope needs to be changed because of a misunderstanding about its purpose.

## Often Information is Not Forthcoming on a Timely Basis

Typically internal audit needs to review certain background information (e.g. business plans, risk updates, etc.) in order to develop the most value adding assignment plan.

However, some auditors experience difficulties and delays getting this information, for example:

- "Do you really need that?"
- "I need to clear that with my manager."
- "When I get the time next week, I will dig that out for you."

All the while the audit staff are waiting – a very clear sign of Muda.

## Planning Just the Fieldwork Can Result in Issues Later on

Greg Coleman (CAE, ITG) reflects on a common problem:

> "I've worked in teams where there wasn't a structure of tightly planned audits, perhaps the timing of the fieldwork was planned, but not the timing of the closing meeting or final report.

> However, if these final deadlines are not established early on it is very easy to end up with scope creep, with auditors wanting to do more work to be comfortable, or delays in holding closing meetings and long debates about the wording of the final report."

These perspectives illustrate how weak assignment planning can often be a root cause of waste later on in the execution of an audit assignment.

## RECOMMENDED ACTIONS

Lean insights derive from following the Kano insights to maximize value add as well as the use of Heijunka principles to help improve the sequencing of work and also to put greater effort into understanding value and how it is going to flow.

## Invest Sufficient Time in Focused Assignment Planning

A fundamental hallmark of lean, progressive auditing is an ability to purposefully plan each assignment. Here are several supporting perspectives:

Karen Dignan (CAE, Group Head Office, OMG):

> "Planning an assignment is key because when I see things going wrong, including delays in delivery, it is often because we didn't think enough up front. It can be as simple as not recognizing a key contact is travelling or on holiday for 2 weeks during the assignment.

> Unless people have really thought about what they want and sufficiently planned and been rigorous in engaging the business, problems will arise."

Andy Weintraub (experienced internal audit leader):

"I love issuing an audit report at the end of an assignment, and getting management to improve the business, but good planning is a crucial step to ensure this happens.

In an earlier company I worked in, the CAE said planning should represent two-thirds of the time for the assignment. Of course, it depends where you draw the line but his message was that it was extremely important to have a good assignment plan if you wanted to deliver a valuable assignment."

Chris Baker (Technical Manager, IIA UK):

"Good audit departments put a lot of effort into thinking about and agreeing the scope of their audits so they are addressing important points; and as a result key findings will then be meaningful to the organization."

That said, assignment planning should be focused and purposeful and not be a black hole of wasted audit time.

Actions for Internal Audit to consider:

- If assignment planning is relatively quick, or rarely affects the planned scope and resourcing, consider whether the planning process needs to better consider value-adding questions;
- If assignment planning is taking a long time, pay close attention to what is expected in the assignment methodology as well as how staff are interpreting these requirements.

## Be Explicit about the Added Value of Each Assignment

Taking a fresh, value-added perspective to each assignment will typically encourage audit to look at each assignment beyond simply assessing risks, controls and processes. One CAE explains their perspective on the value-adding mindset:

"Before you start an audit, you've got to ask yourself, when you come out the other end, what might be the particular outcomes from this audit? Look at that and say, will anyone care? For example, if you've issued a red report and everyone goes, 'So, what?' you should ask yourself: why did we look at that? Finding a risk that is not well controlled is not adding value if the risk doesn't really matter to the organization.

The question to ask is – if we come up with a finding will it be a unit level issue, a regional issue or a group issue? If you know at the start it's unlikely going to be more than a business unit issue you should think hard about whether the audit is worthwhile and properly scoped. It might add value to a particular unit's management, but is it right for the Group as a whole, in terms of resource allocation? It's all about understanding IA's role in assessing the control environment at the correct level.

There may still be a valid reason to go and audit a unit level issue, perhaps to do some root cause analysis and share that more broadly. So the value of this assignment is going to be greater than addressing specific issues in that location."

Taking a value adding perspective links closely to the question of understanding management's risk appetite; progressive ways of working pay close attention to potential differences between auditors and management in relation to risk appetite at the planning stage, rather than seeing these differences manifest themselves in the "so what" reactions of management described earlier.

Jonathan Kidd (CAE, UK Met Office) provides advice about planning that seeks to head off these sorts of difficulties:

"I think it's really important in the planning stage not just to focus on what controls we expect to see. Think ahead also about what we think good might look like, and what would bad look like? If this was going to be a report rated unsatisfactory, worthy of senior management or audit committee attention, what kind of things would we expect to see?

The answer would be more than just whether a specific system is not being password protected, because it would all depend why it was not protected. It would probably be more serious if audit discovered problems around the culture and attitude of people within that part of the organization."

Taking this approach means that if management don't believe that certain controls are needed, or don't believe that monitoring is important, or don't believe it needs to be documented, audit may already have potential "design level" or "risk and control culture" observations that may be of real value to key stakeholders.

Developing a theme discussed in an earlier chapter on the audit planning process, thinking about the likely value add of the potential outputs from an assignment can be helpful when considering what resources to allocate to the assignment. If an audit is going to cost (say) $10,000 is there a good chance that points with a value in excess of this are going to be found?

How to quantify the value of audit outputs can be straightforward in some instances and more judgmental in others. The most popular progressive approach I see is to be clear whether findings are going to be of significance to just the unit or process being examined, or to the organization as a whole.

Having a mindset of "what is the value of this finding?" requires auditors to be grounded in the organizational context, raising their sights towards important matters and moving audit away from "nit picking" – unless there is a clear connection with something that really matters.

Actions for Internal Audit to consider:

- Ask what the value from each assignment is going to be and make this specific (e.g. unit level importance or organizational level importance);
- If appropriate, engage management or other key stakeholders on the potential outcomes of the assignment and see whether they would regard these as being of value.

## Engage with the Assignment Sponsor During the Assignment

Earlier in this book I discussed the importance of being clear who is the customer of audit work. Ideally, the needs of senior management and the board should be gathered during audit planning, so that any assignment delivers their needs (and, ideally from a lean perspective, the needs of the external customer).

I also explained that for key assignments one increasingly popular practice is to agree an assignment sponsor at least one management level above the "auditee", so that audit does not miss an opportunity to deliver value to other stakeholders. However, it is important that once a sponsor is identified they are properly engaged. One CAE explains:

> "I ensure that every single audit we do has a sponsor. I'm not expecting them to be that involved in everything, but I want them sufficiently involved in what we are doing so we don't get a value gap. We always have an opening meeting where they are invited and we will liaise with

them at intervals during the assignment so that we can get feedback concerning the extent to which we are providing insights of value."

The sponsor can also play a helpful role in driving a timely assignment. David Whitehouse (experienced audit professional) explains:

"If you have a senior sponsor it gets the attention of the person being audited, it also provides an excellent reminder that things can be escalated quickly if there are any doubts about the timing or the scope of the assignment."

Actions for Internal Audit to consider:

- Where possible, select an assignment sponsor and engage them on questions of the value that the assignment will deliver;
- Engage sponsors during the assignment as issues emerge to explore the "so what?" aspects of what is being found;
- Use the sponsor if there are any uncertainties about accountabilities in the area being audited, or delays in the progress of the assignment.

## Think about Key Risks and Key Controls

A useful approach to help internal audit gain clarity about the scope and value add from an assignment is to clarify the key risks, rather than all of the risks, and the key controls, rather than all of the controls, that should be examined during an assignment.

Greg Coleman (CAE, ITG) offers the following advice:

"I think it's useful, during the assignment planning process to consider explicitly up front: what are the key risks we need to address and what do we expect the controls to be to manage the risk to the risk appetite that has been set?

We generally use template Risk & Control Matrices, but it's important these are not used simply as checklists, because it is so easy to miss the issue of: what is the key risk on this occasion and what controls must be working really well at this point in time? We then share our view of key risks and expected key controls in the draft scope document, which goes to senior management and other managers, giving them the opportunity to add or remove controls.

Obviously, when we go and do an assignment, if there are controls that we haven't thought of in the expected controls, we'll assess those and test them as necessary."

The ability to focus an assignment on key risks and key controls is becoming an increasingly common hallmark of progressive auditing. Lean encourages auditors to look at them from the perspective of what will add value to stakeholders and the external customer. In particular, are the key risks and controls for an assignment important for just *this* assignment, or *are they important from an overall organizational and external customer perspective as well*? (Consider the notion of the "key key" controls to highlight the most important control activities for the whole organization).

Being clear about the "key key" controls can help significantly when an audit function is seeking to connect the results of individual assignments to any overall assurance opinion that might be required. In particular, this approach challenges the practice of taking an average control effectiveness rating (from audits across a range of more and less material areas), and thinking that this can be used to extrapolate the effectiveness of risk management and controls effectiveness for the organization as a whole.

Actions for Internal Audit to consider:

- Do audit assignments make a clear distinction between all of the risk areas and controls and the key risks and the key controls?
- Where it is helpful, make key risks and expected key controls clear in the assignment plan, so that management can comment on these at an early stage;
- Ensure there is clarity about the overall organizational importance of key risks and key controls and consider ways of making this clear on an ongoing basis (e.g. using terminology such as "key key");
- If required to offer an overall opinion consider the extent of the audit coverage or other assurances in relation to "key key" controls to ensure it is based on the effectiveness of the risks and controls that matter the most.

## Consider an Initial or Working Hypothesis

When I was CAE of AstraZeneca, taking a lean approach offered many fresh insights in relation to our standard auditing practices. A particular approach that we developed was the use of a "working hypothesis" for each assignment.

The origin of this idea came from David Powell, one of the Audit Directors, (who started us along the journey of lean), who looked at an earlier assignment and analysed how we had spent the time on the assignment compared to the eventual findings we had come up with (notice the interest in resource expended compared to added value). His analysis was that only 35% of the time spent on the assignment actually resulted in the most important findings. Of course, we recognized that all assignments will have a degree of waste and it was not wasteful to establish that an important risk or process was working effectively. However, there was something important in what David had found, particularly since we realized that we already had a good idea what the findings would be before the assignment had even started!

The audit management team realized that, if we could make better use of our hunches, there was a good chance we could drive more productivity in assignments. We called these hunches the "working hypothesis". As a result, when we were revising the internal audit assignment methodology to be more oriented towards lean principles we incorporated a step that was to ask the auditors working on an assignment to consider whether they had a working hypothesis concerning what the key weaknesses might be (see Figures 13.1 and 13.2). We subsequently discovered that this technique is used by consulting companies (such as McKinsey) where an "initial hypothesis" is encouraged.

**Figure 13.1**   Metaphor for auditing without a working hypothesis

**Figure 13.2**    Metaphor for auditing with a working hypothesis

Phil Gerrard (CAE, Rolls-Royce) explains why the use of a hypothesis can be of value:

> "The reason a hypothesis is important is twofold. It helps clarity as you start and progress the assignment because it makes you ask yourself the 'So what?' questions. If you hypothesize about the petty cash getting stolen, you need to be clear whether it's important in the scheme of things. It makes you really think about what matters. It can help you to do a sort of reverse stress test."

The power of the working hypothesis in an audit context goes beyond helping to fast track assignments, it can also help auditors become clearer about whether they have preconceptions (or even prejudices) in relation to what might be uncovered during an assignment. The benefit of this can be to make the auditors more mindful of a lack of independence and objectivity during the assignment. That said, a hypothesis must be used with care; Rania Bejjani (CAE, Colt Technology Group) explains her approach:

> "Sometimes I do express my concerns and views about an audit to the team when they are planning their work. However, at times when an assignment is complex where there could be a range of issues, I would

explain the context and the interdependencies, but I may not always voice my hunches upfront to the team. The reason is that I do not want to influence the objectivity of my auditors or insert a bias and undue influence in their judgment. I want them to assess the situation objectively, independently with an open mind.

However, my questioning about the progress of the assignment and what is being found would be informed by my hunches. I won't necessarily put these on the table upfront for each assignment, but they are present in my mind and I would voice them when I believe it is appropriate. Again, that's because I want the team to do a thorough diligent job and I want them to have an open mind when looking at an area rather than pre-judging the situation or jumping too early to unsubstantiated conclusions."

The source of a good working hypothesis will normally be developed by good audit planning; considering relevant key performance indicators and other intelligence, combined with the insights of experienced auditors. Using a range of inputs to inform the working hypothesis will normally help to reduce the risk of personal auditor biases about what the issues might be. The role of gathering and assessing intelligence as a key source of audit added value will be discussed further in a subsequent chapter.

Actions for Internal Audit to consider:

- Pilot the use of a working hypothesis to prioritize the work done in assignments and review the results obtained;
- Recognize that the working hypothesis may also reveal auditor pre-conceptions and may not be correct, so try to establish whether there is a factual basis for the concern.


### Revisit the Scope and Resourcing of Each Assignment as a Fundamental Part of Assignment Planning

A common practice in lean progressive audit functions is to adjust the scope and approach of each assignment in accordance with what emerges during the assignment planning process. Nicola Rimmer (former President of the IIA UK) explains her preference:

"I prefer an approach in which, when we have done some planning work, we will rethink the size of the assignment ahead and the likely completion deadlines. At one end we might realize we're going to finish in 15 days, so that goes into the plan and our completion milestones. Or you might realize there is a big issue to be addressed across a number of departments, or more work is going to be needed to look at root causes, which may take you twice as long, in which case we plan for that.

The discipline of managing an assignment as a series of mini-projects is good, but it needs to be based on the actual needs of the assignment that emerge from assignment planning and not some standardized resource allocation set at the time of the audit plan. The benefit of this approach is also in the savings you can get when you recognize the original resource allocation was too generous."

Thus, a fundamental part of planning an assignment should be to give consideration to its purpose, value and resource the assignment accordingly.

Actions for Internal Audit to consider:

• Ensure that an integral part of the assignment planning process includes a reassessment of the correct resources and milestones in the light of the benefits being sought.

## Plan Assignments like Projects Throughout

One of the key changes we made when we transformed our approach to internal audit in AstraZeneca was to plan assignments all the way through to an issued report, and not just a closing meeting. Each stage had a milestone and auditors reported progress at each stage that helped to keep assignments moving forward, and allowed for the early escalation of issues that were causing delays. This practice is gaining ground and Greg Coleman (CAE, ITG) explains the benefits that result:

"I favour having very clear structure for most assignments, particularly an agreed date for the closing meeting and then the final report. We put proposed dates into people's diaries quite early on in the planning of an assignment, so they have it in their diary. They are then told that they will get a draft of the report 24 hours before the meeting, and they're encouraged to make sure they've got some time to review it.

Occasionally we do have to move this closing meeting, but it's rare. Generally speaking we're able to hit the deadline. It does mean sometimes that the audit team has to work quite hard in the two or three days prior to the meeting, to make sure that the draft report is ready for the 24 hour deadline. But I don't think that's a bad thing, and I think it keeps people focused on the key areas. In previous organizations where there was no firm assignment plan, in addition to scope creep, it was common to see meetings slipping since people weren't always available if you tried to book them at the last minute, and you can end up in a situation where audits just drag on."

Phil Gerrard (CAE, Rolls-Royce) also adopts this approach:

"We aim to set an end date after our assignment planning and get time in the diary of key stakeholders, because on a practical level if you don't get it in the diary up front you won't get the right people there. So you set the milestones early and manage achievement of them actively. We will explain that we plan to issue a draft audit report on a given date, so it's important management are not on holiday, or away then."

Of course, the planned timescales for delivering each assignment will differ based on the likely complexity of the assignment and other factors, and some deadlines will slip, but the lean, progressive approach to auditing is about creating a forward pressure in relation to the need to bring assignments to a conclusion without unnecessary delay. When this sense of purpose and energy is an integral part of the auditing process, it becomes visible to management, typically resulting in reduced prevarication and fewer delays on their part.

Actions for Internal Audit to consider:

• Set milestones for all key stages of the assignment and track progress;
• Create a discipline in which key meetings with management are booked well in advance and papers circulated ahead of time wherever possible;
• Within audit, champion a sense of purpose and energy in the auditing process in order to create a culture in which audits are delivered on time as a rule, rather than as an exception.


## CONCLUDING REMARKS

A key dilemma to manage at the assignment phase is to navigate between too little and too much planning. It is also to balance between the use of standard assignment resource allocations for an initial guide but to have the confidence to amend this as the assignment purpose and assignment plan becomes clearer.

Lean, progressive ways of working regard assignment scoping and planning as a key part of each assignment during which:

- The value from each assignment can be validated or updated with a sponsor typically at a level above the person being audited;
- There is clarity about the breadth and depth of what the assignment will cover;
- Known issues and other intelligence is weighed up to help guide the likely assignment plan and testing needs;
- Each assignment is set up as a mini-project, with updated resource requirements and milestones.

Phil Gerrard (CAE, Rolls-Royce) sums up the progressive mindset:

"Always ask yourself why am I doing the assignment? And the answer should not simply be 'Because it is in the plan'."

---

### SUMMARY OF KEY POINTS FOR INTERNAL AUDIT

- Carry out focused planning for each assignment – it will pay dividends;
- Be explicit about the value from each assignment;
- Update the resource allocation for an assignment based on the value being sought;
- Select an assignment sponsor and engage them on questions of value during the audit assignment;
- Be clear about which risks and controls are going to be addressed and make greater use of key risks and key controls to focus the work of audit;
- Use a working hypothesis as a way of fast-tracking key focus areas for the assignment, where findings may arise, but also be mindful of potential biases;
- Plan assignments as mini projects from the beginning to the end to maintain momentum, and track progress at key stages;
- Create a culture of purpose and energy in the auditing process, which will become visible to management and should reduce prevarication and delays on their part.

## RECOMMENDATIONS FOR SENIOR MANAGERS AND BOARD MEMBERS

- Ask Internal Audit to advise whether each assignment has a clear value proposition;
- For key assignments, understand what value will be delivered and offer input concerning the points likely to be of the greatest significance;
- Look for appropriate senior management sponsorship of key assignments;
- Gain a greater understanding of the breadth and depth of audit assignments: which assignments in the plan will look at all risks and controls, and which just the key risks and key controls;
- Establish whether internal audit and management are *jointly* committed to deadlines for producing a finalized assignment report;
- Obtain updates at intervals whether there are any issues that delay the flow of assignments.

# 14
# Assignment Delivery – Managing What Really Goes On

Planning for value adding assignments is important, but unless each assignment is executed to deliver that value in an efficient and timely way, the assignment will not deliver its full potential. As discussed in the last chapter, a good starting point is to regard each assignment as a mini-project, with a clear sense of its value and with key milestones along the way, and then to track progress. However, the reality (Gemba) of assignment execution is often filled with difficulties and complexities that may cause delays or impact the value delivered.

## COMMON PRACTICES AND IIA STANDARDS OF NOTE

There can be a range of approaches to delivering audit assignments, depending on their purpose (e.g. whether it is a design effectiveness review or detailed audit), complexity (e.g. multi-location or multi-department) and other factors (such as the use of co-source or specialist skills or the requirement to meet specific deadlines).

Common audit practice is to work through the assignment plan that has been prepared to deliver the assignment scope and objectives. Depending on the precise nature of the assignment plan, auditors may carry out any or all of the following tasks: obtaining and analysing relevant data, reviewing documentation and information, walking through processes and activities, carrying out interviews and carrying out more detailed testing as required. This work should help the auditor form a view about the different areas in the assignment, and to understand the likely remediation actions that should be undertaken. Better audit functions try to probe the underlying reasons for their findings; with the IIA recommending the use of root cause analysis techniques to do this.

## COMMON CHALLENGES & DILEMMAS

CAEs become interested in lean auditing for a number of reasons, but it is quite common for me to see CAEs and audit terms after they have had a "scare" in relation to their assignment productivity and delivery. At one extreme this can be due to a major shortfall in plan delivery, or just a growing sense that things are "slipping", with a number of audits running over budget, or a sense that within the time allotted auditors are not always getting to the heart of key issues.

Where an audit function develops a culture of regularly requesting additional time for assignments, or finds itself challenged to deliver the audit plan, lean ways of working are likely to make a considerable difference. Lean ways of working pay attention to the Gemba (reality) of why delays arise, at a more structured and granular level than might be achieved through benchmarking or general best practice discussions. The most common challenges are summarized below:

### Getting Data and Documents in Advance is not Always Straightforward

As I spend time with different audit functions I see a wide range of different cultures they must operate within. Each organizational culture will be influenced by a number of factors, including the country, the type of organization and sector, its history, senior management style, and also the current challenges the organization is facing.

Against this backdrop some audit functions find it takes a lot of time and effort to get the documentation and information they require for the assignment, whilst others encounter little or no difficulty.

The reasons for delays in getting information are manyfold and can include the fact that some audit staff do not communicate early enough with management concerning what information they need. This may be due to a lack of planning on the auditor's part or because the auditor was only recently given the audit assignment by audit management. Either way, unless "auditees" are given sufficient notice of the information that needs to be provided, it is likely that delays will arise, partly because of the other priorities and resource constraints that "auditees" work within, but also because of practical factors (such as the need to run tailored system enquiries or obtain documents from a filing room).

Additional problems auditors face can include finding that the information supplied is not complete and therefore having to request more information, often just before or at the start of the planned fieldwork. Inevitably, delays in getting data and documentation can result in a lot of effort "chasing after" relevant files and even delay the start of the fieldwork: all constituting Muda.

## Process Mapping

Another challenge I hear in relation to the early stages of an audit assignment is the time it can take "making sense" of processes and controls before they are audited in detail. A practice for some audit functions is to engage management about key activities and processes, through discussions or a process walkthrough, and then produce some process mapping documentation that sets out the "as is" situation and the important control activities that then need to be tested in more detail. This process mapping by audit can consume several days depending on the extent of documentation already in place, the complexity of the process, and the auditor who is assigned the task.

## Managers and Staff are Often Busy and have Limited Time to Engage in the Audit Process

As assignments progress auditors tell me about the feeling that management and staff are "squeezing in" their support for the audit alongside their day-to-day work. Thus, auditors can often experience being told: "You will need to wait until later today," or "Can I look into that issue and then perhaps we can discuss it tomorrow?"

The best auditors plan meetings with key staff in advance, but managers and staff are not always reliable in making these appointments, or auditors can find that the time for these meetings is squeezed. Looked at from the perspective of line managers, some comment: "The audit staff were poorly prepared and I spent half my time educating them" or

"The auditor kept coming back with additional questions and information requests."

Even where audit functions are more disciplined with their ways of working, one of the dilemmas auditors experience about "pushing" for information, is the feeling that it will adversely impact relationships with management. There is no doubt that a way to create dissatisfaction is to ignore the reality of the pressures facing managers and staff. However, underlying this can be a question of what constitutes sufficient notice for information requests, and how quickly audit requests should be turned around.

If auditors regularly experience managers and staff struggling to provide information, this can provide important clues about Muda, either within the audit process or management processes. It can also yield clues about potential control environment issues (i.e. over-stretched managers and staff regularly in fire-fighting mode, or poor information management disciplines, or a weak risk and control mindset).

## The Impact of Auditor Preferences on Testing

Testing is clearly a fundamental part of what an auditor must do and yet, time and time again, I hear of CAEs who are concerned about this area. Their concerns can range from finding that some members of the team have a tendency to do "auditing by anecdote", and not do enough detailed fact-finding. At the other extreme can be auditors who get lost in the detail of a particular area out of all proportion to its real importance. Richard Chambers (President & CEO, IIA) makes the following observation:

> "I think part of our problem as a profession is that sometimes we have a tendency to over-audit. Sometimes we do things in the audit process to validate things that aren't really going to be important."

(See Figure 14.1).

One of the reasons for this can be that some auditors have "pet topic areas" that they like to focus on. These focus areas may be justified, but sometimes the time devoted to a specific area can be influenced by an auditor's personal interests, or reflect areas they have expertise in, or enjoy, auditing. This is an important topic and comes up regularly in workshops and consulting assignments; the key point being that an

**Figure 14.1**    The auditor challenge of maintaining perspective

auditor's preference to look at some areas may not match the reality of what is truly important to the organization at that point in time, and therefore constitutes Muda.

## "Innocent Until Proven Guilty?"

Another common point that emerges from discussions regarding testing is the question of who has the onus to demonstrate that there are risk assurance issues? Often auditors tell me that they will find a problem, based on a sample of information, but when this is shared with management they will retort with comments such as: "Your sample is too small, I'm sure that's just a one off problem" or "Yes, but I don't think this is a problem elsewhere." And as a result, internal audit can find it is being asked to do more testing, with a bigger sample size about the extent and impact of the issue they believe they have uncovered.

The mindset seems to be that management is "innocent until proven guilty" (as commonly understood in many legal systems), and therefore the burden should fall on audit to prove "beyond reasonable doubt" both: i) there is an issue and ii) that the issue matters. This mindset can result in audit having to devote a considerable amount of time and effort to addressing these questions; raising the question of whether this effort is really adding value.

## Audit Tools: A Blessing or A Curse?

I have been fortunate to spend time with a number of audit functions looking at their audit strategies and I also get the opportunity to look at audit functions through my work on External Quality Assessments (EQAs). On occasions I might recommend the need to better leverage audit tools such as audit software or data analytics, since these can save a considerable amount of time and enable audit to "zoom in" on key areas of potential weakness.

With larger audit functions audit tools are normally in place, but may not be delivering all that was hoped for. One auditor summed up the problem by observing:

> "Often my assignments are as much about 'feeding the machine' as they are about doing the audit."

I have even seen audit functions, disappointed with one audit software, that then put a lot of effort into migrating to another software only to be confronted with many of the same issues!

## Waste Associated with Meetings

At the lean auditing workshops I run, we look at the difficulties that can arise in relation to meetings with management during the course of an assignment. Difficulties can include meetings being cut short or meetings being cancelled, or managers explaining: "I'm really not the right person to speak to about that, you need to speak to Joe."

Auditors also speak of "side tracking" by managers, who do not answer a question directly and instead talk about other issues. After meetings are completed, some auditors may take several hours to write up the minutes of what happened, or find that a key follow up action that they thought they had agreed with management is not delivered on time.

Another issue that regularly comes up at my lean auditing workshops and during consulting work, is an awareness that sometimes a key point in an assignment does not get properly pinned down, causing disagreements and delays towards the end of an assignment. This can include staff disowning comments made earlier in the audit when in the presence of a senior manager.

## What Is a Finding?

Even when auditors have successfully established facts that demonstrate there may be a weakness in control, various further challenges can arise, each of which can undermine audit's position, or result in additional work:

- A statement that there is a compensating control that "covers" the gap in control that audit has found;
- A statement that whilst there could be a weakness in control, the problem is not that serious and therefore no remediation is required because it is within management's "risk appetite"; and
- An argument that audit has raised a hypothetical issue that management doesn't have the time to worry about given other more pressing priorities.

Karen Dignan (CAE, Group Head Office, OMG) offers the following reflections on risk appetite:

> "I think that auditors generally could be better at thinking about risk appetite. Because it's easy to raise points and then hear management saying 'Why are you raising that point as a finding? We're not really concerned about that. We are happy to accept that risk and we don't see it as a key risk'."

When this is the outcome of an auditor's work there is a real question whether the audit has added value, especially if management's views would be shared by board members and/or external customers.

These challenges highlight Muda that can be commonplace during audit assignments: delays, wasted time and effort, with a good portion of the assignment that is actually delivering very little value.

## RECOMMENDED PRACTICES

Lean demands an awareness of, and focus on, all forms of waste (Muda) and areas where value is not being added. Henry Ford (Founder of the Ford Motor Company) provided the following observation, highlighting the kind of mindset that paved the way for lean ways of working:

"Time waste differs from material waste in that there can be no salvage. The easiest of all wastes and the hardest to correct is the waste of time, because wasted time does not litter the floor like wasted material."

This mindset can often be missing in some organizations and some functions (including audit), where a sense of urgency can so easily be lost, and highlights one of the changes in mindset that needs to take place to drive lean ways of working.

Other approaches that have been successful are summarized below.

## Make the Assignment as Painless as Possible

Lean encourages us to be sensitive to those who are directly, or indirectly, involved in delivering customer value. As a result audit should consider the impact of its assignments. Richard Young (Director, UNIAC) gives his perspective:

"When our best auditors are working on an assignment most staff in the area concerned hardly realize an audit is underway. The auditors understand the context those people work in, being mindful of how they use their time and cutting out the things that aren't going to add any value. This mindset is crucial when you think of lean auditing."

Thus, preparation by audit, being mindful of management priorities and being very focused on what really matters are all hallmarks of progressive ways of working. Linked to this is the importance of encouraging management to advise audit about any known or suspected issues or concerns they have and what they are doing about these – it doesn't add much value for audit to spend time and effort unearthing an issue that management are already aware of!

Actions for Internal Audit to consider:

• Discuss good practices in terms of preparation and assignment approach to ensure that managers are not unnecessarily disrupted during the assignment process;
• Ensure management are explicitly asked to outline known issues or areas of concern and existing or planned remediation actions – paying close attention to what this means for the execution of the assignment.

## Aim for a Flow of Data and Documents Through Direct Access

A specific good practice by progressive lean audit functions is the way they get information for assignments, with the minimum of disruption to management and without delays. Different approaches can be adopted, as outlined below:

- Requesting key information and data at the time the assignment scope is issued (e.g. many weeks ahead of the field work);
- Requesting read-only access to key systems and folders, so that audit can access this information for itself;
- Already having direct read-only access to a range of key systems and folders, so access does not need to be requested.

The "direct access" approaches of options b) and c) are likely to be the most efficient. Option b) can sometimes require the audit function to negotiate with a system or data owner to get access to data and information. Option c) can be achieved by agreeing a protocol with senior management and the board that the IT department will, as a matter of routine, grant audit access to systems that are most used or will be covered as part of the agreed audit plan.

Both options b) and c) enjoy a further benefit over option a) since direct access to data and folders gives audit an insight into the Gemba of information storage "in the wild". This avoids the problem of management doing "window dressing" or "tidying up" before or during an assignment, which is a worry a number of auditors have when they are waiting to receive information.

Actions for Internal Audit to consider:

- Seek direct access to data and documents wherever possible, in order to more closely see the state of information as it is "in the wild";
- Agree an access protocol with senior stakeholders for systems and key folders if time is being wasted negotiating access on a case-by-case basis.

## Consider an Audit Liaison Role and Agree Expectations Around Timelines

As discussed earlier, having a senior sponsor for an assignment can be a powerful way to focus and cut through disagreements and delays associated with scoping and scheduling an assignment. Another role that can greatly smooth the assignment process is an audit liaison role. This will typically be a person nominated by the assignment sponsor or the manager of the area being reviewed. The person nominated to act in a liaison role should support audit before and during assignment fieldwork by organizing meetings, helping to get information and data when needed and supporting audit by escalating issues to the sponsor.

At one of my lean auditing workshops an audit manager said that she had encountered a department that created a liaison role, but observed, half joking, that the "liaison person seems to specialize in keeping us away from anything sensitive, rather than helping us". Needless to say, if there is a risk of this, the role and responsibilities of the liaison role may need to be explicitly defined.

Alongside a liaison role, it may be necessary to spell out a protocol for the provision of information during an audit assignment. This can relate to the time allowed for a management response to a draft audit report, for example, but can be extended to time expectations for all stages of the assignment – for both managers and auditors. Tellingly, one auditor once remarked to me: "I'm not sure about this timelines protocol idea; of course it would be good to get management to give us information on a more timely basis, but if it applies to both sides I'm not so sure how easily our audit function would meet its side of the bargain!"

Needless to say, being lean in assignment delivery is something that requires improved discipline by both management and audit. Where there is repeated slippage audit functions need to be prepared to escalate this upwards so that timelines are adhered to.

Actions for Internal Audit to consider:

- Within audit, determine the preferred timelines for the key steps of an assignment;
- Seek senior manager or sponsor endorsement of typical timelines;
- Discuss role expectations and timelines with key management contacts at the start of each assignment;
- Agree liaison contacts where this is going to be helpful;
- Note and escalate repeated delays or difficulties.

## Prioritize Scope Delivery and Use "If Time Permits"

In the last chapter I discussed the importance of having a clear focus on what, exactly, in an assignment is adding value. However, unless this is very clearly communicated and managed throughout the assignment, it can be easy for an assignment to slip "off track".

A simple way of keeping a clear focus on what matters the most is to ensure that any assignment scope that is documented is ranked in terms of the importance of the areas under review. Thus, an audit methodology that is lean should encourage auditors to focus, in the first instance, on the most important items within the assignment scope. Auditors should be warned about the pitfalls of starting work on areas they regard to be straightforward (or that they enjoy working on) in order to "get off to a good start".

Taking a value approach, the early stages of the assignment should be focused on what is most valuable for the organization, and move to other areas of scope when it is clear that the key areas have been properly addressed.

The advantage of this approach, which was adopted by internal audit in AstraZeneca after our work on lean, is that it enables more assignments to deliver to time. This is because, if an assignment runs into difficulties, the areas remaining to be done are likely to be the less important ones, and therefore can be more easily dropped.

Some audit functions explicitly address the fact that the assignment should focus on what is most important by stating that some areas of scope will be covered "if time permits". Of course, the best auditors will usually deliver all areas of scope within an assignment, but this approach allows for some explicit contingency if there is a risk of an assignment running over budget.

Using this approach can also have some interesting spin off consequences; for example, I have heard of instances when management have asked: "What do you mean, 'if time permits'? I was hoping you were going to look at this area for me. I want to know what is going on!" This can then allow for discussions about the assignment purpose and value add as well as the role of audit and management's monitoring role, e.g. "It's not the role of audit to carry out your monitoring role for you."

Actions for Internal Audit to consider:

- Rank the assignment scope based on value add;
- Create clear expectations about what areas should be looked at first;
- Consider stating "if time permits" for less important areas in audit scope documents to allow audit to meet its resource and timeline plans.

## Deriving Value from Process or Systems Mapping, and Clarifying the Role of Audit in this Regard

It is clearly sensible that auditors should understand the areas that they are working on, and it will often make sense for them to walk through key processes, systems or other activities – assuming these address key areas of potential value loss.

However, if process or systems documentation does not exist, or needs to be significantly updated, there is an important question about whether it should be the role of internal audit to pull together this documentation. Conversely: what accountability do management and staff have to maintain up to date documentation of processes and procedures?

Several choices arise in relation to systems and process documentation:

- To agree that it is management's role to keep this documentation up to date, and if this is not happening audit can raise a finding immediately that this should be done and documentation updated on an ongoing basis;
- To agree that in the long run it is management's role to keep this documentation up to date, but that audit will develop a "starter for 10" process or systems maps, which management must then own and keep up to date, (and if they do not do this in the future, audit can raise a finding);
- To agree that in the long run it is management's role to keep this documentation up to date, but that audit will i) help advise what good process or systems documentation will look like and, perhaps, ii) work jointly with management to prepare this.

My advice is that internal audit should be wary of writing process and systems documentation on a regular basis without considering the question of roles.

However, if auditors do go to the trouble of writing or updating systems and process documentation, this should not just be done "for the audit file" but shared with staff or managers in the area for their ongoing use. "The audit file" is not a customer as far as lean is concerned!

Actions for Internal Audit to consider:

- Agree as an audit function whether the accountability for keeping process and systems documentation is clear;
- Establish a way of working in relation to system and process mapping, ideally moving towards management ownership of this task;
- If audit does any work to update or improve systems or process maps, this work should be shared with management, with an expectation they will keep it up to date in future, as far as possible.

## Managing Auditor Pet Topics and Risk Control Matrices

In the last chapter I discussed the role of risk control matrices. These can be used as a tool to help assignments focus on the most important risks and controls (i.e. the key risks and the key controls). They can also be very helpful during assignments. Here are some reflections from a senior audit manager:

"You've got to recognize that auditors will feel more comfortable auditing some things rather than others. What you mustn't have is an audit that's driven by what an auditor feels most comfortable looking at.

You have to sit down as part of planning and go through with the auditor what's the risk in this process, what's the risk in this business unit, whatever it is you have to be looking at. What are the key controls that address those risks? And how would we test for them?

That way you don't end up testing things that don't matter."

Risk control matrices are one tool that can be used so that assignments stay focused on what matters the most. (See Figure 14.2).
However, some words of caution:

- Pre-prepared risk control matrices may not cover key risk areas that have been identified during assignment planning;
- Pre-prepared risk control matrices may include risks and controls that are not really key in the context of the assignment purpose or management risk appetite.

As a result, it is vital that during the assignment planning stage, risk control matrices are modified to:

- Incorporate key risks and controls not included in a standard risk control matrix;
- Exclude risk areas or controls that are not relevant to the scope, or the agreed risk appetite.

The sign of a value adding assignment, without waste, is often the intelligent editing of risk control matrices, rather than slavishly sticking to pre-prepared formats.

| Risk | Ref | Expected Control | Actual Control | Work to be performed / work completed | Issues arising / observations |
|---|---|---|---|---|---|
| **Communication with Central Functions Regarding Fixed Assets Purchases by the Entity** | | | | | |
| Fixed asset transactions may not be accurately recorded in accordance with company's accounting policies and procedures. | | Written accounting policies and principles on fixed asset transactions (acquisition, physical control, disposal, transfer, depreciation, etc.) are in place and are being implemented. | | Obtain the current policies and procedures over the Capital Investment and Asset Management process and review for adequacy/ appropriateness over the process. Assess whether they have been formalized and communicated to staff. | |
| | | A fixed asset register (FAR) is maintained. All assets are recorded together with descriptions, depreciation rates, cost and asset locations. | | Confirm that a fixed asset register is maintained and this records all relevant asset information, such as:<br>• Asset number<br>• Description<br>• Date of purchase<br>• Original cost<br>• Accumulated depreciation<br>• Written down value<br>• Rate of depreciation – percentage or expected useful life<br>• Location / department<br>• Serial or other identification number | |
| **Evaluation Process and Capital Expenditure** | | | | | |
| Unbudgeted / unauthorized capital expenditure occurs. | | A capital investment plan, which includes suspension of an operation or a disposal of major fixed assets, has been approved by the Board. | | Ensure that a rolling investment plan is reviewed annually and the annual investment plan has been approved by the Board. | |
| Assets are purchased without a thorough selection process & sufficient authorization. | | All new capex requests have undergone a formal evaluation process and a investment application has been completed. | | For a sample of newly acquired assets to the FAR confirm that:<br>• a formal evaluation process has been undertaken.<br>• a capex application has been completed and authorized in line with the delegated financial approval limits. | |

**Figure 14.2** A risk control matrix (illustrative)

Actions for Internal Audit to consider:

- Discuss as a team the use of risk and control matrices;
- Agree disciplines to ensure risk and control matrices are properly focused for each assignment.

## Step Up Meeting Disciplines

As outlined earlier, time can be wasted in relation to meetings, either beforehand (e.g. the meeting is cancelled), during (e.g. the manager going off topic or the auditor missing a key point) or after (e.g. as a result of poor follow up). To drive out Muda, auditors need to adopt a proactive approach to address the areas of most concern.

Auditors often find that some of the improvement areas discussed earlier, such as the creation of a sponsor for each assignment, will help reduce significantly instances of meetings being delayed or cancelled. In addition, auditors who want to enhance the value add from meetings tend to prepare better for what they are going to ask. Andy Weintraub (experienced internal audit leader) offers the following advice:

> "Do your homework. Go into meetings with an agenda and consider providing it to the audit customer in advance, including some of the detailed questions. That way everyone's had a chance to think about what we're going to talk about."

Phil Gerrard (CAE, Rolls-Royce) highlights additional benefits from better preparation:

> "It enhances the credibility of audit when management say 'I can see from your analysis you've done robust planning'. It can also lead to management agreeing to take action, in which case there's no point doing loads of testing to prove something when management has already accepted it."

If an auditor finds that meetings are often being cancelled, be prepared to discuss any patterns of cancellations. For example: "I realize that John's team are busy, but over the past quarter there have been four occasions when they have had to cancel meetings. This is significantly out of line with other departments who are also very busy. What should we do about this?"

The key to this approach is: i) to keep the factual details of what has happened (even a log of meeting bookings and cancellations); ii) to spot the pattern, rather than the individual cancellations, and iii) to use the fact that regular cancellations or rescheduling is out of line compared to other areas, to bring pressure on them, and iv) if necessary, be prepared to escalate further, focusing on the impact on wasted audit resource.

Some CAEs I have worked with on these issues have noted that managers rarely cancel meetings with the external auditor because they will be charged for the lost time. As a consequence, some internal functions have started to threaten charging for cancellations in order to highlight that it is wasteful.

During meetings, the number of auditors in attendance needs to be weighed up. Some audit functions just allocate one auditor to a meeting, and use voice recorders to record what is said. Clearly recording conversations can affect the dynamic of a meeting, and there may also be legal and privacy issues, but it is clearly an efficient way to use time. In other audit functions a second auditor will be a note taker, with the best making notes directly into a computer, so little time is lost writing up notes afterwards.

Thinking about Muda should make auditors mindful of writing up long minutes of meetings. One audit function I have worked with has a rule that the minutes of a meeting should take no longer to complete than the length of the meeting itself. Another audit function has a rule that the key points from any meeting should be summarized in bullet point form and sent to the interviewee within the hour! Some auditors look stunned when I explain this, but I think many managers (and external customers) would be equally stunned to find some auditors can spend half a day writing up minutes of a 90-minute meeting! If we are concerned with maximizing value and eliminating waste there can be no blank cheques, or free resources. Remember Parkinson's law: "Work expands so as to fill the time available for its completion."

Finally, one practice we implemented after the lean review of Astra-Zeneca's internal audit function, was to spend more time thinking about the quality of our interview questioning and follow-through. In one assignment, I remember sitting in on an interview between an audit manager and a business manager. I explained that I was there to take some notes, but my main purpose was to coach the audit manager after the interview. I also said I would ask a few questions at the end of the meeting if I felt something needed to be clarified.

The interview progressed and I observed and took notes. Towards the end of the interview I asked a couple of questions for further clarification, one of which opened up an important line of enquiry. After the interview, I sat down with the audit manager over lunch and we discussed what had happened. We discussed the new line of enquiry that had opened up at the end, and I explained: "You did the groundwork for that. The manager hinted at the issue in response to your earlier questions, but you seemed to be keen to move on to other areas, so you missed the follow-up question. All I did was to make sure it didn't get lost."

Afterwards, we discussed the challenge of knowing when to distinguish between unimportant "noise" and a key "signal" that needs to be pursued. The audit manager recognized that "getting on with the questionnaire" sometimes needs to be put on hold when a key point needs to be resolved.

Similarly, I have observed interviews in which auditors tense up, lean forward or rapidly scribble down notes as a reaction to something that a manager has said. When this happens I can see the manager spotting the auditor's interest and starting to become more careful about what they say. This sort of subtle behavioural signal would never appear in the minutes of a meeting, but can be one reason an auditor was unable to get to the heart of certain issues. It can also explain why some managers may dislike being audited, since they may feel they are being judged.

My experience is that better meeting management disciplines can *significantly* impact both the efficiency and effectiveness of an audit function and also improve relationships between auditor and managers. Training courses in this area can be useful, but I strongly recommend coaching "on the job" as well. This has the power of focusing in on the specific strengths and improvement areas of individual auditors and typically has a very notable, immediate impact, alongside improvements to the audit assignment itself.

Actions for Internal Audit to consider:

- Discuss best practices and areas of difficulty in relation to managing meetings;
- Plan questions and identify which are most important before the meeting starts;
- Agree expectations around note taking – encourage quick feedback to those involved, a clarity of key points discussed and actions agreed, and a proactive approach to following up on open points;
- Observe and coach staff on the effectiveness of their interview techniques.

## Utilizing Data Analytics

When I discuss lean ways of working with internal auditors, it is often not long before auditors want to talk about the use of data analytics tools (which can, among other things, analyze large quantities of data with a view to finding exceptions and other useful information). There can be no doubt these tools can be useful in the right context and I am sometimes surprised by audit functions that make little use of these tools, when reasonably priced options are increasingly available. Here are the reflections of one CAE:

> "I think it is absolutely mandatory that audit should have some capability in audit tools, especially if you are doing financial compliance work. We have saved a lot of time in the team by much more automated testing. It's stuff that we are asked to do each year so we just run it and report."

However, the most progressive approaches I have seen exploit this technology, not just simply in routine areas, but as a way of identifying important value opportunities. Leigh Flanigan (CAE, CSIRO, Australia) explains:

> "When people talk data analytics their mind immediately goes to financial data. However, there is a lot more data in an organization than that which is financial. Analyzing operational data you can do all sorts of interesting things with data analytics that tell you things about your key performance indicators, operational and strategic."

Thus, the more progressive audit functions are able to use data analytics outside of the financial area and also to use them as a tool to aid audit planning, not just speeding up testing.

However, the extensive use of data analytics does not automatically equate to being lean. Norman Marks (GRC thought leader) explains:

> "Data mining and analysis is just a set of tools. But by the same token talking to people is a set of tools, probably more important than even analytical routines.

> You need to have the right mindset. Whether it's the analysis of big data or going around talking to people, that comes after you've identified what you are trying to achieve."

Thus, an essential message in relation to data analytics is the ability to use these tools in order to deliver value to clients and stakeholders (and ultimately external customers) and not to regard them as "playthings" within the audit function. Linked to this is the need to think carefully about whose role it should be to deploy data analytics. Here are the reflections of Jonathan Kidd (CAE, UK Met Office):

> "My ultimate aim is to embed a data analytics capability into finance and purchasing. I believe that management should be doing continuous monitoring and we should just be able to go to them and say okay, it's that time of year again. Show us your exception reports and what you have done with them. We would get a more continuous controls monitoring culture and proactive approach to remediating issues."

Encouraging greater accountability in the first and second lines of defence is an important ingredient in improving the risk and control culture of an organization; after all, stopping a fraud is something that is mostly achieved "on the ground" in real time by finance or purchasing procedures, or management supervision. All too often the work of internal audit will take place after a fraud has taken place, which is clearly less valuable than stopping the fraud in the first place.

Actions for Internal Audit to consider:

- Discuss the use of data analytics tools – are these being underused?
- Are any auditors using data analytics as a toy rather than a tool?
- Consider whether the ownership of data analytics should be extended, so that continuous monitoring and auditing can be deployed by other functions (such as purchasing, finance and payroll, etc).

## Taking a Step-by-Step Approach to Testing

The use of a prioritized assignment scope and objectives, an understanding of key risks and key controls, and leveraging of data analytics tools can considerably help assignments to be both more efficient and impactful. However, "in the trenches" of an audit assignment, good plans can easily get bogged down in detail and "rabbit holes". One former senior audit manager makes the following observations:

> "There isn't really any business – large or small – where you can look at the detail of everything, so deciding what to look at is really critical.

And the scale of activity means that often times random sampling isn't really going to be very helpful. You've got to be much more focused to say where it would be best to look – and stay focused, as much as possible, in delivering that."

Leigh Flanigan (CAE, CSIRO, Australia) offers his reflections about how auditors should manage the detail:

"Something I tell my staff is that more work can always be done, but you can't undo work you've already done. If you've done some work and you think you've found an issue, communicate it up; don't just do more work and leave the communication to the end.

If you think there's an issue, you can look into it better by engaging with the right people in the organization. Then, if more work needs to be done, you can do it; but if no more work needs to be done, it's down tools."

Andy Weintraub (experienced internal audit leader) continues:

"From my perspective, every stone doesn't have to be uncovered. Every single detail doesn't have to be figured out. If you're testing and you run into a question or something's not adding up then you've got to use your judgment and know when to dig a bit more and when to let go.

To help strike the right balance it can really help to have checkpoints in the audit team. Here's what we found so far and this is what we're planning to focus on now. Great. Go design your tests. Great. How many are you going to look at? What are the attributes you're going to look at? Great.

It's not micromanaging an assignment, but rather it's having key checkpoints to make sure that auditors are on track, that they're going down the right direction and not getting bogged down in details."

Chris Baker (Technical Manager, IIA UK) provides the following perspective:

"IIA Standards say that you need to gather sufficient evidence and have sufficient relevant information to be confident about what you are concluding and in order to be able to express an opinion.

The basic principle is clear: you've got to do enough work and gather enough information and interpret and analyse that information to form a view.

That's often translated into a whole load of advice about how many records you need to look at and how many tests you need to do to substantiate everything, when, in point of fact, when we are focusing on risk and adding value it should be different from that.

It's wrong to stick to sample requirements in a rigid way."

Actions for Internal Audit to consider:

• Review the audit methodology and practice in the audit function around testing;
• Encourage early engagement with management;
• Instill discipline in the testing process to appropriately balance rigour and efficiency.

## Keeping Your Eyes Open for "Killer Facts"

Whilst one of the key ways to drive efficiency in audit assignments is to adopt a more focused and step-by-step approach to testing, it is important to recognize this does not mean audit should abandon working in the detail. An experienced Health & Safety auditor provides the following reflections about the challenge of auditing to the right level of detail:

> "If you regard lean auditing as simply a 'doing less' approach, you might fail to test something in sufficient detail and therefore give false assurance. I can think of at least two or three examples in my career where simply doing a high level review would have suggested a management system in place, but below this were quite serious issues. As auditors we know that sometimes it's only by doing the deep dive down to the transactional level of analysis that you are going to uncover some gaps in control, or improvement opportunities.
>
> In a nutshell, you can have the wool pulled over your eyes if you don't go deep enough, but this fear does not mean you should check absolutely everything."

Richard Chambers (President & CEO, IIA) offers his perspective on striking this balance:

> "I would never advocate that internal audit ease its vigilance for fraud or other irregularities, even in the course of narrowing objectives or scope.

However, all too often we end up trying to tell someone how to build a watch – when all they really need to know is the time of day."

Another perspective on the dilemma of keeping your eyes open, without getting distracted, is to look out for a "killer fact" that will grab the attention of stakeholders, over-turn counter-arguments, and galvanize appropriate action. To illustrate, one CAE explained that for some audit reports he would ask his auditors to include copies of key documents (e.g. key documents with missing signatures), or photographs (e.g. confidential documents visible on a desk), to demonstrate that audit had found something indisputable and important, that needed to be discussed and/or remediated.

A "killer fact" need not simply be a piece of conventional audit evidence. It could also be other internal data and information, or even come from external sources. For example, if audit finds a problem with disaster recovery arrangements, a typical management response can be: "Well you've just highlighted a hypothetical issue, why should we spend time and effort on something that might happen?" The "killer fact" response could be: "This is not a hypothetical issue. In our organization, in the last year, there were six occasions when systems experienced service interruptions" or "This issue is not hypothetical. Major continuity issues have happened in three organizations in our sector in the last year, with the following impact..."

Thus, having a value oriented approach to audit testing and findings recognizes that value does not simply come from having bigger sample sizes: finding 40 issues out of a sample of 100 is not necessarily twice as valuable as finding 20 issues out of a sample of 50. In fact, sometimes it's about finding the right 10 issues out of 25 that will enable audit to: i) find the root cause of an issue and ii) persuade management to take action.

Actions for Internal Audit to consider:

- Never underestimate the power of a good example (i.e. "killer fact") to highlight an area for improvement and generate management action. These should be captured in even the shortest audit reports;
- Review some recent audits and identify how clearly these "killer facts" are reflected;
- Discuss ways of working when doing testing work to maximize the use of "killer facts".

## Using Root Cause Analysis to Add Value and Streamline Reports

With one of my CAE clients we noticed reports that were becoming too lengthy. I discussed this with the auditors concerned and we identified – amongst other things – the need to improve the way in which findings were being examined for their root causes. In one case we reduced 25 "findings" down to seven key root cause issues, and as a result slimmed the report in half.

Root cause analysis has become an increasingly important area in my consulting and training. Shagen Ganason (former Chief Assurance officer at Department of Conservation, New Zealand) has seen the same benefit from using root cause analysis:

> "Root cause analysis reduces the number of findings. Because instead of having ten findings you probably have three findings with common root causes. If you are able to identify the proper root causes you can then actually combine a lot of the findings, which leads to shorter more impactful reporting."

A related point is that audit actions allocated to relatively junior staff are often unlikely to be addressing root causes. At AstraZeneca we had a minimum level of seniority within the management structure that we aimed to agree actions with to try to ensure: i) the right level of management engagement and ii) that the underlying causes for issues were considered and dealt with.

Norman Marks (GRC thought leader) considers other more strategic benefits from root cause analysis:

> "I think that reporting the findings in terms of symptoms and then stopping is ridiculous. If you just report the reconciliations are not being done, without asking five or six more questions that may be needed to identify the root cause, the issues don't go away. You're actually not curing the patient. You're just pointing out the problem."

Thus, root cause analysis, if done well, can not only result in streamlined reporting, but also start to get to the heart of important issues in relation to GRC and assurance matters. This is also why an analysis of common themes from audits can be powerful, since it might point to common root causes in the risk and assurance culture. Addressing these can drive improvements in organizational efficiency and effectiveness, for the benefit of all key stakeholders.

Of course, root cause analysis can sometimes add time onto an assignment so there may be judgments to be made about how best to do this. However, if auditors approach their assignments with a root cause mindset this does not need to be a significant additional burden. Here is some advice from Phil Gerrard (CAE, Rolls-Royce):

> "When planning an assignment think about what the root causes might be and implant those in the minds of your auditors. So at least they are clear about what you mean when you discuss this with them."

Actions for Internal Audit to consider:

- Look at some recent audit reports and consider whether the real root causes have been clearly identified;
- Consider how clear the audit methodology is on root cause analysis and how clearly it is understood and applied by auditors in practice;
- If relatively junior persons are normally tasked with actions, consider whether this is a sign that root causes are not being identified;
- Pay close attention to issues, incidents and audit themes since they may point to underlying cultural issues that have not yet been addressed in the organization.

## CONCLUDING REMARKS

I acknowledge that every assignment is different and the application of my "Actions for Internal Audit to consider" will vary depending on current practice and the organizational context. In particular, where there are regulatory or compliance obligations, there may be limited room for manoeuvre to implement a number of lean ways of working. However, even with compliance or regulatory related assignments it has been my experience that the principles of value add and eliminating Muda can be successfully applied (if necessary by discussing planned changes with key stakeholders (including regulators) outlining the benefits that will result).

I also recognize that some of the other challenges and inefficiencies faced by audit functions are a result of other pressures and constraints and my recommended actions suggested need to be considered within this context as well. However, having worked in this field for a number of years, my experience is that notable productivity improvements can be made in relation to what is done in relation to assignment fieldwork. I also recognize that in the real world a degree of "Muda" is almost inevitable in order to validate that important areas are working well during an audit assignment. However, the key is keeping any waste to a modest level with the minimum number of dead ends.

A recurring theme is the importance of being purposeful during each assignment and never regarding the testing stage as something that can be done on autopilot. Of course, autopilot moments will arise from time to time, but if this becomes a regular occurrence, alarm bells should be ringing about whether audit is really delivering value. This may include considering whether audit is taking on management's monitoring role.

Finally, it is worth emphasizing the importance of good communication within the audit function. Slowing down to discuss what has been found and what needs to be done next, can – paradoxically – speed up the assignment delivery process in the long-run, as will be examined in more detail in the next chapter. Phil Gerrard (CAE, Rolls-Royce) sums up the lean approach to assignments:

> "When you're doing lean auditing you really have to say 'So what?' all the time, through every stage of the assignment process."

---

## SUMMARY OF KEY POINTS FOR INTERNAL AUDIT

- Take care to manage the impact of the assignment on management;
- Always ask management up-front about known or potential issues or risks of concern and what they are doing about these;
- Obtain data and information directly wherever possible;
- Agree timelines (on both sides) for the delivery of information during the assignment;
- Create an audit liaison role in relevant departments where this will be helpful;
- Intelligently manage risk control matrices to focus the assignment on what is most important and avoid auditor pet topics;
- Recognize effective meetings management and interview techniques as a key source of value add;
- Leverage data analytics as a tool, not a toy, and encourage their use by other functions;
- Test on a step-by-step basis and don't be afraid to stop when a finding looks clear;
- Check for "killer facts" that bring to life a problem, and galvanize the need for action wherever possible;
- Incorporate root cause analysis into audit ways of working to get to the heart of problems (and – often – as a way of streamlining reports).

## RECOMMENDATIONS FOR SENIOR MANAGERS AND THE BOARD

- Ask the CAE to explain what the normal timelines are for information requests and obtaining responses and to report on any significant instances of delay;
- Establish what management self reporting or self assessment processes exist in the organization, and how audit leverages this information during the assignment process to avoid repeating what is already known;
- Understand what training and coaching auditors receive on interview techniques and the extent to which senior audit managers join assignments and participate in interviews to assess their quality (not just closing meetings);
- Enquire about the use of data analytics to help target audit's work and also understand how these tools are deployed outside of audit, e.g. in payroll, finance and purchasing;
- If repeat findings appear to occur enquire about the work audit does on themes and also what process is in place to consider root cause analysis;
- Encourage real examples to be provided when audit reports its issues;
- Clarify whether there is a minimum level of seniority to which actions are allocated (on the basis that this is more likely to communicate the importance of what audit is doing and ensure root causes are being considered and addressed).

### References and Other Related Material of Interest

Paterson, J. (2013) Delivering Root Cause Analysis – webinar for the IIA UK. https://www.iia.org.uk/resources/delivering-internal-audit/root-cause-analysis-webinar/

Root cause analysis – IIA Practice advisory 2320–2

# 15
# Using Communication and Quality Standards to Maximize the Added Value from Assignments

The last chapter covered good practices for driving both value and efficiency during the fact-finding and testing stage of an assignment. However, at some point audit findings need to be validated (e.g. against quality standards), communicated to management and then appropriate actions agreed. After all, from a customer perspective, it is the agreement, and implementation, of value adding actions that generates meaningful benefits from an assignment, not just issuing a report!

## COMMON PRACTICES AND IIA STANDARDS OF NOTE

As an audit progresses, and moves towards a conclusion, the work of the auditors will normally be supervised by audit management. This may include checking the audit file to ensure there is the required documentation to back up what is being said. Key points from the assignment will be shared with management at various stages, typically culminating in a "closing meeting" to discuss the findings and possible management actions.

Depending on the specific methodology of the audit function, a draft report will usually be prepared, often including an executive summary of what, if anything, has been found, along with more detailed points and then recommendations for management action. After the draft assignment report has been produced it will then be shared with relevant management for their comment, normally resulting in a written summary of agreed actions, the person accountable for implementing these and the timescales for completion. In many instances, an audit rating or other opinion also accompanies the report.

## COMMON CHALLENGES & DILEMMAS

### Management Disagree with Audit's Judgment about Findings and Remediation Needs

As the assignment progresses, auditors will share their findings with management. However, it is not unusual to find that, on hearing that audit have a concern, management may offer counter-arguments. These can include:

- The existence of another process or control, that compensates for the weakness audit has found (often referred to as "compensating controls");
- A belief that the issues audit is raising are within management's risk appetite, so no additional action is needed (which can include the argument that additional action is not justified on a cost/benefit basis);
- That they recently became aware of this issue and "are working on" it, so should be given credit for this;
- That the issue has recently been fixed.

I have heard many auditors explain that assignments would run to time, were it not for these frustrating, often last minute, challenges from management. The impact of these challenges often results in auditors having to "run around" for additional information, as well as having to decide whether management should be given credit for areas that are being, or have been, remediated. This can be particularly frustrating for auditors when they suspect that during the audit assignment, managers have been busy "building their documentation" to demonstrate that some or all of the auditor's concerns are either not founded or have now been addressed.

## The Audit Quality Process Introduces Delays and Frustrations

Depending on the approach taken to quality control by the audit function, the review of audit work papers and the draft audit report may require auditors to carry out additional testing and obtain additional documentation to justify key conclusions. From one perspective this additional work is not wasteful if it helps to ensure audit comes to robust, value adding, conclusions. However, from the perspective of management, it can appear that audit is having a "second bite at the cherry", and drawing out the assignment.

In addition, the audit quality process can introduce delays towards the end of an assignment as auditors share working papers and draft audit reports up the chain within the audit function. Delays are sometimes due to the fact that audit managers and/or CAEs are very busy and therefore work papers and draft reports can sit on their desk for several days, even weeks, before they are signed off.

In some instances, this audit quality control process can be considerable. Here is a reflection from Jonathan Kidd (CAE, UK Met Office):

> "At its worst you used to have situations where the audit methodology would state that, if a report was drafted by a junior auditor it would need to be checked by a senior auditor, and it would then need to be reviewed by an audit manager, and then it would require sign off by the CAE."

In addition to introducing delays, multiple reviews within the audit function can create a culture in which auditors feel that "someone else will check or change what I have done to suit their needs", reducing the sense of personal accountability for quality.

Ironically, despite the fact that an audit quality process is intended to add value, it is very often cited by auditors as a time when significant value can be lost – after all, small changes in a report may not be noticed by a manager, but they will notice the fact that the audit report has been issued a month after the fieldwork was completed! In addition, morale within the audit function is typically reduced when there is extensive "tweaking" of audit reports – something I have been guilty of myself.

## Challenges without (and with) Audit Management Software

There are some audit functions that I speak to that make limited use of audit software to capture the work performed during the assignment. As a result, time is spent filing papers, copying extracts from certain documents into an audit folder and then into the audit report, resulting in a lot of administrative tasks for the auditors. Needless to say, the time and effort spent on such tasks is waste (Muda).

At the other end of the spectrum, there are some audit functions that make extensive use of audit software, where work papers are stored and exceptions noted and an audit report can be produced at the push of a button. However, the use of an audit system may not be waste free since I have heard many auditors speak about the amount of time they spend "feeding the system".

In addition, whilst one of the attractions of an audit system is that it can quickly generate an audit report, there is a danger that this automated approach to reporting may not be the most value adding. One CAE explained:

> "I don't always like the push button to generate a report approach, because it drives the auditor away from what is really important and what is going to be of most value to your customer, be it audit committee or management.
>
> If you generate a report by system you are in danger of getting an exception report, which you might get from a compliance team. This is not the same as a proper audit report that tells you what your real risks are. Furthermore when you press a button to get a report, you run the risk of missing root causes and deskilling your audit function.
>
> Of course we should improve the efficiency of the reporting process, but there is a trap when we press the button that we miss the really important issues in relation to the GRC framework, accountability and resource issues. You can go too far on automation."

Thus, being a lean audit function does not simply mean rolling out audit software. This is the superficial version of lean thinking where efficiencies ignore questions about the insightfulness of the report, its impact on management, and the value it will deliver to the end customer.

## Report Findings, Wording and Ratings

Another area identified as wasteful by auditors is when managers challenge audit over what they believe to be minor points, either in terms of the organizational importance of the issue, or the way the points are contextualized or explained in the report.

Furthermore, whilst it might appear that having a greater number of points in an audit report is the sign of comprehensive work by audit, management may share the opposite view. Helen Maneuf (CAE, Hertfordshire SIAS) observes:

> "I am increasingly aware that low level recommendations about minor issues can be used to discredit any more serious points we are trying to make."

Roger Timewell (former Head of R&D audit at AstraZeneca, now consulting in clinical trial auditing) has an interesting "war story" that highlights the problem of overly lengthy audit reports:

> "I had an experience a few years ago where I was asked to sit alongside an auditor to give the company comfort about the quality of auditing. It was one of the worst audits I have ever seen. The auditor wrote a 25-page report about a site with a massive list of detailed facts, with no focus on what the real issues were. For me, there were two really big issues. But when you read the report – and even I who was there at the site – I couldn't see the important issues get clearly captured – so it certainly wouldn't come out to a reader who hadn't been there.
>
> Sadly a number of auditors have got a box-ticking mentality and find it hard to dissect out what really matters.
>
> This is key because most senior managers who get audit reports are not going to do this sort of sifting. They either don't have the time, or they don't have the ability, but in any event we shouldn't be expecting them to do this."

Richard Chambers (President & CEO, IIA) offers some interesting reflections in relation to the difficulties auditors have with brevity:

> "I have thought about this a lot over the years. It's drilled into us from the earliest days as a profession that the single most important attribute of an audit is accuracy.
>
> But think of the audit process as an inverted pyramid. If you break it into three parts, the widest is the accuracy of the report, the middle is its usefulness, and the bottom is its timeliness. So, it's almost like timeliness is the least considered of all of the attributes.
>
> I've seen some ridiculously long audits in my time. On one occasion, we got an audit report for an area that had been deactivated two years earlier! That's how long it had taken them to issue the audit report.

We have an insatiable obsession with being accurate. The cardinal sin would be to put something in a report that's erroneous. But I think that also tends to make us loquacious. We spend so much time auditing, we feel we must spend a lot of time talking about what we found. In fact, the longer a report is, the less likely it's going to be read."

Associated waste (Muda) in relation to audit reporting can include an extensive "to and fro" of interactions between audit and management around the wording of the final report, management comments, proposed action items, accountabilities and timescales and – sometimes an even more contentious issue – the proposed rating of the report (if applicable).

## The Closing Meeting Becomes Difficult

Many auditors will recognize that meetings to close an assignment are bound to be contentious to a greater or lesser extent, especially if audit identified many issues and areas for action.

The reasons for difficulties are many-fold, but an experienced Health & Safety auditor highlights a key problem area:

"It's not great when audit pulls a rabbit out of the hat in the closing meeting. That makes for a much more difficult time at the end and will probably extend the audit because management can start to say they now need to find evidence that the auditor has not found and so on."

The key point is to recognize that it is to be expected that management will challenge audit during the closing meeting, not simply if there is a factual disagreement but also if there is a disagreement around the seriousness about what has been found or how best to remediate it. Of course, the audit perspective is often: "I told them about these issues during the assignment," but the management version of this is often: "What you have written down in the report is not the same as what you said to me verbally."

## RECOMMENDED PRACTICES

A number of the points recommended in earlier chapters can help to address the difficulties outlined; for example, determining who should be accountable for delivering action points is often much easier when there is an assignment sponsor. However, there are a range of other good practices, outlined below, that can significantly reduce rework, delays and frustrations towards the end of an audit assignment.

### Address Compensating Controls Early on and Be Clear about How Control Remediation Will Be Regarded

In addition to my work on lean auditing, I also do work as an External Quality Assessor for the IIA UK. In both capacities I am asked to look at the audit methodology of an audit function. In several instances where there has been a pattern of carrying out additional testing at the last minute, I have found that the question of compensating controls is not explicitly addressed in the audit methodology. My advice is simple: auditors should always be mindful of the problem of encountering compensating controls, and therefore this is something that they explicitly addressed when developing and discussing test plans of key risks and key controls. From my perspective, good practice in an audit methodology is to include guidance on how to "head off" issues with compensating controls.

In addition, senior management (and the board if necessary) should be engaged on the question of how management efforts to remediate faulty controls should be regarded. I have seen a distinction being drawn between remediation that was already underway before the assignment started as part of the normal management process, and remediation that is started when audit said they were going to visit. This is why it is important to ask management about "known or suspected issues" or control improvement initiatives planned, or underway, at the start of an assignment. If this question is asked early on and then documented (e.g. in a short note of meeting), it can make it less easy for management to say later in an assignment: "Come to think of it, I've found out that we have actually been working on improving that area for a few weeks now."

Audit rating criteria should also explicitly address the issue of how to rate an area that is in the process of being remediated, or has just been remediated. Some audit functions adopt the principle that, if an issue has been remediated it need not be reported, on the basis that management and the board value things being fixed, and only need to know about open issues. Other functions adopt the approach that whether or not an issue has been remediated, the key point is to ensure all key weaknesses are known, even if just recently remediated, so that questions of root causes and wider lessons for the organization can be captured. My personal preference is to ensure that key issues and weaknesses are logged, even if remediated, on the basis that the external customer would want the organization to learn lessons to ensure their needs were met and other problems headed off.

Actions for Internal Audit to consider:

- Address how to approach compensating controls in the audit assignment methodology;
- Clarify how improvement actions should be regarded for the purposes of audit findings and any final audit ratings.

### Ensure that Criteria for Rating Findings Is Understood Early in the Assignment

Earlier on in this book, I discussed the importance of tuning in to management's risk appetite early on in an assignment. Another important step auditors can take is to be more up-front about the basis upon which assignments will be rated (just discussed in the context of remediation progress). Two key points need to be considered:

- The criteria by which facts will be judged and translated into "findings";
- The criteria by which any findings will be rated.

For standard assignments in relation to compliance or financial control issues, the criteria for judging facts will often be a policy, procedure or stated risk appetite (e.g. additional approval will be needed above a certain threshold). In these instances an absence of a process, or documentation will clearly become a finding (or part of a finding) because the facts differ from the approved policy process or procedure.

However, for non-standard assignments, (e.g. the management of an emerging risk area), the criteria for rating the facts may be less clear, resulting in time-consuming disagreements (i.e. how good should the risk assessment of the emerging risk area be? How quickly should actions be implemented?).

In order to create a more streamlined, value adding, assignment process it is vital that auditors should engage management at an early stage about the criteria for judging facts if there is any doubt about what the criteria will be. In the case above; what expectations, if any, have been set for the risk assessment of an emerging risk and the timeliness of actions? The timing of audit engagement with management on appropriate criteria matters, because, if audit raises an issue towards the end of an assignment without being clear about the criteria up front, there may be a tendency for management to say that what audit has found is not a real problem, and that it is within their risk appetite (especially if nothing bad has happened up to that point).

If auditors are expected to rate an audit (e.g. Good, Satisfactory, Poor, or Red, Amber, Green), this should be based on criteria agreed in advance with senior managers and the board. Good practice is that ratings criteria should be known by, and accessible to, management, so that any audit rating is not a surprise. This can be achieved by posting the criteria for assignments ratings on any intranet site maintained by audit. Good practice is to try to align any audit rating criteria with any other key rating criterion in use in the organization (e.g. that of risk or other key assurance functions). However, human behaviour is often to deny that the specific facts audit has found apply to this particular assignment, often resulting in wasteful discussions. Therefore, it is good practice for the audit team to explain assignment ratings during staff and manager briefings, using concrete examples of how ratings were decided. It is also good practice to specifically discuss ratings at the start of an assignment, for example: "These are the criteria that management and the board want us to use, so that means that if we found X, it would be rated Amber; does that make sense to you? Do you think any of the areas we are about to look at could be rated Red or Amber?"

It is worth noting that sometimes the criteria for assignment ratings can be a cause of disagreements and difficulties, because the audit ratings system is not in line with the way management thinks. When I was CAE of AstraZeneca, following our work on lean ways of working, we implemented a new approach to rating audits that was more in tune with key questions about value and risk. In particular, we implemented a distinction between our assessment of risk management and control effectiveness ("How bad") and our assessment of how important the issues were in organizational terms ("How big") (see Figure 15.1). This new approach was cited as a best practice by the Audit Director Roundtable in 2008, and is something I regularly explore with CAEs who are trying to take some of the "heat and light" out of the assignment ratings process.

Work very recently with one CAE has resulted in us raising the bar in relation to ratings, supported by senior management and the board. The new ratings system has revised its Green rating from "Satisfactory" to "In control". The change is intended to signal that

| Impact  Control effectiveness | Low (e.g. local) | Medium (e.g. region) | High (e.g. group) |
|---|---|---|---|
| Unsatisfactory | | | |
| Needs improvement | | | |
| Good | | | |

**Figure 15.1**   Assessing what has been found:
how big and how bad

a basic level of compliance and control is not sufficient in the modern risk and regulatory environment. Instead being "In Control" requires genuinely embedded, adaptive and improving risk management. The result of these changes will be many more Amber and Red audit reports, but this action has been taken consciously as a way of overcoming a degree of management complacency in relation to risk and control matters (see Figure 15.2).

Actions for Internal Audit to consider:

• Consider how much waste is caused by disagreements on findings or ratings and consider the reasons for this;
• Create a manager's guide explaining how ratings are determined, seeking clarity concerning how this is aligned with other ratings criteria (e.g. risk);
• Provide examples of how assignments have been rated to bring this to life and ensure this is communicated to key managers, especially at the start of assignments;
• Consider whether the current ratings system is really adding value in terms of its impact on the organization – ensure that audit ratings make sense in the wider organizational context (e.g. by distinguishing between control effectiveness and organizational impact), and are not engendering a sense of inappropriate complacency.

| Areas | UNSATISFACTORY<br>There are some important areas of performance management, risk identification or control operation that require urgent action | NEEDS IMPROVEMENT<br>Whilst there are several satisfactory areas management is not clearly demonstrating it is able to effectively identify and mitigate relevant risk areas | NEEDS DEVELOPMENT<br>Demonstrates satisfactory risk and control, but development needed to manage emerging risks and/or support future business/control needs | "IN CONTROL"<br>Demonstrates Risk and Control that should meet immediate and future business needs |
|---|---|---|---|---|
| Financial controls including Reporting, Capex and Procurement | | | | |
| Exposure to financial loss, fraud | | | | |
| Management reporting and forecasting | | | | |
| Controls to maintain acceptable levels of confidentiality, integrity and availability of information, IS and IT. | | | | |
| Legal and regulatory compliance | | | | |
| Code of Conduct and policy compliance | | | | |

**Figure 15.2** Ratings template, using the notion of being "In Control"

## Identify Opportunities in Relation to Audit Software

The key lean message is that audit tools and software are a means to an end, not an end in their own right. Audit software should help the audit function focus on the most important issues and drive efficiencies. The audit methodology should emphasize that a value adding report may require careful thought and not just pushing a button to get a list of exceptions.

Actions for Internal Audit to consider:

• If the audit function is not using audit software, examine options for using audit software, or even the functionality in existing software available to the audit team;
• If audit software is in use, discuss what is working well/less well;
• Ensure that any automated reports are properly considered for their insight and value add, including the identification of root causes.

## Audit Work-papers Should Not be an Objective of the Assignment

A fundamental hallmark of a value-oriented approach is to have a balanced approach to working papers. Andy Weintraub (experienced internal audit leader) sums up a progressive approach:

> "Work papers are important – there's got to be enough to substantiate your findings, and if there are no findings you've got to have enough to substantiate why the area is clean.

> However, I don't believe auditors should just write pages and pages of notes without being very clear what this is for. Of course, you've got to have evidence noted against key areas of scope, but to document every single meeting in detail? I'm not so sure. Maybe document who you met with and when and some of the key points and actions that arose in a brief note, but I'm not looking for documenting for the sake of documenting. Often information from meetings, etc, can also be captured in risk control templates."

One CAE offered an interesting perspective about working papers:

> "I'd probably say that, after working in internal audit for over twenty years, I don't think I've ever had an audit sponsor say, let me see the audit file so I can judge how good the audit was. It just doesn't happen."

They also observed:

"Sometimes less good assignments can have quite a lot of the audit file, but the danger is that making the file look good has been the focus of the auditors, not engaging the business, thinking about what the findings really mean, or properly preparing for the closure meeting."

Actions for Internal Audit to consider:

- Consider the time spent on audit work papers and the audit file. Is there waste?
- Agree the core requirements for working papers, but try to drive a culture in which working papers are seen to be a means to an end, not an end in themselves.

## Think Carefully about the Audit Quality Process and Emphasize Quality Control "In Flight"

It should be self-evident that "getting it right first time" is one of the key objectives of a lean approach. As a result, the audit quality control process should be aiming for this and – as far as possible – built into the way assignments are managed. QC or quality assurance (QA) after the assignment is completed runs the risk of rework, or not delivering the better assignment in real time, which is where value is added. This is a change we made in the audit function at AstraZeneca, paying more attention to "in flight" quality control, rather than QA some time after the assignment.

In addition, the amount of QC should depend on the specifics of the assignment and the staff allocated to it. Jonathan Kidd (CAE, UK Met Office) explains his approach, which is typical of progressive practice:

"One of the things I did was make the methodology a lot more flexible round QC and made the QC process a bit more dynamic, and made it more dependent on the situation. Say you've got an audit that's been done previously. It's following a testing method we've done before, and the person doing it is experienced and they know what they are doing, then really we probably don't need that much QC at all. We just need someone to check they've not completely messed up and are we comfortable.

If it's a new area, an audit that is particularly strategically placed, it is very high risk to the organization in terms of what it is looking at, then you might want to have the level of QC ramped up. That's something you decide at the planning stage.

We have changed our QC approach so that you don't get to the end and go, right, now we've got to do five days of QC. What we want to do is fold it into the audit process and make sure that the QC is proportionate to the importance of the audit itself."

Jonathan's approach highlights the key shift in leaner ways of working, carrying out QC on a proportionate basis, in real time. Ivan Butler (CAE Denbighshire County Council) uses the analogy of formula one racing, calling QC during an assignment "pit stops".

In addition, the QC should not just focus on documentation and compliance with standards, but also look at progress against the assignment timeline and the value add emerging from the assignment.

Norman Marks (GRC thought leader) highlights the shift that arises when thinking with a progressive added value mindset:

"When it comes to assignment quality control, personally, I prefer to talk to the auditor. And have a discussion about what has been happening, what they did, what they found. What is not in the work papers is perhaps more important than what is documented in the work papers.

Sadly, filing work papers is often a defensive cover yourself activity. This is again coming back to what lean is all about. What are we trying to do? Let's make sure we really understand what we need to do, because if we can focus on the key set of actions necessary to deliver the best value to our customer, then we can eliminate so much of what we traditionally do."

I have encountered a few instances where assignments are completed, but audit files (and draft reports) are then sent for review to the CAE or an audit manager, and this then takes days or even weeks (I wish I was joking). The reason for the bottleneck is that the manager or CAE is so busy they don't have the time to review the file immediately.

Two root causes need to be addressed here. The first is booking ahead the time for the management review (cf. earlier comments about managing assignments as projects); the second is agreeing a maximum time that a file can await a quality sign off and reconsider whether all of these files require sign off in this way.

Remember, as time passes some managers may be wondering where the report is, whilst others may be delighted it is being held up. However, an external customer would expect the report to be done as quickly as possible.

Further insights in relation to bottlenecks can be found in articles concerning the *Theory of Constraints* by E M Goldratt.

Actions for Internal Audit to consider:

- Ask the audit function what value they are getting from the current quality control process and what value the stakeholders of audit are getting;
- Consider how to make the amount of quality control proportionate to the value of the assignment;
- Examine options for more real time quality control activities, (rather than post assignment quality assurance) focusing on value and efficiency questions as well as other quality related issues;
- Identify and address any bottlenecks or constraints in the quality process (especially in relation to audit report reviews), so that time is not lost.

## Engage Management Throughout the Assignment

In a recent External Quality Assessment (EQA) review for the UK IIA, I looked at the audit methodology of a large UK audit function and found just one mention of the need to engage management during an assignment. It stated: "Management should be advised of any significant audit findings before the closing meeting." Readers should not be surprised to learn this audit function was experiencing "slippage" in assignment delivery due to late disagreements with management about what audit was finding. One of our conclusions from the EQA was that a much greater level of management engagement should be expected throughout assignments, and made much more explicit in the assignment methodology, as well as a focus of assignment supervision. An experienced Health & Safety auditor sums up a better approach:

> "I like the no surprises approach, bringing the management team with you.
>
> I prefer a completely open and transparent communication approach. The only exception is when you are looking at potential fraud or corruption, but an investigation is a very different beast from an audit assignment."

One CAE explained:

"It's so important to listen and to communicate regularly with managers because you might be technically very strong but if you don't tune your communication and your analysis to the perspective of key managers and stakeholders, what you will come up with risks the danger of being in a bubble."

Thus management engagement should include asking them whether any compensating controls have been missed (as discussed earlier) and also sharing the proposed wording of sections of the audit report, to allow them to acclimatize to the words that audit is proposing to use, and to consider the actions that should be taken as the assignment progresses, rather than leaving this all to the end.

Actions for Internal Audit to consider:

- Ensure the audit methodology requires ongoing, timely communication with management about what is being found as assignments progress;
- Follow up in writing at appropriate points in relation to audit findings, so that management can comment early on the way issues are being described and start to consider action steps to be taken;
- Coach those auditors who have a tendency to keep things to themselves, drawing lessons from issues that have arisen as a result, so they can understand the importance of this way of working.

## Be Clear about the Purpose of Any Report before it is Written

In order to avoid the painful, time-consuming and demotivating process of auditors drafting audit reports that are then rewritten, it is vital for auditors and audit managers to *agree, as much as is practical, the proposed contents of any assignment report before the report is written*. Andy Weintraub (experienced internal audit leader) explains:

"Before we put pen to paper and waste our time, let's write up a list of findings and first of all decide whether we agree these are all important.

After that we can look at the findings and the proposed corrective actions and start to see whether there are patterns, so that they can be combined.

This approach makes sure that audit reports are more focused, with less need of rewriting. It also helps you to combine points making reports as concise and readable as possible, and also helping stakeholders better judge the relative significance of what is being found."

This approach requires that audit managers who supervise assignments should keep sufficiently close to what is being done so that they can guide auditors to step back and determine what is important. Often this requires greater discipline to summarize the work in progress during assignments, and setting aside time, towards the end of fieldwork, to go through key points before the audit report is written.

At AstraZeneca auditors were asked to plot their proposed findings from each assignment against the framework of "How big" and "How bad" before the report was written. This was an excellent tool to focus discussions about the key points to be made in the audit report, since it would enable us to adjust perspectives on the importance of specific points as well as to spot root causes and the need to aggregate issues. In addition, this approach was invaluable when it came to assignment ratings.

Actions for Internal Audit to consider:

- Set aside a time towards the end of fieldwork to go over all key points before the audit report is finalized;
- Consider findings in a structured way (e.g. How big and How bad) and consider their root causes and respective importance;
- Agree the key points that should be made in the assignment report to reduce time spent composing it, and to avoid rewriting it.

## Properly Prepare for and Manage the Assignment Closing Meeting

Experienced auditors recognize that if there is appropriate preparation before the closing meeting, the less problematic the closing meeting is likely to be. Ideally key facts, the criteria by which they should be rated, and proposed actions, action owners and timescales should be mostly agreed before any closing meeting.

I recommend that auditors should carry out their own risk assessment ahead of the closing meeting to consider the extent to which any sensitive matters are still open. Sensitivities might include the way a point is described or positioned, the nature of the action being proposed or the organizational or political context that may influence the staff and managers involved. Once these risks are understood, auditors can then agree a plan of action of preparatory meetings or lobbying, to maximize the chances of a comparatively smooth closing meeting.

Of course, it is not always possible to lobby key stakeholders in advance of a closing meeting. When this is the case, and there is a concern that the closing meeting is going to be "interesting," auditors should consider rehearsing the meeting. The rehearsal should be run as if it was the closing meeting, using another auditor or audit manager to act in the role of the key manager who needs to be persuaded at the closing meeting. The idea is to focus on what the likely real life dynamics of the closing meeting are going to be about, not just the straightforward factual issues. The outcome of these rehearsals can be to help the lead auditor be much more careful about the language they are going to use in the closing meeting, and to have thought through the supporting evidence and documentation or other evidence (e.g. "killer facts"), that they will need to bring the meeting to a satisfactory conclusion. It can also help the auditor who is leading the assignment to become clearer about their negotiation strategy if there is push back (e.g. what can be conceded and what key points must be defended).

When I coach auditors at pre-closing rehearsals, I often ask them to "rewind" what they have just done, so they can have a second, or even a third attempt at presenting a key point. The result is often to help auditors build up greater awareness of how to position key points and to increase their confidence and resilience in relation to what might happen.

Of course, these rehearsals never quite match what actually happens in the real closing meeting, but my experience is that the time invested upfront (which may seem wasteful at face value) normally pays dividends in terms of both the speed of coming to a mutually satisfactory conclusion as well as maintaining good relationships between management and audit. It also builds a greater awareness in the auditor in terms of their style and strengthens their ability to manage effectively in key meetings. From a range of perspectives, therefore, this can be a value-adding thing to do.

Actions for Internal Audit to consider:

- Carry out a risk assessment of the way in which audit points are going to be received;
- Lobby on key points as needed before the closing meeting;

- For the most high stakes closing meetings carry out a rehearsal, concentrating on not just what is going to be said, but how to say it and what counter arguments should be prepared for.

## The Report Wording and Word Count Does Matter, but so Does Balance

Whether or not a draft audit report is available for any closing meeting, it is clearly going to be of value to share any written conclusions and proposed action plans as soon after the closing meeting as possible. Some audit functions are able to issue the final version of the assignment report (with agreed actions) within five days of any closing meeting. To write a report in the most efficient way, with minimal delays, a number of good practices are worth highlighting.

Karen Dignan (CAE, Group Head Office, OMG):

"Put yourself into the mind of the person that you are writing your report for. What is the business language and the business context we need to tune into rather than just our audit speak?

It should be about substance not form. The temptation as an auditor is to list what you have done in a very prescribed way, but you have to move on from that to consider: what does this all mean? And how do we best get that message across to the client?"

Phil Gerrard (CAE, Rolls-Royce) explains:

"Assume the reader is a reluctant reader, is how I'd phrase it.

The readers of most audit reports are senior people. They don't have a lot of time. So just psychologically if they see 20 or 30 pages land on their desk or inbox, it won't be encouraging for them to read. Keep it concise, to the point; it needs to join the dots for the reader so the business impact of issues is clear."

Helen Maneuf (CAE, Hertfordshire SIAS):

"The goal is to present a report in a way that's going to make people pay attention to it. If you fill it up with trivia nobody's going to give it any attention. The important things that you might be saying will get overlooked.

I recently read an audit report, it had nine recommendations and one key thing in the report was the ninth recommendation. By the time you got to it you would have given up."

(See Figure 15.3).

**Figure 15.3**   What many stakeholders value from reporting

Timeliness is another key theme. Norman Marks (GRC thought leader) notes:

"It really comes back down to, what is it we need to deliver? It's not just the assurance that is valuable, but how quickly that assurance is delivered and how it is packaged.

So do you want to give the CEO a 15-page report? Or do you just want to say, 'Everything is good except for these, one, two three, issues'. And 'I've talked to management about fixing these points, and they'll work on them over the next few months'."

Greg Coleman (CAE, ITG) continues this theme:

"On balance, in most cases, I would much rather have an audit report issued in a timely way, than have a report which drags on and only is finalized weeks or months afterwards. The process may not be perfect, and sometimes there are areas that, with the benefit of hindsight, we think we could have spent more time. But the benefit is we have a report with a series of agreed actions that's issued and being worked on. If we do feel that there's an area where additional work would be useful we can always do that later."

It is worth saying that driving an efficient, lean, approach does not mean only exception based reporting. This is something we considered at AstraZeneca but we agreed that a brief amount of context and balance was needed to add value to senior stakeholders. Phil Gerrard (CAE, Rolls-Royce) endorses this approach:

> "Reports should have context, so if I just listed out the 10 things that I thought were wrong, that wouldn't be fair. You have to take the responsibility for setting hares running quite seriously. You've got to put yourself in the reader's shoes."

The key message is to write a report that is meaningful and clear to key stakeholders, with minimum waste and being mindful of the time this is taking.

Actions for Internal Audit to consider:

- As a general rule assignment reports should be as short as they can be, without losing key value adding information;
- Structure the report in a way that will grab the reader's attention: key points first with the relevant context;
- Timeliness is important, see this as a counterbalance to the desire to write longer reports or to polish reports to perfection;
- If some stakeholders want longer reports, don't hide from them how much resource and time this would take.

## Address Any "To and Fro" of Audit Recommendations and Management Comments

I have emphasized that good practice in auditing is to engage management on an ongoing basis throughout an assignment. However, even if an auditor does this, progress on an assignment can slow when final actions have to be agreed. A particular source for delay can be a "to and fro" of comments as audit makes recommendations, management provides comments, and then getting agreement to write up the final actions, allocate ownership and determine suitable timescales.

I contrast the written "to and fro" of audit recommendations and management responses to what it is like when I go to see my doctor. If I see the doctor, I just want to discuss key points face-to-face and agree what I should do there and then! The traditional audit approach of lengthy written reports seems to be a throwback to the times of Charles Dickens, when gentlefolk would correspond with one another, in eloquent prose.

To address the problem of audit recommendations and management responses being exchanged, an increasing number of audit functions are streamlining their audit reports to highlight just agreed actions. The key point is that, from the perspective of key stakeholders (and the external customer for that matter), what matters the most is that appropriate actions have been agreed, within a suitable timescale.

Of course, auditors can and should make verbal recommendations to management about what might be done, but the lean progressive approach is to encourage *direct engagement and dialogue to finalize what should be done*, rather than correspondence. Furthermore, a number of CAEs have remarked to me that the inclusion of management comments about audit points in addition to the proposed actions can actually *dilute* what audit has found and what should now be done.

If, for cultural or practical reasons there is a need to exchange draft reports, a practical way to make this flow better is to schedule meetings or telephone discussions to address comments and also to agree timescales for responses (I recommend no more than a week, and preferably the next day). In addition, if management responses remain in the audit report, they should be requested to be as brief as possible.

If audit and management cannot agree certain actions, then this should be noted so that more senior management, and the board if necessary, can determine what should be done. However, the progressive, lean approach is that recording recommendations and management responses would be the exception rather than the rule.

Actions for Internal Audit to consider:

- Move towards "Agreed management actions" in the audit report and seek to secure this through discussion, rather than correspondence;
- Only record audit recommendations and management comments where audit and management do not agree, or there is an explicit regulatory need to do this;
- Schedule meetings or telephone conversations to progress the document, wherever possible;
- If management comments continue to be included in the audit report, work to limit the length of what can be said, and be mindful of management comments that dilute the actions that are being agreed.

## A Few Words Concerning Timelines for Remediation

One source of tension between audit and management, as reports are finalized, can be the timescales within which audit findings should be addressed. Some audit functions adopt the approach that they should be realistic, recognizing business pressures and resource constraints and therefore adjust milestones for delivering actions accordingly. This pragmatism on the side of audit may be appreciated and valued by management (e.g. "They understand the real world we live in"). However, the downsides can be:

- An implicit sense that audit accepts that its findings cannot and should not be fixed more quickly; and
- A risk that an issue may emerge whilst an issue is still to be remediated.

As a consequence, I would encourage auditors to consider compromises and constraints to remediation from the perspective of whether this meets the needs of the most senior managers and the board and/or key external customers.

As I see it, there is a balance to strike between being pragmatic, maintaining relationships and being independent. My advice is that it can be a useful discipline within the audit function to expect remediation to be completed within (say) one, two, four or eight months. Then, if management request longer than this in relation to a key risk area a discussion can progress along the lines of:

> "I understand why you want to wait and address this risk area when the new system comes along in 12 months, but I want to be sure that senior management and the board accept that this is an area that can wait, because if something were to go wrong in the meantime we could have a big reputational issue, or difficulty with a customer."

Actions for Internal Audit to consider:

- Agree typical timescales within which issues should normally be remediated (e.g. one, two, four or eight months) and what would influence the need to complete remediation more or less quickly (e.g. the importance of the issue and risk appetite in relation to the area);
- Agree a process for escalating timescales outside of the agreed parameters to senior management and the board, so that resource and other constraints are clear and that risk appetite sign-offs are clear.

## Effective Reporting Often Involves a Degree of Branding

Whilst lean encourages auditors to create "short and sweet" reports it is important to recognize that the way reports are written and the way they look is also important. Stephen Foster (CAE, Cargotec) explains:

> "It seems a contradiction to efficiency and lean processes, but actually if you say that our role is to communicate issues, and to gain agreement to improvement actions then we need to be able to communicate well. People are far more receptive to ideas and suggestions when it's done in a very professional and consistent manner.
>
> Subconsciously you recognize that if someone has taken the care to write a professional report, they are likely to have taken the care to make sure the contents of the report are right. The form is important, because people are human and the form is a way of making a good first impression. But, if you don't have the substance behind it then ultimately good form will fail. If you're going to be successful you have to have the full suite, form and substance."

I see an increasing number of audit functions writing reports in landscape format, and giving them a "newspaper feel". This sort of format can encourage shorter reports and will often follow good branding practices that can be seen in external auditor or consultant's reports.

Actions for Internal Audit to consider:

- Compare audit reports to reports from other respected sources and look for ways to improve the internal audit brand through improved reporting formats.

## Communicate with a Focus on Adding Value and Minimizing Waste

Earlier I discussed the way in which management appreciates not being surprised. Thus, if an audit report has been agreed and is about to be issued, it is worthwhile thinking about the best way of communicating this to the organization. Just sending an e-mail with a long list of addressees is not always valued, especially by those who are copied in. Phil Gerrard (CAE, Rolls-Royce) provides some advice:

"Think about the distribution of audit reports. It's so easy to waste people's time by copying them in on a report that is only marginally relevant. My advice is don't c.c. the world. Don't fall into that trap."

Norman Marks (GRC thought leader) adds:

"If we are going to be successful, just putting something in somebody's inbox is not going to get them to listen, to think about what audit has said, to understand it and move forward. Not nearly as well or sympathetically as if you sit down with them and talk about what you have found, why any change is necessary, what's in it for them and how it will help them and the organization to succeed.

It comes down to what is the product. The product is not the memo. The product is to generate change, or to provide assurance."

Thus, staggering the communication of audit reports, including personalizing communications (e.g. a personal note or e-mail: "No action for you on this report, but we should pick up point 5 when we next meet"), or organizing a meeting to talk stakeholders through what audit has found, can be much more valued by management, and helpful for audit, than just sending e-mails. Some audit functions organize monthly or quarterly meetings with key senior stakeholders and use this as the opportunity to talk through what they have done, and what they have found, in order to have a deeper dialogue with the managers concerned.

Actions for Internal Audit to consider:

- Think about the circulation lists for audit reports – keep them relevant and personalized;
- Do those who receive a copy of the report find this helpful? Explore other ways of communicating with them more effectively.

### Evolve any Reports as Needed

From the foregoing discussion it should be clear that I do not believe there is one "correct" way to report the outcome of an audit assignment. After all there can be some stakeholders and some situations where a more detailed report is clearly going to be of value, and other situations and stakeholders where just the headlines will suffice.

In all circumstances, the hallmark of good practice is to engage management and the board about the different options and what would be most valuable to them. In my experience, a useful additional angle to take is to explain how much time a longer report takes to write:

"You want a 20-page report as a rule, rather than 10 pages? We can do that, but you will lose on average two days of fieldwork if we do that. Are you sure that is that what you want?"

Shagen Ganason (former Chief Assurance Officer at the Department of Conservation, New Zealand) sums up his perspective on the value of an audit report:

> "A report is only valuable when management and the board use it and see that it helps them.
>
> If they briefly look at it and then put it aside, then it is basically useless in my view. On the other hand, if they look at the report and say 'yes, this is something I think will help me manage my business' or if they discuss the contents of the report with other parts of the business, then it is a good sign.
>
> My measurement of the value of an audit report is not about the contents or the number of issues raised but by how management and the board use it to manage their business."

Jonathan Kidd (CAE, UK Met Office) goes on to explain how the feedback process can support the ongoing improvement of audit reports:

> "I would expect to see a regular feedback process from stakeholders, and this should cover assignment reporting. As a result of this I would expect to see things gradually change. Six months ago we were doing this report, we don't do that any more because that's no longer necessary."

As a concluding comment it is worth noting that I have even heard some CAEs (in larger audit functions) speak about recruiting professional report writers into their audit functions. The idea is to use this specialism to drive improvements and innovations in the way internal audit communicates with the organization.

Actions for Internal Audit to consider:

- Ensure that senior stakeholders understand the trade-off between the length of an audit report and the impact on time available for fieldwork;
- Be prepared to try different approaches to reporting, if only on a pilot basis, to see what reaction that gets;

- Consider engaging professional report writers for a period to drive a step up in the audit reporting process;
- Regularly engage stakeholders in relation to how useful they find audit reports.

## CONCLUDING REMARKS

I have covered a lot of ground in this chapter and combined report writing with the later stages of fieldwork and quality control. This has been done deliberately to highlight the extent to which issues in the later stages of an assignment can end up impacting the closing meeting and agreement of the assignment report. In addition, I hope that by joining up management engagement with the reporting process it becomes clear why this is needed to achieve a flow encompassing gathering facts, identifying root causes, prioritizing criteria, leading to a value-adding outcome, with minimum waste. Norman Marks (GRC thought leader) notes:

> "The standards do not require us to have a formal audit report that is written. It says we need to communicate."

Of course, the challenge facing most audit functions is that an audit report is required, and is expected to be backed-up by sufficient evidence. However, the danger is that the audit report and audit file to support it starts to take on an importance, and absorb time, that is not in line with its true value. Crucial throughout everything I have said is the spirit of an audit function that "wants to get on with it"; that wants to engage management with a sense of urgency. The progressive, lean, function regards what it is doing as just as important and urgent as anything else the organization is doing, because it sees a clear connection between its work and the delivery of added value. As a result, the delays and disagreements at the latter stages of an audit assignment are not just "one of those things", but symptomatic of a culture of waste, inefficiency and a non-value add focus that needs to be addressed in both audit and the wider organization.

Driving through debate and discussion does not mean audit will get everything it wants, or that it should ignore political and practical sensitivities, but it should ensure timely consideration by senior management and the board of key hot spots and trigger a decision about whether these need to be addressed or whether risks are accepted.

As a concluding reflection, Richard Young (Director, UNIAC) sums up the lean, progressive audit mindset:

> "Forget about the audit report, the question is, did audit's work make a difference?
>
> Talking about reports and saying they are well structured, useful and concise is great, but that is peripheral in the grand scheme of things.
>
> The bigger questions are: did audit's work add value, did it improve controls or did it give appropriate assurance?"

---

### SUMMARY OF KEY POINTS FOR INTERNAL AUDIT

- Ensure the issue of compensating controls is adequately addressed in any assignment methodology;
- Ensure the criteria for audit ratings has been considered from the perspective of its alignment with other criterion (e.g. risk) and the risk appetite of the organization;
- Look out for warning signs that current audit ratings may be creating a culture of complacency around risk and control;
- Recognize audit software as an important tool, but not a toy, and leverage its use by other functions;
- Remember the objective of the assignment is not to create a good report or audit file, it is to achieve the right change on a timely basis;
- Carry out "in flight" quality control and address any bottlenecks that delay delivery;
- Err on the side of engaging management more during the assignment rather than less;
- Prepare for closing meetings taking into account sensitivities, rehearsing beforehand if necessary;
- Develop a clear approach to expected remediation timescales in order to ensure risk appetite perspectives and resource constraints are understood;
- Consider the look of any reports, their length and any other ways in which they can be more impactful – always engaging management in relation to the value they get from audit reports.

---

## RECOMMENDATIONS FOR SENIOR MANAGERS AND THE BOARD

- Ask audit for details of negotiations over assignment ratings in the past 12 months, tracking the original ratings and the agreed ratings and ask audit to explain the reasons for the changes;
- Understand the way in which audit agrees timescales for remediation and the grounds for lengthy timescales. Clarify when remediation timescales might need to be escalated upwards;
- Ask your CAE whether the current criteria for audit assignments are i) aligned with other ratings criteria (e.g. risk) and ii) driving the right behaviours in the organization;
- How much are you using the reports audit issues? What would make them more useful?
- If reports are lengthy ask for clarity about the amount of time these reports take to write.

---

### References and Other Related Material of Interest

Goldratt, E. M. (1990) *Theory of Constraints*. North River Press, Great Barrington Massachusetts.

# 16
# Assignment Follow-Up and Follow On

In the last chapter I discussed ways in which audit functions can drive through assignments so that they deliver valued outputs (in the form of briefings or written reports that make a positive difference). However, strictly speaking, real value add from a lean perspective is not achieved until action items have actually been implemented in the organization (at which point they may then be adding value to key stakeholders and/ or external customers).

## COMMON PRACTICE AND IIA STANDARDS OF NOTE

Standard practice for audit, and as set out in the IIA's standards, is that they should play a role in keeping track of "the disposition of results".

## COMMON CHALLENGES & DILEMMAS

The best audit functions will regard their involvement in keeping track of the remediation of open points as a relatively straightforward matter, taking up only a minimum amount of time. However a number of audit functions I have worked with experience issues in relation to keeping track of remediation and following up open points. The most notable challenges appear to be:

## Audit is Expected to Drive the Process for Tracking Remediation

Some audit functions find they spend a lot of time notifying management of up and coming remediation deadlines, and chase them for comments as well as adjusting deadlines if these are not going to be met. In some cases this is recorded in audit software and in others it is recorded in a spreadsheet, absorbing quite a lot of time for an administrator or junior auditor.

In these circumstances, if audit does not chase management, remediation may be delayed, and I have heard of instances when audit has been blamed for failing to notify management of up-and-coming deadlines.

It is still quite common to find that audit functions have a performance metric that is based on remediation progress (by management). In addition, I know of some CAEs who have been reprimanded by the board and senior managers for issues with remediation progress. To my mind this highlights a misunderstanding about who is actually accountable for ensuring actions are completed: it is the role of audit to make and agree sensible actions with management but surely it is the role of management to actually implement these within the agreed timescales?

## Role and Process Clarity Regarding Remediation

An additional burden in relation to tracking remediation is the amount of time and effort that some audit functions spend on follow-up auditing to validate whether issues have been effectively remediated.

This can result in audit functions "chasing after" information and evidence to verify agreed actions have been completed. This can involve going back to management and staff to get them to pull together relevant information and documentation. Having obtained evidence from management, there can also be disagreements about whether this is sufficient to demonstrate that issues have been properly remediated. All of this can amount to a noticeable amount of the annual audit budget. In the case of audit in AstraZeneca, back in 2005, we estimated this was as much as 10% of the audit budget in some areas.

## RECOMMENDED PRACTICES

The first key point to make is that verifying that actions have been remediated is an important area. After all, what could be more wasteful than going to the trouble of identifying areas that need to be addressed and then not actually seeing this through?

The second key point is that manual approaches to tracking remediation progress need to be carefully considered in terms of the impact on audit time and effort. It is quite easy to set up an automated follow-up process with automatic reminders that flow directly from what has been agreed with management at the end of an assignment. There is audit software that can do this, but other modern office software can mimic much of this functionality.

### Management Should Be Clearly Accountable for Remediation Timescales and Confirming What Has Been Done

The most fundamental shift we made when we adopted lean ways of working in auditing at AstraZeneca was to be much clearer about whose role it was to verify remediation had been completed. The best audit functions have a streamlined process to follow-ups, and in my lean auditing workshops and consulting assignments, this is often one of the key "quick win" areas for improvement.

Chris Baker (Technical Manager, IIA UK):

> "The emphasis in the Standards is for the CAE to make sure that there is a process of follow-up. The worst-case scenario is that internal audit assumes responsibility for monitoring the implementation of recommendations and spends a lot of time chasing managers to get their responses. In this case auditors are assuming more responsibility than the standards want internal auditors to have.
>
> I still see a fair bit of that. I think more enlightened organizations understand that it is a management responsibility to ensure follow-up of audit actions and they will grasp the nettle and make sure that these recommendations and actions are being implemented."

One CAE explains how he has made this shift, offering a degree of support, but ensuring a sensible role for audit.

> "My feeling on follow-up process is that audit shouldn't be doing much there.

Our starting point is that we bring reports finalized to the audit committee with thought-through management actions. That really is the foundation and therefore follow up has to be the responsibility of relevant
management. We encourage management to stay on top of what is happening and to give updates to key stakeholders. At one level you can say:
'It's not really to do with audit. Management agreed to do this, so where
are they?'"

Thus, there is an important cultural shift for some organizations to
make: audit should facilitate the process for remediation in tracking,
but should not be compensating for a lack of ownership on progress
tracking or – worse still – covering up management's lack of ownership.

In the most progressive organizations timely management remediation is actually a key performance metric for managers; it is not a target
for the audit function.

Actions for Internal Audit to consider:

• Ensure the accountability for following up audit actions rests with
  management;
• Revisit any remediation metrics within internal audit;
• Create performance metrics for management in relation to remediation.

## Audit Should Follow up Selectively

In addition to a shift in the ownership for tracking remediation, there is
an important question to address in terms of the value added by verifying all issues have been remediated. Here is the perspective of Chris
Baker (Technical Manager, IIA UK):

"I see the better audit departments selectively deciding which issues to
revisit by way of follow-up, and that would invariably be around the high
priority risks and areas where there is particular interest.

I recommend to audit functions that you don't have to re-check everything, you can leave some things to the next time you audit this area, or
just follow up on the most important areas."

This is precisely the change we made in audit at AstraZeneca; it is
now in place in many other audit functions. Here are the comments of
Jonathan Kidd (CAE, UK Met Office):

"I only do follow up audits if it is absolutely necessary. It's about the impact. If it's important I'll plan our follow-up for an appropriate time period, but it's usually a focused check, I'm not going to review the whole area again.

We just look at the material and the strategic points. We check they have been resolved effectively and we will do testing, but only in the specific areas that we feel we need to."

Of course, if there are indications that, as a result of a more focused approach, management is ignoring the remediation then this can be selectively examined by audit and flagged for discussion with senior managers and the board. However, there are other ways of managing this difficulty explained in the next recommendation.

Actions for Internal Audit to consider:

• Explore ways of following up selectively on the most high impact issues, rather than on everything.

## Agree What Remediation Means and Pay Attention to Where Verification Evidence Is Stored

The root cause of a number of the difficulties in verifying the remediation of audit findings is often due to a degree of uncertainty about what, exactly, it means to remediate an audit point. In particular, what evidence is going to be required to demonstrate an issue has been addressed effectively. As a result, better audit functions work to agree with management, at the time they are identifying an action, what evidence will be needed to demonstrate that remediation has been completed. On occasions, this process of clarifying what verification evidence is needed will flush out disagreements about the proposed actions and whether they are realistic (e.g. management may plan to fix a specific issue whereas audit is expecting improvements in a whole process and the way it is monitored).

In addition, audit can also encourage greater interest within the management chain of command in relation to who should sign off that remediation has been completed before it is communicated as being closed. When a more senior manager is asked to sign off that an issue has been closed, it is much more likely to be done properly than if it is just down to a lower level management self-assessment.

There are also ways to streamline the process of checking evidence that actions have been completed. One CAE explains the approach their function has implemented:

> "The onus that issues have been closed off rests firmly with management, and we carry out selected verification. Management have access to the system in which audit issues have been recorded and they log into the system to update progress, the audit function then pulls together the overall picture and quality checks the status from time to time.
>
> In addition, we expect management to file the evidence they have gathered to demonstrate issues have been closed into our system, so we don't need to go running around to chase for evidence".

Actions for internal audit to consider:

- Agree what verification evidence is going to be needed to demonstrate that key audit actions have been remediated;
- Encourage a culture in which more senior managers sign off that actions have been completed in order to encourage a degree of rigour in the closure process within the management line;
- Examine ways for audit to have easy access to the evidence that shows that issues have been remediated (e.g. through a shared folder).

### Think about the Value Add from Follow-up If You Visit a Location Again

Whilst putting the emphasis on remediation tracking and verification on management, key stakeholders may still value some selected audit follow up. This may require audit checking verification evidence remotely, or it may require a visit to a specific location.

In the cases where a visit is justified, audit functions can consider whether there are other important, value added areas, that might sensibly be addressed while they are on location. For example, if applicable, to gain insights into an emerging risk area of growing importance.

Taking a variant to driving value add to the follow-up process, Karen Dignan (CAE, Group Head Office, OMG) explains the approach of her audit function:

"If we've raised an unsatisfactory report for a key risk area we go back within a defined period, it might be six months or a year, when the actions are done.

When we make these visits we look at the whole risk area again, assuming it is material. We don't only look at what needed fixing, but we look at other important areas. Because in fixing things, a common problem is: did management take their eye off the ball on the other stuff?

We do this because it's common to find that when you know you've got a problem on one area, you might not be dealing with other things, or new things."

Chris Baker (Technical Manager, IIA UK):

"I still see people literally re-auditing everything just to make sure that it's working properly.

I think you've got to be more savvy and understand the relative importance of things."

Actions for Internal Audit to consider:

- Question what follow-up audits are needed, consider following up only high impact points routinely;
- If a follow-up visit is needed, examine any associated material risks at the same time (e.g. looking for slippage in a key area whilst effort was being put into remediation).

## CONCLUDING REMARKS

Whilst the tracking of assignment remediation is very important, lean progressive ways of auditing encourage management to take up a greater assurance role, with greater clarity of what it means to sign off remediation, and a clear understanding of where to record this. As a result, audit can take up a much more value-adding role, looking at the overall remediation process, the completion of the most material issues, as well as any new risks that have arisen while remediation was taking place.

## SUMMARY OF KEY POINTS FOR INTERNAL AUDIT

- Ensure that the process for tracking remediation is owned by management;
- Ensure the criteria/evidence for closing issues is clear;
- Exploit software solutions to streamline chasing issues, and also to store remediation evidence;
- Create a risk and value based follow-up approach to follow-up audits;
- Question any audit function targets that include management remediation; the accountability is management's, not audit's.

## RECOMMENDATIONS FOR SENIOR MANAGERS AND THE BOARD

- Recognize that progress on remediation is a management accountability – as a result it should be a target for management, not audit;
- Clarify what evidence and level of sign off by the management chain is needed to close open audit issues;
- If remediation is delayed, invite management (not audit) to explain why this has occurred.

# PART 3
# Looking at Key Underpinning Capabilities, Processes and Ways of Working

# 17
# Measuring Performance and Driving Improvements in Audit Ways of Working

In earlier chapters I outlined good practices for both audit planning and assignment delivery and a follow up process that has a focus on maximizing the added value from audit, and on reducing waste. The next stage is to ensure that the audit function has:

- Measures that enable the audit function to: a) drive efficiency and flow and b) understand the value that is being added; and
- Measures that clearly communicate this to management and the board; and
- Measures that are collected as efficiently as possible in terms of time and effort.

## COMMON PRACTICES AND IIA STANDARDS OF NOTE

Most audit functions recognize the need to measure their performance and to drive continuous improvement. Performance metrics often include the delivery of the audit plan against budget, how staff time has been used, and – incorrectly in my analysis – the status of issue remediation (discussed in the last chapter).

Improvement initiatives for audit (and associated metrics) vary from case to case, but may include making improvements to staff utilization, making better use of audit software, and training and development for the audit function.

These activities reflect IIA standards that auditors should: "improve their proficiency and the effectiveness and quality of their services". In addition, the current IIA standards state that internal audit should have a quality assurance and improvement programme, and should submit themselves to an external review no less than once every five years.

## COMMON CHALLENGES & DILEMMAS

### Learning After each Assignment Is Limited

As mentioned before, when I work with audit functions I will often review their audit methodology to offer advice about how it can be amended to better drive added value and reduce waste. In around 50% of the cases I see, there is very little written in the audit methodology about learning reviews after each assignment.

When I talk to the CAEs concerned they explain that, although a learning review may not be explicitly required, they nonetheless expect their audit managers to consider the key learning points from each assignment and debrief their staff accordingly. However, even where this is the case, some CAEs accept that they have limited insight into the detail of what happens, and several CAEs I have spoken to have confessed that they suspect this is an area that is not done particularly well as a result of workload pressures.

### Audit Methodologies and Software Have a Range of Shortcomings

As readers will appreciate, lean ways of working are concerned with defining value adding and waste free processes as well as being concerned about the Gemba of what is happening in practice. In an audit context often an audit methodology (if it exists) may be intended to help auditors know what they should do during an assignment. However, it is not unusual to find auditors have a range of concerns about the audit methodology they are expected follow:

1. A sense that the methodology is principally about completing a series of key documents or meeting the needs of audit software requirements.

Reading the audit methodology becomes a lengthy "how to" guide in relation to which forms to complete and how to complete these properly, or how to use the audit software (and which drop down boxes to use).

2. A sense that the methodology has a limited appreciation for the reality of the difficulties and dilemmas that may be encountered when delivering an audit assignment.

It is almost as if by not discussing the challenges in assignment delivery they will not happen! In addition, many audit methodologies underplay the practical (Gemba) difficulties of navigating between quality, time, and the completion of the audit file alongside managing relationships with management.

Note that these concerns can arise whether or not there is an extensive audit methodology or a very brief methodology. In any event, there is a significant risk that an audit methodology is neither an enabler to the delivery of added value, nor a tool to drive productivity in the audit process, but instead it is inadvertently a barrier to both.

## Metrics Are Not Collected At All, or Are Collected to Little Practical Effect

I see a wide variety of practices in relation to measuring audit performance. When I speak to auditors at workshops or training events, a number are frustrated with the amount of time they spend recording how they have spent their time, or are concerned about the time they spend explaining detailed variances, with no obvious benefit that they can see. I know of a number of instances where a metric to deliver an audit report within a set timescale has auditors rushing out reports, only then to result in negative feedback for failing to properly engage management on the remediation plan.

In addition, auditors can sometimes feel pressured into doing other dysfunctional things, for example, delaying the assignment closing meeting, or calling it something else ("a pre-close meeting") so that they can meet a target they have been set in relation to the time between the close of the meeting and the issue of the final report.

Phil Gerrard (CAE, Rolls-Royce) shares the following perspective on dysfunctional aspects around time recording:

> "I've seen teams completing timesheets with very little coming out of it. Worse still I suspect some of the data was flawed, with people

estimating how they were using their time. Moreover, it wasn't being used as an active management tool.

So think very carefully about what you collect."

I also see CAEs encountering difficulties with plan delivery towards the end of the audit year who admit their audit function metrics have not really helped them anticipate these issues, or drive better delivery performance during the year. What value do metrics have if they do not help the audit team to manage the key things that would be of value to key stakeholders and the external customer?!

Chris Baker (Technical Manager, IIA UK) provides a more general observation about typical audit metrics:

> "Many audit functions should move away from the traditional things that we see, like number of audits completed, time lapses to issue audit reports and all of the things we are familiar with; and develop a broader set of metrics. Because I think there's a much wider way of understanding how effective internal audit is."

## Quality Assessments Are Done Reluctantly and Not Seen as a Tool for Driving Added Value

I remember, after becoming CAE for AstraZeneca, requesting an External Quality Assessment (EQA) for the audit function after six months in my role. I wanted to get input on whether we were on the right track with the changes we had started to work on. The process was very helpful and I will never forget a Big Four partner saying to me:

> "It's great to do an EQA for a CAE, it makes it much more collaborative. The majority of EQAs we do are at the request of the CFO or Audit Committee, and this can be a sign that they are concerned with what is going on in audit. Indeed it's not unusual to see the results of our review lead to a change in the leadership of the audit function."

To this day, based on my experience as an EQA assessor for the IIA UK, there appear to be a number of CAEs who still have serious doubts about the need or benefit of having an EQA review, perhaps based on problems in the past. I have some sympathy with this view, since it is easy to be reviewed by someone with limited real world experience managing an audit function, who takes a rather idealistic approach to what needs to be changed. However, with some of my colleagues on the IIA UK EQA panel, we have also wondered whether there is something in the culture of audit that enjoys auditing others, but is less comfortable when it is being scrutinized itself?

## RECOMMENDED PRACTICES

Lean ways of working demand that we measure the performance and added value of audit and continuously drive improvement, using processes (such as the assignment methodology) and systems (such as audit software) as an important way of supporting productivity and value add, but not as an end in their own right.

### Post Assignment Learning is Essential

The starting point for driving a mindset of value add and efficiency within the audit function is to recognize the importance of the "Voice of the Customer" and this means taking regular soundings from the sponsors of audit assignments, as well as other key stakeholders. At Astra-Zeneca, gathering feedback from key internal customers (assignment sponsors, senior managers and the audit committee) became a central foundation of our new way of working.

In addition auditors were asked to do a "lessons learned" review after each assignment. Things that had gone well were just as important as things that could be done better, since this is a way of building good practices and not just seeing the review process as negative. Post assignment reviews could result in: affirmation of the audit methodology (e.g. "It was great that we clarified the criteria for assessment early on, because that seemed to help later"), individual coaching points for auditors (and pin-pointing further training needs, if there was a recurring need for improvement), or even lead to clarifications or improvements in the audit methodology.

Following the lean mindset of delivering value to customers, it is good practice to supplement feedback from the auditee after each assignment with feedback from time to time from key stakeholders, such as assignment sponsors, senior management and the board.

Actions for internal audit to consider:

- Regard post assignment reviews as a fundamental engine for driving continuous improvement in the audit function;
- Do these reviews on a timely basis, focusing on what went well as well as what could be improved;
- Use learning reviews to drive auditor coaching as well as enhancements to the audit methodology or the way it is communicated;
- Ensure that feedback from assignment sponsors, senior managers and the board is also obtained, recognizing their role as key stakeholders – and not just auditees.

### Revisit the Audit Methodology and Ensure it is Guiding Good Practice

At AstraZeneca one of the key changes we made after our lean review of audit was to overhaul the audit assignment methodology. The goal was to make it much easier to understand what good practice looks like, and to allow for flexibility, within a framework of having a small number of key mandatory requirements and to concentrate on value and driving productivity. The new audit methodology was much easier to follow, which made it easier to refer to on a regular basis, more straightforward to train new audit staff and guest auditors, and much easier to keep up to date.

Since then I have worked on the upgrading of a number of audit methodologies with CAEs to better focus on efficiency and value add. Here are the observations of Stephen Foster (CAE, Cargotec) about the benefits of such an upgraded approach:

> "First of all I wanted to provide a consistent approach which is the same across the audit team. I think it's important that an audit function has a solid base in relation to its key assignment process, the business would expect that.
>
> The second reason is to get everybody on message in terms of the way we want the business to be looked at in order to add value during assignments.
>
> Finally if we are trying to educate the business about the value of a structure and discipline in its processes, we need this sort of approach built into the audit way of working as well. It can help us say: 'You

should be looking at processes in this way – and this is how we ourselves do it.'

Updating our manual along lean principles has helped me, as the CAE, clarify how we can best add value.

As a consequence we have found ourselves, as a team, talking more and more about how we approach assignments and what value we are getting out of doing certain things. How do we justify that something is worth doing?

It has acted as a catalyst to actually put value-adding principles into practice."

Actions for Internal Audit to consider:

- As an audit function, discuss the strengths and weaknesses of the current audit methodology (is it a useful tool, regularly referred to?);
- Does the methodology address the Gemba of real assignment challenges and guide auditors to navigate their way through challenges of delivery to time, completion of tasks and the need to add value?

## Revisit Metrics for Their Usefulness and Focus on Value and Productivity

Whilst some traditional audit metrics have their place, lean ways of working encourage audit functions to focus on metrics that really drive added value and efficiency. This can mean enhancing some metrics significantly and dropping others. John Earley (Partner, Smart Chain International) summarizes the essence of what it means to have metrics that are lean:

"If you can't make a direct line back to measuring customer value then you've got a question whether that metric is actually effective, or whether you are just filling in a box for the sake of it."

At audit within AstraZeneca we dropped a number of metrics after our lean review, but improved our metrics around assignment delivery. One CAE explains their approach to managing assignment delivery:

"I know exactly where the audits are at any one time. As soon as they pass a deadline date, I will get an amber flag and expect the reasons to be chased, if slippage increases we step up our efforts to identify the reasons for this and the actions we need to take to progress the assignment without adversely impacting quality."

Phil Gerrard (CAE, Rolls-Royce) outlines his approach to assignment metrics:

"I think managing budgeted times on audit, by key stage, can give you lots of intelligence around where your bottlenecks are. Look at these metrics regularly and look at the variation between what you planned for each assignment and what has happened and then try to understand the reasons for differences. Why did we get that wrong? What should we do differently? How can we be smarter? Or, oh, that was clever, what did we do there to deliver the assignment ahead of expectations"?

Good audit metrics should also address questions of adding value, Karen Dignan (CAE, Group Head Office, OMG) offers her reflections:

"We have a questionnaire after each assignment which is very short, just five questions. The main questions are narrative, rather than scoring. However, there's an overall value rating that we ask the audit client to score and what's more we ask 'If you had to pay for the assignment, how much would you have paid for it?'

We also have a basket of other measures. Some of these are around how quickly we get our reports out, but we set different targets between local and group-wide audits, since the latter are typically more complex to land. Also we aim for 85% achievement of various targets – we try to recognize that there will be exceptions to simple time based targets."

Greg Coleman (CAE, ITG) offers his reflections:

"The metrics that are used to measure internal audit functions often focus on areas such as 'How quickly do you issue reports, how much money are you spending, how many audits are you issuing in a year?' But really, they can be superficial. It doesn't really speak to whether you are adding any value. Because anybody can issue 50 unimportant audits, if that's your target.

In terms of adding value, it's more about what audits you do and also being flexible regarding bringing in new audits if required, and helping out on projects, change initiatives etc.

I think adding value is as much about the feedback after assignments and how the organization reacts to you overall. If management come to you with requests and engage with you on a regular basis, I think that is a good start to ensuring you are a value adding audit function."

Actions for Internal Audit to consider:

- As an audit function discuss whether current metrics focus adequately on value add and productivity;
- Is the time taken collecting metrics justified in terms of the benefit they are providing?
- Engage key stakeholders in a discussion about how metrics are helping to serve their interests.

### Regard External Quality Assessments (EQAs) as a Performance Improvement Tool

My experience of working on audit External Quality Assessments (EQAs) is that if care is taken in engaging the right team to carry out the EQA, a good deal of added value can be obtained. I recommend that CAEs take a proactive approach to initiating EQAs since this should allow them to use the EQA to validate progress made on areas already identified as requiring improvement as well as highlighting key new areas for improvement. As much as possible, I recommend any EQA should always go beyond questions about compliance with IIA standards.

I start all of the EQA reviews I work on with the maxim: "No audit function is perfect" and with a view that the purpose of the EQA should not be to pinpoint all of the minor flaws in the operation of audit, but rather to focus attention on the most important opportunities (if they exist) to make a step change in relation to adding value or productivity.

I also start my work on EQAs with the view that those CAEs who request a quality review are showing a good degree of maturity since – sadly – many audit functions do not use this process to "step up their game". I am certain that increasingly the best audit functions will be the ones that carry out quality reviews on a regular basis; after all, if we believe that internal audits can act as a catalyst for improvement in organizations, the same should be true for the audit functions, provided that the EQA itself is done from a progressive, value adding frame of mind.

If an audit function has not had an EQA for a while, I recommend carrying out a "pre-EQA" review comprising some self-assessment alongside some independent input, but not amounting to a full EQA; this helps to put the audit function on the right track before having a full EQA review.

I believe a good EQA should also be used to name issues about board and management engagement with audit, so that the EQA can help start important conversations about the risk and control culture of the organization and the appropriate role and focus of audit.

Actions for Internal Audit to consider:

• Take a proactive approach to EQAs;
• Take care to select the right EQA team that goes beyond compliance to look at value add and productivity;
• Act as a role model so that key stakeholders can see the value of independent assurance in practice;
• If it has been a while since the last EQA, consider a pre-EQA review to help gear up the audit function for a full EQA later without the cost and effort of a full EQA immediately.


## CONCLUDING REMARKS

Progressive ways of working require auditors to take a fresh approach to thinking about what a good audit methodology looks like and to have a strong interest in the measurement of value and productivity. This often creates a tension between what has been in place in the past and what may still be in place in other audit functions.

However, the lean, progressive mindset is to regard the audit methodology as means to an end, not an end in itself. Likewise, lean encourages internal audit functions to get a much greater grip on some issues (such as driving through the flow of assignments, and validating the value add they are delivering), whilst recognizing that collecting some metrics is not helpful and – at its worst – actually a source of inefficiency and dysfunctional behaviour.

In addition, I hope I have conveyed that External Quality Assessments can be a powerful source of value add, provided they are carried out with the right mindset. As touched upon, EQAs can sometimes be a key way of unblocking stalemates between the audit function and key stakeholders. For example, I have seen many EQA reviews drawing out shortcomings in:

- The link between the audit plan and key risks;
- The absence of a joined up risk assurance picture;
- The impact of capability and resource constraints within the audit function.

Another benefit of having a regular EQA is that when a manager challenges an audit and says: "Well, who audits you then?", you can honestly reply: "Well actually, we were audited last year!" (I used this response on more than one occasion at AstraZeneca).

---

**SUMMARY OF KEY POINTS FOR INTERNAL AUDIT**

- Consider how much the audit methodology acts as an enabler for productive and value adding assignments and recognize the extent to which it is constraining;
- Enshrine post-assignment learning as an engine for driving a continuous improvement culture and personal development within the audit function;
- Consider current metrics – are they addressing key value and efficiency questions? Are metrics leading to any dysfunctional behaviour?
- Embrace EQA reviews, taking care to ensure these are carried out by reviewers with the right experience and mindset.

---

**RECOMMENDATIONS FOR SENIOR MANAGERS AND THE BOARD**

- Are you being consulted in relation to the value you are getting from internal audit?
- Understand the other feedback that is being obtained in respect of audit work – is it asking about the value that management are getting from the process?
- Ask when the last External Quality Assessment was carried out and the progress made on actioning key improvement points.

# 18
# Using Lean Audit Principles to Underpin Cultural Change in the Wider Organization

I mentioned at the beginning of this book that properly embracing lean ways of working is much more than just about following a check the box approach to a series of efficiency oriented good practices. My experience, as a CAE, and working with other audit functions, is that those functions that follow the spirit of lean can become important catalysts for improvements across the organization. In fact, I would go so far as to say that the best audit functions can trigger a recognition of the need for certain cultural changes in the wider organization. This may seem a rather grand claim to make, and it was not initially something at the forefront of my mind when I started implementing lean ways of working. However, over the years, I think those functions that operate in line with these principles exemplify the best of what internal audit can be and demonstrate how audit can effectively operate at the top table. Phil Gerrard (CAE, Rolls-Royce) captures the progressive, value adding mindset I am talking about:

> "My view is I'm here to make this a better business tomorrow than it is today, through better understanding of the risks the business is taking, leading to better decision-making and overall a control environment that manages to a level of risk that management has set, as opposed to a woolly, we are improving and we'll get there in the end, type of approach."

I don't want to say that it is *only* by following lean practices that audit can be this sort of catalyst; I am sure there are many progressive audit functions that may not have thought about lean explicitly. However, what I would claim is that lean can give a useful insight into the sort of mindset, and the sort of practical approaches, that drive a value adding, productive and influential way of operating as an audit function.

However, to put this into practice auditors need to be aware of some of the cultural and behavioural factors that can impede progressive ways of working. I have discussed a number of these barriers during the course of this book, but will now offer an overview of what the key difficulties seem to be. I will also more explicitly outline the sort of cultural change that lean, progressive audit practices can support.

## COMMON PRACTICES AND IIA STANDARDS OF NOTE

Going back to basics, the essence of the internal audit role is to provide independent and objective assurance and advice to key stakeholders in a manner that adds value. Over time, the scope of the internal audit role has grown from a focus on financial controls to a focus on compliance with laws and regulations, to increasingly looking at the effectiveness and efficiency of processes, procedures and systems. More recently, there has been a growing recognition of the need to adopt a risk based approach to internal audit work, and to examine the way key risks are being managed, giving consideration to governance and cultural questions as well.

## COMMON CHALLENGES & DILEMMAS

Despite making it clear that internal audit should have a broad role, there still appears to be a considerable inertia within the profession towards traditional ways of working, focusing audit's work mostly on financial controls, regulatory compliance and operational processes and procedures.

The challenges to audit taking up a more comprehensive role to look at risk and governance areas are multifold and have been discussed at intervals in this book. The main reasons the status quo is reinforced include:

- Differences between stakeholder views in relation to what they want from internal audit.

Some stakeholders can be conscious that the audit function could take on a wider role, but might be reluctant to "push" for this, partly for fear of antagonizing other stakeholders, but also from a sense that this might be too much of a stretch for the audit function. As a result, audit work on financial controls and compliance auditing may represent something of a "lowest common denominator" role that can be agreed between senior management and the board. That said, taking up this role will result in a self-fulfilling prophecy that audit's work delivers limited added value.

- A poor understanding of the three lines of defence model.

Sometimes internal audit is seen as a quality checking function (in the second line of defence), rather than a quality assurance function (in the third line of defence). As a result audit is encouraged to carry out routine monitoring work and to look into management areas of concern; and of course the audit function is likely to be good at doing this, justifying the status quo.

- A perception, that improved disciplines in risk, governance and assurance are likely to impede organizational performance rather than improve it.

If management has had negative experiences of audit in the past they may be concerned about audit being involved in key risk and performance issues. Keeping audit focused on financial controls and compliance therefore allows management to "get on with" their work without potentially unhelpful distractions from auditors who might only be able to make recommendations of doing things "by the book".

- A mindset that, because an organization has been successful to date, there are only likely to be minor surprises ahead.

If things have been going reasonably well for a period of time, there is a risk that management can be complacent and as a result, suffer from "a failure of imagination". However, unless audit can focus on areas of key risk and offer insightful findings, the problem is that the status quo will be maintained up to the point when something goes seriously wrong.

- A tendency to overreact to real, or imagined issues, leading to risk "fads."

A pattern that you can see in some organizations is that if something goes seriously wrong, or there is a considerable fanfare of concern about a specific risk area (e.g. the millennium bug, anti-bribery legislation) which particularly resonates or is required, then the organization may find itself in the grip of taking actions that may be out of proportion to the real risk. In other words, for some organizations problems or potential problems, can take on the characteristic of a fad. Addressing topical issues can give those involved in improving things a sense of achievement, but the danger – over time – is that this can lead to a degree of governance fatigue (e.g. "We put all that effort into new policies, processes and procedures but what did it really do to improve things?")

Organizations that have this sort of cultural trait are at risk of being at the mercy of fads and potentially miss the real risk that may be most damaging to them. To put this at its most extreme you can sum up this culture as follows: "Are we the sort of organization that is reluctant to react when there are minor audit findings and that only takes serious action when things have already gone badly wrong, or are mandated by regulation?"

## Processes and Procedures (and Audits) Can so Often Get Lost in the Detail

After applying lean ways of working to internal audit in AstraZeneca, we started to recognize potential Muda in relation to the length and complexity of corporate policies and procedures and worked to streamline what was in place. Increasingly, I see audit functions that recognize that the length and complexity of policies, processes and procedures can actually make it harder for all staff to understand what they need to do. The root cause of this may be in part due to the complexity of regulatory requirements (e.g. financial services or pharmaceuticals), but can also be due to a "layer upon layer" growth of policies (sometimes written in haste to respond to a regulatory need), that are not fully integrated or pruned.

Phil Gerrard (CAE, Rolls-Royce) considers the shortcomings of not stepping back when looking at control and compliance procedures:

> "If I look at many businesses, they have standards coming out of their ears. The standard for buying an inexpensive piece of IT kit at £5,000 can sometimes go through the same process and approvals as for investing £500,000. It's a process. Tick, have you followed the steps? You get lost in the detail.
>
> You need to focus on what matters and ensure everyone is clear on that and has easy-to-follow guidance.
>
> So everyone's signing everything. And we say, yes, that's been done. Okay, but to what purpose?

When you look at the detail, they are only signing things because a previous person signed them. And you realize there's no control because the first person signing a form knows other people are going to sign it after them. So no-one's taking accountability."

An additional dimension to this problem is a lack of agreement of what it means, in practice, to "roll-out a policy". When issues are found, staff can often say "I didn't realize, no one trained me" and management can respond in turn, "Well we published the requirements on the intranet."

## "Groundhog Day" is Alive and Well

One of my favourite films is called *Groundhog Day*, a comedy in which the lead character Phil Connors (played by Bill Murray) is destined to live the same day over and over again until... (no... I'm not going to spoil the plot if you haven't seen the film).

I often ask auditors attending my courses and workshops whether they experience Groundhog Day in the context of their work as an auditor. This question normally gets a few smiles as auditors explain that they continue to find the same issues year in and year out, or similar issues across different departments. This picture of no, or patchy, progress in relation to risk and compliance in some organizations can be attributed to issues around "tone at the top" or a "poor risk culture". However, where audit has been operating for a period of time, it probably says something about the difficulties there can be in identifying and naming the true root causes of control failings and compliance shortcomings, and making effective inroads into an organization's culture.

## Other Lines of Defence Are Weak and Audit Has Limited Involvement with These Functions

Organizations in some sectors can have a relatively strong second line of defence (e.g. financial services, pharmaceuticals and utilities) because compliance and risk management functions have – by and large – stepped up their role in the wake of a crisis, or an extensive regulatory regime. However, as discussed earlier, it is still quite common to find organizations with a relatively weak second line of defence. Shortcomings can range from:

• Limited and/or inconsistent upward reporting by these functions in relation to risks, issues and incidents;

- Monitoring or audit programmes, that may not be risk based and with limited coverage of all key risk areas due to resource constraints;
- Weak follow-up disciplines to track remediation.

An experienced Health & Safety auditor outlined to me another weakness he/she has encountered in the past in the context of certain compliance activities:

> "I've seen examples where organizations have said they have a compliance programme, but it's mostly a façade. It's a tick box, and they have not taken it to heart and really internalized what needs to be done."

In some instances these shortcomings in other compliance functions can be invisible to the internal audit function (until, perhaps, there is work on assurance mapping and assurance co-ordination). Indeed I have seen compliance functions that gather valuable information about issues and incidents, but have not made it available to the internal audit function. There can be a range of reasons for this, including the view that the information will not be of value to internal audit (which internal auditors may think also), or a view that such information should not be shared for confidentiality reasons.

The danger of some risk and compliance functions being something of a blind spot to internal audit is that valuable intelligence may be wasted and also that potential allies in risk, control and governance are not combining their collective insights and influence. This can result in internal audit being one of the few (or even the only) independent and objective voices in the organization.

## RECOMMENDED PRACTICES

### Take the Opportunity to Prune and Strengthen the Policy Compliance Landscape

After our work on lean auditing, the AstraZeneca audit function spent time with colleagues in compliance to look at the company code of conduct and a range of policy areas, with the aim of creating a clearer, more structured, set of expectations for staff and managers. My recent experience is that progressive audit functions recognize that sometimes "less is more" when it comes to the policy environment.

Alongside a streamlining of policies, it is important that any legal or compliance functions have a good understanding of what the real world is like in terms of trying to apply policies (i.e. they should have a Gemba perspective).

If there is any indifference to this question, internal audit can ask managers and staff what they (really) think of these policies and the associated training and guidance, and feed this back to the policy owners: and often there will be concerns. The key message is that policy owners must understand that the policies they issue need to be understood and applied by busy staff who have limited time to read lengthy guidance, are not superhumans with a law degree, or individuals who have nothing else to do!

As discussed in Chapter 8, the "Seven elements of an effective compliance programme" framework, which is in extensive use in the US, is an excellent way of helping organizations understand the essential ingredients to drive compliance with policies and procedures. My experience is that, if implemented on a pragmatic basis, with appropriate policies, this framework can help staff, policy owners and compliance functions to understand their roles and responsibilities, so that many of the common issues are not encountered.

Actions for Internal Audit to consider:

- Consider how many audit findings are a result of the complexity of the policy landscape and suggest a rationalization of what is in place;
- Establish whether staff "on the ground" have a voice in relation to the clarity of policies, if not encourage this, so that policies operate in the real world;
- Review the "Seven elements of an effective compliance programme" framework and consider whether it could add something to your organization.

## Look to Streamline Systems, Processes and Controls Where Possible

In the same way that the policy compliance landscape can often be streamlined, this is also true of systems, processes, procedures and control activities. At AstraZeneca, we worked to develop a key set of financial and IT controls, which was invaluable in relation to our work for Sarbanes–Oxley compliance. I know many other organizations have found the same to be true. Indeed, I sometimes tell CAEs who have not had to worry about Sarbanes–Oxley compliance, that it has some very powerful and helpful ideas that can be useful to build a better control environment.

One former CAE explained what they had done to streamline controls:

"This is something which we worked on a few years ago. We had a sense that we could be smarter about what was really important in relation to financial controls. We held various meetings with key people and came up with a list of key financial controls. It focused everyone's efforts.

I think it really helped audit, since when this approach was implemented it stopped comments that we were looking at things that were of no interest to anybody."

Phil Gerrard (CAE, Rolls-Royce) explains a similar approach:

"Audit can work with finance to decide what a finance control framework should look like. It can create some great discussions with senior finance staff to get a shared sense of what is really important.

In fact you don't even need to do any auditing and already finance management are getting engaged and endorsing what is really key, and we in audit are supporting the development of that. It will never be 100%, but the aim is to ensure there are no big gaps."

This approach need not only apply to financial and IT controls. It can be applied to a range of compliance and control areas (e.g. purchasing and crisis management). Phil Gerrard (CAE, Rolls-Royce) continues:

"It's worth spending time with the business to encourage them to develop proper frameworks to help their management manage the business. To think about how they might use the data they have. The aim is to help them manage the business better and pre-empt issues, rather than audit going in and finding problems.

I believe audit should be proactive. Go to the business and say, in this area, have you thought about this way to focus what you are doing and head off problems?"

An experienced Health & Safety auditor explains:

"You can put together relatively simple systems and processes that are extremely effective. So often it's about leadership and commitment. If you haven't got leadership and commitment that's driving it through and making it the way things get done around here, you're probably not going to have a good control environment in practice."

This underlines one of the most fundamental points that the Sarbanes–Oxley legislation made back in 2002: it is management (starting with the CEO and CFO) that is responsible in the first instance for the risk management and control processes over disclosures and financial reporting, not the auditors.

Actions for Internal Audit to consider:

- If you are not familiar with Sarbanes–Oxley regime, talk to someone who can explain it in simple terms, and consider how it could improve financial and IT controls in your organization;
- Share the principles of key risks and key controls as a way of encouraging the organization to streamline core processes and control activities in areas such as finance, purchasing and IT systems.

## Assurance Coordination and Assurance Mapping

In the earlier chapters on audit planning, I explained the importance of taking a risk and assurance approach to the audit plan. Beyond this is the wider question of how to leverage any other sources of assurance through assurance mapping and assurance coordination. This is an area I have been consulting on for a number of years and it is worthy of a book in its own right, but for the purpose of this discussion about lean, progressive auditing, a few key points are worth making:

A) Audit should clearly understand the overall assurance picture for the organization and play a role to ensure this is properly coordinated.

Phil Gerrard (CAE, Rolls-Royce):

"If I started driving what other assurance providers did or their relationship to the business, I think that's going too far. However, our legitimate role is to:

i) support the business in really understanding its assurance provision, and

ii) help manage the impact on the business of such assurance. It's so easy, if we don't talk to each other, to find they'll get an audit one week from one function and then another audit next week from internal audit. That's not helping the business, and creates barriers.

In trying to understand the overall assurance picture, audit should understand what it looks like because it's a jigsaw puzzle. If there are gaps, are they gaps I want to cover or, to be frank, maybe they don't pass the 'So what?' test. And then making sure that the board is aware of that."

B) Audit should gain a good understanding of the level of assurance being provided by other functions.

It was a significant step along my journey as CAE when I decided to probe the effectiveness of other compliance and assurance functions, such as: health and safety, product quality etc. This is increasingly being adopted by progressive internal audit functions often yielding opportunities for improvement and, most importantly, deepening audit's appreciation of what these functions are – and are not – doing. Phil Gerrard (CAE, Rolls-Royce) explains:

"Audit should feel able to independently look at what the other functions are doing, for example quality and health and safety, in order to give comfort to stakeholders about how much this can be relied upon. Indeed, I think our reporting should be more holistic, and capture assurance provided by others, so that senior management and the Audit Committee understand better how risk is being mitigated."

C) Audit should encourage a coordinated approach in reporting to senior management and the board from a range of compliance and assurance functions

As efforts in assurance coordination progress it should be possible to pull together a risk assurance dashboard, with inputs from management and a range of risk and compliance functions. Such a dashboard, which we implemented at AstraZeneca, consolidates separate information flows from a range of functions to provide a more joined up "continuous assurance" picture to senior management and the board.

Efforts to deliver a continuous assurance dashboard require collaboration on reporting processes and reporting criteria across a range of areas. However, work in this area can deliver – sometimes for the first time – an up to date, comprehensive, consistent and concise message about the state of risk and compliance across the organization. As a result, senior management and the board can have a complete picture about all of the key issues that need to be addressed at a given point in time.

To avoid any misunderstanding, I am not recommending that internal audit take the sole lead on assurance coordination, since it could lose its ability to assess the quality of the overall risk assurance picture. However, I do believe audit should be a clear advocate and key advisor about the way this can be done properly. This leads me to a brief "side bar": who should lead an assurance mapping process? I think there is no simple single answer, but as a rule I have found that assurance mapping needs to involve those persons in the organization *who have the authority to drive forward the benefits being sought.* Failure to engage the right level of sponsorship for assurance coordination efforts invariably leads to the creation of "talking shops" with little real progress.

Actions for Internal Audit to consider:

- Play a proactive role in promoting the development of an assurance map and driving improved assurance coordination;
- Be prepared to look at the work of other assurance providers;
- Examine opportunities for coordinated reporting;
- Think about the benefits to be gained and the sponsorship that will be required to deliver those benefits.

## Be a Role Model for Lean and Collaborative Ways of Working

Building on the topic of assurance coordination, audit functions keen to maximize their added value in the most efficient way are not afraid to step up to facilitate cross-functional working on certain issues. Richard Young (Director, UNIAC) gives an explanation of a progressive approach:

"In the old days an auditor looking at information security would visit, perhaps, 15 departments, speaking to one person at a time, asking specific questions.

The modern auditor meets them all in a room together, makes it very clear what the purpose of the meeting is and encourages 15 people to talk about it. The auditor understands human dynamics and is experienced. When it's done well, the managers attending the workshop will stand up and say, for example 'This is what I do in my department on data assurance and this is what I do less well'. Before you know it, you've got everyone chipping in, sharing best practices and highlighting areas where a co-ordinated response may be needed."

This dynamic approach to getting things done can always be complemented by more conventional assurance work, but is symbolic of lean ways of working: a small amount of effort and a high return for the organization.

Actions for Internal Audit to consider:

* Pilot new approaches (workshops, surveys etc.) as a way of gaining insights that can enable your organization to make progress;
* Make special efforts to bring together different parts of the organization that may have best practices to share.

## CONCLUDING REMARKS

It is possible that some more traditional internal audit functions feel safe in their role by being the expert at checking controls and compliance. There is certainly a role for this work in some industries and organizations. However, the risk is that if audit starts to become a substitute for the second line of defence, root causes for difficulties can easily get missed. In addition, whilst it is completely understandable for audit to want to act in a supportive mode towards any legal, compliance and risk functions (because they are often the allies of internal audit), this can result in audit "pulling its punches" when these functions themselves have shortcomings, and as a result this can limit the effective development of the overall control environment of an organization.

With more progressive, lean, internal auditing the internal audit function is striving to add value and eliminate waste to the extent that it is prepared to do itself out of a job. Thus, if management or a compliance function can take care of some areas on a day-to-day basis, then fine, audit will only look at these areas selectively based on risk and value.

Paradoxically, an internal audit function that is confident enough to want to push for its own redundancy in certain areas, acting selflessly for the benefit of the organization and its customers, is – in my analysis – more likely to guarantee its future, since there are always going to be new areas that will benefit from an independent and objective perspective. This is the essence of what lean encourages internal audit to aspire to and I hope that comes across throughout this book.

## SUMMARY OF KEY POINTS FOR INTERNAL AUDIT

- Review the policy environment and look for opportunities to integrate and prune what is in place – less can genuinely be more;
- Benchmark policy roles and accountabilities against the "Seven elements of an effective compliance programme" framework and identify key areas for improvement;
- Encourage a mindset of key risks and key controls so that the work of management and compliance and audit is better focused at what matters the most;
- Establish the case for assurance mapping and assurance coordination, but with a clear eye on the benefits and who should lead these efforts in addition to audit;
- Recognize the importance of audit working "on" the organization so that audit may potentially be out of a job in some areas, rather than staying trapped "in" the current organizational norms and expectations.

## RECOMMENDATIONS FOR SENIOR MANAGERS AND THE BOARD

- Ask when the policy framework was last reviewed against an independent framework (such as the "Seven elements of an effective compliance programme" framework) and whether it is so complex it can't be easily understood on the ground;
- Ask whether key processes and systems have clearly documented key risks and key control areas so that people know what they must do;
- Ask management whether assurance mapping or assurance coordination have been considered and what benefits could be obtained;
- What evidence is there that audit is evolving its role, and moving into new areas, rather than creating a culture of dependency on its work?

# 19
# Leading the Audit Function

I hope it is clear from all of the foregoing chapters that a progressive internal audit function that is intent on delivering value and eliminating waste cannot operate quietly on the sidelines. It must take up a key role in any organization focusing on key value areas and making timely, insightful and impactful recommendations that can positively drive the effective management of the organization across a broad range of areas. To take up this value adding role requires excellent leadership, combined with well-trained staff and appropriate ways of working that are capable of delivering added value on a day-to-day basis.

This chapter addresses the leadership qualities necessary in a CAE to deliver a progressive, lean audit function. The next chapter then looks at team capability, development and ways of working to support this.

## COMMON PRACTICES AND IIA STANDARDS OF NOTE

As mentioned at the outset of this book, a CAE is expected to lead an audit function in order to add value to senior managers and the board. He (and when I say "he", I mean "he" or "she") will normally lead the audit planning process and oversee the delivery of the plan (for quality and productivity). They will oversee the delivery of assignments (directly or through their management structure), managing any sensitive issues, and presenting the results of audit work to senior managers and the board.

A number of CAEs provide overall opinions on the state of risk management and control for their organizations, and are expected to highlight to senior management and the board any areas where there is disagreement about the remediation action that should be taken (so that the risk appetite can be formally considered).

The IIA emphasizes that internal auditors, including CAEs, should only engage in delivering services for which they have the requisite knowledge, skills and experience.


## COMMON CHALLENGES & DILEMMAS

### Being Disconnected from Senior Management and the Board

I run leadership workshops for CAEs in which we explore ways to be more influential. Clearly different CAEs have different styles and different relationships with key stakeholders, but there are three areas which consistently crop up as important challenges:

- Simply getting access to the diaries of senior managers and the board;
- Not fully understanding the evolving agendas, motivations and political sensitivities of these key stakeholders;
- Determining whether and how these stakeholders can be constructively challenged without adversely affecting working relationships.

Audit may not be alone in having problems of access. However, CAEs can sometimes sense that there *is* an inner circle of senior leaders who do have time for one another to talk openly about a range of issues, but it seems hard to break into this group. Chris Baker (Technical Manager, IIA UK) offers some reflections from his experience carrying out External Quality Assessments (EQAs):

> "Having informal discussions with senior managers and audit committee members is a great thing to do. But I still don't see that in a number of instances, sadly."

When thinking about being in a position to add value, a CAE who finds himself relegated to the margins of senior leadership interactions, cannot just accept it as "one of those things"; he must proactively take steps to remedy the situation.

## Having to Play Constant Catch-Up in Relation to Planned Strategic Developments and Key Operational Challenges

A number of CAEs and auditors find themselves regularly in "detective" or "catch up" mode, trying to find out what is going on in their organization in relation to key operational achievements and challenges, and especially in relation to strategic developments.

I have spoken to several CAEs who have heard about major systems and process changes "out of the blue" without being consulted or informed. This is despite the fact that they were most likely one of the most well-informed and impartial senior managers who could understand the key risks and opportunities in relation to what was being proposed.

The reason that CAEs and auditors may find themselves having to play detective may be due in part to their relationships with senior management; however, it can also be due to a management view that "this is not an issue of concern for audit" or "this is not an area audit will be able to help".

## CAEs Thinking "They Have Seen It All Before" and Sticking to Traditional Ways of Working

At various audit leadership workshops, I see CAEs from a wide variety of backgrounds and with considerable differences in experience. Some of the most experienced CAEs are engaged and interested in new ways of working that might enhance the value adding contribution of audit. Often these CAEs are actively engaged in auditing high value, strategic areas.

However, other CAEs I have met say they have stopped attending most professional update meetings because they: "rarely get any fresh insights". However, at the same time, it does not surprise me to learn that often their audit functions carry out a traditional role and are not particularly well resourced. John Earley (Partner, Smart Chain International) highlights the mindset that can be a barrier to effective lean working:

> "If you're satisfied with the way things are, you're not there. Your head is in the wrong place."

## CAEs Who Have Difficulty in Taking a Lead and Making a Real Difference

I see an enormous range of CAE styles; I do not believe there is a simple formula for being successful, since it depends on a range of factors, including the organizational context, culture and the preferences of senior managers and the board. However, I have seen a number of instances where even long-standing CAEs have lamented, in private, shortcomings in the risk and control culture of their organization. When we have then examined this in more detail, we have identified missed opportunities to educate and influence senior stakeholders (although I recognize we cannot be certain they could have been persuaded if they were challenged by the CAE). Richard Chambers (President & CEO, IIA) offers an interesting reflection on this topic:

> "If you appear tentative, if you appear intimidated, if you appear uncertain, your detractors will seize on that, and that undermines internal audit's effectiveness."

Thus, a CAE may achieve personal security by holding on to their role for a period of time, but this can sometimes be at the expense of the organization making real progress in relation to GRC and assurance disciplines. From a lean perspective, no external customer is going to be satisfied with someone who is just interested in collecting their pay cheque.

## RECOMMENDED ACTIONS

### Ensure You Are Properly Plugged in to What Is Going on in the Wider Organization

John Earley (Partner, Smart Chain International) explains:

> "In any kind of lean environment communication is fundamental. It has to be. If information is not flowing, in the same way that everything else should be flowing, then you have a major problem. Because people need to understand what is going on, and why they are doing what they are doing."

Marcin Godyń (Head of Internal Audit, USP Group) explains:

> "If management aren't involving you in everything that's going on how can you build the right audit plan and work on the key issues that right now may need to be better managed?
>
> Being fully connected is fundamental to value adding ways of working.

I believe that we need to understand things as they progress, being a partner alongside management, so that we can add value on a timely basis. Making comments after things are done can add value, but rarely much as giving real time input."

Karen Dignan (CAE, Group Head Office, OMG) has been working on this area and explains the changes that have taken place:

"A key change recently has been the level and quality of information I am now getting about what's going on, about big strategic changes, etc. This increase has followed a recognition that we might get involved in issues that in the past wouldn't have seemed relevant to us."

Such a flow of information can be achieved by ensuring the CAE is included in senior management circulation lists, key performance updates, and is also informed about the agendas of key meetings. When this happens, the CAE can meet with senior managers and the board far better prepared, and as a result, better placed to explore questions concerning risk and assurance in more depth. Karen Dignan (CAE, Group Head Office, OMG) goes on to emphasize:

"Having more information is a good thing, but if everyone's on a treadmill with no time to consider what it means, it's a waste. So you've got to explicitly make sure you've got time to digest information and also to engage with the right people."

In practical terms this can mean that the audit function should nominate roles within the function to distil key messages from internal and external sources and stimulate discussions within the audit function about the practical implications going forward.

Actions for Internal Audit to consider:

- Consider what information exists within the organization and the extent to which it is flowing easily to the audit function;
- If information is not flowing, work with stakeholders to explain the benefits of doing this in terms of having a better understanding of organizational issues (as well as less time wasted);
- Allocate roles within the audit function to review information and digest this for onward consideration in the audit function.

## Proactively Manage Contact with Key Stakeholders to Build Trust and "Money in the Bank"

Beyond being kept up to date with what is going on, effective CAEs recognize the crucial role they play in proactively engaging with senior managers and the board. Karen Dignan (CAE, Group Head Office, OMG) explains:

> "We actively work to maintain regular contact with key stakeholders. We'll discuss what's happening in the business, as well as relevant developments in the plan and audit findings."

Greg Coleman (CAE, ITG) goes on to explain:

> "I think it's essential that senior stakeholders get to know you well enough to trust you. I think the challenge for many CAEs is that due to their workloads it's so easy not to take the time out to engage them. My goal is to make contact with them frequently enough that they know who you are, and what you can do, and they are comfortable giving you a call.

> At the same time it's important to be conscious of their diaries and recognize there's no point in just having a meeting for the sake of it. If you haven't got anything of significance to really discuss they'll think you're wasting their time."

Richard Young (Director, UNIAC) explains the approach he has taken:

> "Building relationships with senior stakeholders leads you to being more in tune with the business and higher up on the list of: who do I call to have a chat about this? Who do we trust? Who have I got a rapport with?

> We have to be seen as part of the top table. If it doesn't happen ask yourself why are you not attending more senior management team meetings? If the answer is that you are worried that you are going to be out of your depth, you need to get beyond that.

> One approach is to agree to attend some key meetings as an observer and then offer them some reflections, perhaps even in private, after that. That's where audit should be."

If managed proactively, audit involvement in key meetings can create a virtuous circle of being well informed about developments, which in turn enables the CAE to engage with senior stakeholders on a more equal basis, offering insights on issues that matter and ensuring there are no surprises in relation to the work audit is engaged in.

Beyond this it is important that CAEs should work to ensure they and their senior managers stay engaged with a range of key stakeholders across the organization, keeping track of key contacts and the key points that were discussed. Most of all, CAEs and senior audit managers should not simply spend time with those colleagues they feel most comfortable with.

Building closer relationships can be achieved by sharing learning on best practices with colleagues and participating in joint working groups. At an informal level it can involve going to lunch with colleagues and being involved in social events, creating an underlying relationship of friendly interaction that can be a useful backdrop for any more difficult interactions.

Actions for Internal Audit to consider:

- Map out the key stakeholders of audit and consider when these stake-holders were last contacted and what about;
- Be wary of spending too much time with some contacts simply because you get on with them;
- Consider the quality of relations between the CAE and key stakehold-ers – try to build some "money in the bank" so that when issues become difficult there is already a degree of trust and mutual understanding.

## Adopt a Mindset of Continuous Improvement

Properly engaging key stakeholders in relation to what they are looking for and what can be done differently should create a natural pressure to make changes to audit practice, since what is wanted at one point in time is not necessarily going to be wanted the next.

Staying properly plugged in to professional developments within GRC and assurance circles is also likely to help the audit function keep moving forward. Particular favourites of mine are "audit hot spot" updates (which can be invaluable when thinking about planning) and also best practice templates (e.g. to enhance audit reporting and audit committee presentations). External best practice updates, that might address how a topic is being addressed in other organizations, should not only be read by the audit function, but also be shared (in summary form) with senior managers and the board, as a way of educating them on key developments in GRC and assurance. At the same time, their feedback on what they make of these new practices can give the CAE a useful perspective on how stakeholders are viewing audit as well as wider GRC and assurance developments.

As discussed in an earlier chapter, CAEs should take a close interest in post assignment feedback and the outcomes of assignment learning reviews. Phil Gerrard (CAE, Rolls-Royce) outlines his approach to continuous improvement:

> "A value adding function has got to keep moving. You've got to keep challenging yourself. Get your team involved, because they will often come up with some great ideas: What should we stop doing, what should start doing? What should we change?
>
> I'll do this every year because you need some fresh perspectives. Some of the best insights are from the people who have been in the function three weeks. They say, I don't understand why you are doing this? And I'll realize they're absolutely right: why do we do that?"

Actions for Internal Audit to consider:

- Regard feedback from stakeholders as a key source of fuel for a continuous improvement culture in audit;
- Determine which members of the audit function should take the lead in key areas of audit best practice and regularly share improvement opportunities within audit and with key stakeholders.

## Politics and Influencing Do Matter

Building relationships with key stakeholders is important, but it should be recognized that there is often a degree of organizational politics in relation to what audit does, particularly if it involves challenging the organization on well-established processes, roles and other cultural norms. However, not every CAE fully appreciates the importance of managing organizational politics, or is particularly skilled in this arena. Indeed, research by the Audit Director Roundtable cites this as one of the reasons new CAEs can fail in their role.

An experienced UK audit manager explains his philosophy about influencing and political savvy:

> "Over the years I have come to understand that anything that comes as a surprise is annoying. Anything that gets communicated out of chain generates a lot of sensitivity and negative feedback.

The things we focus a lot of our time on is making sure we tell people what we're thinking as we go along so there are no surprises. We encourage people to go through their chain of command so it doesn't come as a surprise at the top. So you have to put an awful lot of effort into that. Understanding the political dimension of our work is a key component of being effective.

This means you need to think ahead, to give people time to respond, and be able to understand not only what push back you are getting, but the reasons for this, as well as the unspoken clues that can give insights into other problem areas."

Thinking politically also means being able to think ahead about competing agendas and to operate strategically in order to build support for key improvement opportunities. I have been running development workshops for CAEs on influencing and political savvy for several years. My observation is that there is no standard technique to apply, often it is just a question of taking time to think about the sensitivities of certain proposals in the context of organizational challenges and individual priorities, so that what is being offered by audit genuinely seems of value. Over time these opportunities to reflect on the wider context within which audit proposals sit can instill a more mindful approach to influencing stakeholders.

Actions for Internal Audit to consider:

- How often are you consciously thinking politically and devising strategies in order to achieve positive change in the organization?
- Consider coaching or training on influencing and/or political savvy.

### Be a Role Model for Senior Management and the Board through Professional Reporting, Engagement and Transparency

In addition to a good understanding of organizational politics and influencing at the most senior levels, the most effective CAEs recognize that their impact comes from having a range of attributes over and above pure technical skills. Greg Coleman (CAE, ITG) provides a perspective on one of the ways in which CAEs can build credibility and influence:

"It's crucial to focus on being professional in all aspects of the audit process, especially when dealing with senior stakeholders. For example, you might be presenting to the audit committee, and you are sitting next to the external auditor, who has got a slick presentation, where a lot of money has been spent on all the graphics and everything else. I think it's really important that what you present from internal audit looks really good and professional and on a par with them."

Having a good look and feel to an audit report and an audit committee paper is often identified as a key area where for a small amount of effort audit can impress stakeholders and set a benchmark for clarity and transparency for other board reporting.

Beyond working on senior management and board reporting, a good understanding of key facts (e.g. killer facts) is important for the CAE's credibility, and for their ability to influence. Stephen Foster (CAE, Cargotec) explains:

"Relationships are important and we need to be able to lobby and persuade management but at the same time, there is a saying that one fact beats a thousand arguments. Doing work, with concrete facts that show what's going on, which can demonstrate what the weaknesses are, is very important.

Facts aren't really the message but they're the supporter of the message I might need to give. A relevant piece of factual information, which has gone through a proper process, that I can then call on, is a crucial value contribution from the audit perspective. This is because so often, when you are dealing with senior levels of management, it can be the person who is the most persuasive with their argument, who has the greatest charm, who can determine the outcome of a disagreement.

But you can often counteract that very effectively and efficiently by presenting the facts. Calling on hard findings or issues that I'm aware of from other audit reports can be so powerful. In a discussion at an executive level some might say something is not an issue and I can say: it is an issue: we've had a couple of sites where this has happened in the last year.

I couldn't persuade and guide if I didn't have hard facts. But at the same time, just having the hard facts is not enough; you need to find a way of communicating that is more than setting down a set of cold reports."

Whatever strategies are used by the CAE to build trust and influence, it is clearly fundamental that the CAE obtains regular feedback to ensure that they are on the right track.

Actions for Internal Audit to consider:

- Ensure the look and feel of audit reports promote audit in its best light;
- Be prepared: make sure that you have key facts to hand when interacting with key stakeholders;
- Ask for feedback from key stakeholders about your presence at senior stakeholder meetings.

## Being a Leader

Influencing skills, political savvy and having the right presence at senior meetings are all important ingredients to being successful. However, at the end of the day, being effective at a senior level requires an ability to take the lead. Rania Bejjani (CAE, Colt Technology Group) offers a useful analogy:

> "Most CEOs, most CFOs, most heads of business divisions, are people with a strong character and personality. Overall, they tend to be driven ambitious strong leaders, the equivalent of lions in nature. And, a CAE cannot be a mouse talking to a lion. I've got to be a lion to have an equal footing with a lion.
>
> So heads of audit need to be strong, driven and emotionally intelligent characters, who understand the business, and are able to flex their behaviours to build rapport. The aim is to build credibility and gain the trust of management so they see the CAE as an equivalent peer who speaks their language and shares their objectives."

Phil Gerrard (CAE, Rolls-Royce) offers the following perspective:

> "Have confidence in your view. You need to be happy putting your head above the parapet, because if you are not you won't succeed. If you crumble in front of management at the first challenge, your credibility can be lost. So even if you've got really good points, you're fighting uphill after that.
>
> Have confidence, but at the same time listen, if necessary go away, come back, either agree or disagree, but don't fold if you've got something you believe in."

This is a difficult dilemma to navigate through: CAEs with a strong character or a strong opinion on a particular point can sometimes be too rigid and unable to compromise. On the other hand, those who are less confident might tend to underplay their hand, and be disappointed with a lack of progress on GRC issues in their organization. One starting point for some CAEs is to obtain feedback from peers, staff and key stakeholders on their impact, and to build a development road map. Ideally, the CAE should have the courage to share these development needs with close work colleagues so that they can prompt the CAE if they are not managing the balance well.

In the context of progressive ways of working, this feedback can focus on the way that the CAE is leading work on value adding ways of working and also the way the CAE is driving greater productivity. This can sometimes involve readjustments in relation to the way they delegate within the audit function, empowering and coaching audit staff to strengthen their own influencing and leadership skills. Remember that whilst managers are appointed from above, leaders are determined through the consent of those around. Also remember that the best leaders don't develop followers, but other leaders!

Some CAEs are natural leaders; however, even the best may use a professional coach or senior mentor from time to time to help them reflect on what they are doing and how they are doing it. Another mechanism for self-development is the technique of Action Learning. Action Learning was developed in the UK in the 1940s and supports the "development of the self by the mutual support of equals".

I used Action Learning throughout my time as a CAE to examine a number of the key challenges I faced as a CAE, and I am a member of a (different) Action Learning Group to this day. Action Learning helped me hugely on several important issues during my 7 years as CAE. At the influencing workshops I now run with CAEs and audit managers, we use Action Learning discussions to address challenges they are facing. Most find that Action Learning has given them a fresh perspective on the reasons for the difficulties they are facing, as well as new options for moving things forward. At one workshop recently we ran three Action Learning discussions, the last of which concluded the CAE was doing all he could and there were no obvious alternatives, other than accepting the situation or leaving the organization. At the end the CAE commented: "It's interesting that this approach does not always try to 'fix' things. But I now feel a lot better knowing the choices I thought I had are indeed the main choices I have."

My experience is that many of the choices facing CAEs and senior auditors are filled with dilemmas, with no easy answer. However, an

Action Learning group (which has similarities to small work groups in a lean context) offers the opportunity to step back and reappraise a situation, getting multiple perspectives on what may have caused the difficulty and seeing more clearly a range of options for moving forward. Note that Action Learning utilizes techniques that amount to much more than having a chat or giving advice. Indeed one of my main roles when I facilitate these groups is to ensure that the Action Learning Group has an atmosphere of calm reflection and is not judgmental, which can be quite difficult for a group of half a dozen auditors!

Actions for Internal Audit to consider:

- Gather or update feedback on your leadership as a CAE;
- What action plan do you have in place to improve your leadership? How are you progressing? Have courage to ask close colleagues to observe your progress and offer you feedback;
- Consider coaching, mentoring or Action Learning groups to "sharpen your saw" as a leader of the audit function.

## CONCLUDING REMARKS

As I reflect on the challenges that CAEs face, and offer some advice, I am mindful how easy it could be to over simplify what it takes to be an effective CAE. In fact, the reason for the last recommendation about coaching, mentoring and Action Learning is intended to reflect the fact that dilemmas surround the work of a CAE and there are often no simple recipes for success.

In this context, therefore, whilst I am suggesting that we need more leadership in internal audit, this needs to be accompanied by support from other stakeholders. I am not suggesting that a CAE should be a "sacrificial lamb" on the altar of some ideal of good governance and risk management, if key stakeholders are not going to support them.

However, I do worry that some CAEs have lost their way and become disillusioned with their role. Whilst I understand that some stakeholders are infuriating to work with, it is important for us as a profession that we do not allow ourselves to be marginalized or our integrity compromised. If this happens, the losers will be the organizations involved and the customers they serve, as well as the credibility of internal audit as a profession.

In the introduction to this book, I offered a dedication to the CAEs who are striving to do a good job, and this is a sincere sentiment, since I speak as a former CAE. It is so easy for an audit function to feel sidelined, since top level sponsors do not always have the time to fully understand and engage with the CAE, and thus do not appreciate the full spectrum of what audit can offer. In a small way, my CAE coaching and work with Action Learning groups is intended to counteract the sense of isolation some CAEs and auditors feel, but I wonder whether there is more we can do as a profession to help one another? Professional qualifications play an important role, but so many of the challenges CAEs and auditors face relate to dilemmas and difficulties "in the real world" that seem to revolve around personalities, mindsets and cultural issues.

I will leave the closing remarks in this chapter on audit leadership to Richard Chambers (President & CEO, IIA):

> "Tackling your role as CAE from a position of confidence and strength improves your chances of success.
>
> There are very few functions in a company or in an organization that are more personality driven than internal audit.
>
> I spent many years as a national practice leader for PriceWaterhouse-Coopers looking at internal audit departments mainly at the Fortune 500 level. From my experience, there's one absolutely overarching theme. If you have a strong CAE, you will likely have a strong internal audit department. You don't necessarily get a strong CAE because you had a strong audit department. The strong CAE drives the strong audit department."

---

### SUMMARY OF KEY POINTS FOR INTERNAL AUDIT

- Consider whether the audit function is sufficiently "plugged in" to an up to date understanding of what is happening in the organization;
- Have a proactive strategy for stakeholder engagement, which brings value to both sides and creates goodwill ahead of (inevitable) times of disagreement and difficulty;
- Watch out for signs of stagnation, create a culture of continuous improvement, no matter how much experience you have;

- Be a role model in relation to senior management and board engagement in terms of professionalism, a grounding in the facts and transparency;
- Recognize that political know-how and an ability to influence at a strategic level are a fundamental part of what it takes to be an effective CAE;
- Reflect on your leadership and use coaching, mentoring or Action Learning groups to "sharpen your saw."

## RECOMMENDATIONS FOR SENIOR MANAGERS AND THE BOARD

- Clarify whether the CAE is routinely kept up to date, on a timely basis, with all key operational and strategic developments;
- Expect a good CAE to have regular and high quality interactions with key senior managers and relevant board members – both informally and in relation to board level communications. Tell them if you are not happy with their performance;
- Look for signs of complacency and stagnation in the audit function and likewise in relation to the organizational approach to governance, risk and assurance;
- Look for signs of organizational level leadership and influence by the CAE and ensure they have access to executive coaching or mentoring support.

### References and Other Related Material of Interest

Audit Director Roundtable

Chambers, R. *Attributes of Effective CAEs* http://www.dallasiia.org/PDF/030311_Lunch.pdf

IIA and Half, R. 7 *Attributes of Highly Effective Internal Auditors* https://na.theiia.org/news/Pages/IIA-and-Robert-Half-Present-7-Attributes-of-Highly-Effective-Internal-Auditors.aspx

# 20
# The Audit Function: Selection, Training & Development and Ways of Working

No matter how good the CAE may be, without a strong team it will be an uphill struggle to create the sort of audit function that can take the lead in the lean progressive ways described in this book.

## COMMON PRACTICES AND IIA STANDARDS OF NOTE

Many internal audit functions are located within the finance function, with the CAE reporting to the Chief Finance Officer for administrative purposes, with a dotted line to the Chair of the Audit Committee. Variants on this theme will be when the CAE reports into either a head of assurance or a senior legal or compliance officer. More recently, a growing number of CAEs are now reporting directly to the Chief Executive Officer. This has been especially notable in the financial services sector, prompted by various reviews looking at the lessons learned from the 2007–2008 financial crisis.

Against this backdrop, the majority of internal audit staff will be qualified accountants, some of whom may have an internal audit qualification. Depending on the nature of the organization, the audit function may also have specialists in IT, fraud or a background in compliance or risk management. Depending on the organization, the audit function may also include staff with backgrounds in engineering, insurance, banking or project management.

Typically, non IIA qualified staff within the audit function will receive some basic induction training on internal auditing and then additional training on areas that are regarded as important, such as risk management or how to carry out process walk-throughs. Individual development needs will – hopefully – be addressed by coaching on the job, or specialist training and development courses.

The IIA encourages auditors to take professional qualifications in internal auditing, and to enhance their knowledge and skills through continuous professional education (CPE). As discussed before, the IIA expects audit functions to ensure they have the relevant skills for the assignments they undertake and to use other sources of expertise if they do not have the skills needed for particular assignments.

## COMMON CHALLENGES & DILEMMAS

### Problems Attracting Staff

Some audit functions act as a recruitment ground for the finance function. For example, they may take newly qualified accountants and give them two or three years' experience as internal auditors, before they move into other roles. This approach has a number of attractions, since it spreads an awareness of risk and control thinking across the organization, as those auditors move into other roles. However, the downside can be an audit function that is largely filled with inexperienced staff, with a limited ability to carry out work on more complex (and yet potentially more value adding) areas.

Whilst there can be successes recruiting at a more junior level, many CAEs explain to me that they have had limited success in getting more experienced finance staff to join internal audit. This is because many regard internal audit as a sideways or backwards career step, often (incorrectly) associating the work of internal audit with that of the external auditor.

CAEs can find it even more challenging to attract experienced staff outside of finance, risk and compliance to join the internal audit function; not least because this may involve staff having to give up a secure role, and step away from their previously planned career path.

## Selecting the Right Staff

Whether recruited from the finance function, or other functions, another challenge can be that whilst staff may be interested in audit because they are looking for variety, that does not mean they will necessarily be good at auditing! In my experience as a CAE, and working with clients, I have seen many instances of staff who look forward to travelling, learning about new areas and offering advice. However, when it comes to auditing they may be less well suited, either getting lost in the detail, or accepting management representations too easily.

I also think that some people who apply to be auditors at this current point in time would have been fine as auditors five or ten years ago, but for a modern progressive audit function the challenge, in simple terms, is to find auditors who have a "detective gene" (or "sixth sense" as I have heard some say) alongside an ability to work in areas beyond financial controls and regulatory compliance.

## Developing Technical Skills Only

When I work with CAEs on developing their auditors it is quite common to find that there is regular training on technical topics. However, less common are comprehensive programmes of training and development on wider management and leadership skills, not least around listening and influencing skills. Phil Gerrard (CAE, Rolls-Royce) reflects:

> "If you're not able to show empathy as an auditor I think you are lost, because you won't be effective. You may come out with a report and the minimum actions will be completed, but nothing will really change, because you haven't engaged and influenced the organization, and got them to own what's being done."

## Not Playing to People's Strengths

At a workshop a year ago, a CAE explained how pleased she was to have secured the funding to deliver a series of training sessions for all auditors on data analytics, which she wanted to be used more extensively. However, after delivering the training she was becoming disappointed that a number of the auditors did not seem to be particularly interested in using the skills they had just been taught.

During a coaching session discussion about this challenge (which was presented as a problem in relation to the motivation and productivity of some of the auditors who had just had the training on data analytics) we started to wonder whether it was asking too much of some of the auditors to pick up new ways of working.

During the Action Learning session the CAE concluded that she was probably expecting too much for every auditor within the audit function to want to use data analytics on a regular basis. The conclusion was to accept that auditors have different areas of interest and areas of strength and therefore not to expect that all of the auditors should extensively use data analytics.

Continuing the theme of working with the strengths of the audit team, some technical auditors are given management responsibilities when they are poorly suited to the role. This can result in the technical auditors spending time on tasks they do not like (such as stakeholder management and staff coaching) and doing less of what they are good at, and being demotivated at the same time! Needless to say, the negative effects don't stop there: key stakeholders ultimately lose out, as well as the staff working for these managers, who are not properly coached or developed.

## Becoming a Parking Lot

Whilst there are many great audit functions, there are others where there is a good proportion of audit staff who have been in place for many years, without any serious prospect of moving into other roles, who just want to tick over until their pension is due. This "watching the clock" mindset can be found in many organizations and in many departments outside of internal audit, but in a relatively small function like internal audit, it can have a significantly adverse impact.

Rania Bejjani (CAE, Colt Technology Group) sums up a sentiment expressed by a number of CAEs I have spoken to:

> "I think historically our profession has typically attracted people with a more reserved and introverted nature. These characters might have been brilliant accountants and may have excellent analytical skills, but would be more inclined to prefer a lower profile role, and may not always be very comfortable challenging management, resisting business pressure on a tricky issue or voicing their views assertively.
>
> These characters offer many talents and skills to a business but may not best suited to lead an internal audit function that inherently needs to confront management and ruffle some feathers from time to time.

The problem is that across many organizations internal audit is filled with these characters. In these cases, the dynamic between internal audit and management is not necessarily great. The perception of internal audit capabilities may be tarnished and the value they can add may not be communicated."

I have worked with some excellent older auditors, who still have "a twinkle in their eye" and a passion for delivering great results, even in the final years of their career. However, if there are a number of audit staff who are just collecting their pay cheque, it will limit the ability of the audit function to act in the value adding catalytic role I have discussed throughout this book. An audit function is too important to become a parking lot!

## Consequences of Poor Staff Capability Can Often Be Self-Fulfilling

Whilst a number of audit functions have overcome many of the challenges listed above, those that have not been able to do this find themselves in something of a catch-22 position. Chris Baker (Technical Manager, IIA UK) sums up the problem:

"Sadly you'll find entire audit functions who are reluctant to tackle the most important areas, because they can be challenging to execute, and they feel as though they don't have the confidence or the ability to look at them."

In these instances, young recruits may just regard their time in audit as a necessary evil, mostly concerned to "keep their noses clean" and move on into another role. Higher potential staff in the organization may see audit as a dead end function, that is unlikely to: i) offer interesting work, or ii) an interesting work environment, or iii) be good for their future career. Even if good staff join audit, their departure after a short time may be a clue that the audit function is neither currently operating at the right level, nor moving sufficiently quickly in the right direction.

## Poor Value from Co-Sourcing and Outsourcing Support

To address the inevitable capability gaps found in any audit function outsourcing and co-sourcing resources is an important option. However, this does not always go to plan, as the following story from a CAE highlights:

"I had a couple of roles that I needed to fill for a period of time and didn't have the budget to afford some of the better guys I wanted from the consultant. As a result, the consultants sent me a couple of junior guys. They were really enthusiastic, but young and inexperienced. They worked hard and whizzed through assignment tasks, but when we started to review the results we found we needed to ask them to go back and redo certain tests, because they'd missed important issues.

It was annoying because they had a manager who was supposed to look at their work, but he didn't have the time or insight to look at the work properly. In the end I had to put one of my guys to supervise them much more closely. I learnt a lesson there."

My experience is that co-sourcing support can be very useful, but if this support does not provide the right staff or is not properly managed it can easily turn into an expensive waste.

## The Problematic Aspects of an Auditing Culture

I referred earlier to the "detective gene" that I think some of the best auditors have. I sometimes wonder myself whether it is an accident that I am the son of a policeman! Anyway, without getting into a debate about whether or not some people are born to be good auditors, there can be no doubt that effective auditors are often able to weigh up soft and hard data and information to get to key weaknesses that need to be addressed.

Having the right personal attributes can result in excellent auditors, who can spot key issues very quickly. However, an ability to see pitfalls and problems can have a downside, since it can mean the audit function has staff who have a somewhat conservative, cautious and even negative mindset. This can sometimes result in a culture within audit functions which can:

- overanalyse its own difficulties; and/or
- expect others to address these difficulties, whilst taking limited responsibility to address issues themselves.

I have seen this pattern sufficiently often during my work on lean and my work on EQAs to know that this is a trap that even leading functions can slip into.

## RECOMMENDED ACTIONS

### Treating Staff-Related Matters as a Key Priority

A number of CAEs who attend the audit leadership workshops that I run can be rather resigned and downhearted when we discuss staffing matters. They will refer to occasions when they have tried to get staffing gaps or skills shortages onto the agenda of key stakeholders, but have not been successful in securing much change. In some cases CAEs reflect that they had probably not built a compelling "burning platform" for senior stakeholders, connecting staff capability limitations to a range of concrete consequences such as: limited coverage of the audit universe, dissatisfaction with audit's understanding of the business, and a sense of limited value add from audit assignments, and so on.

By the same token, CAEs who take over the leadership of an audit function with a mandate to step up its contribution recognize that addressing staff capabilities will be a fundamental area to address if it is going to change for the better. In my role as the CAE of AstraZeneca, making a number of staffing changes was fundamental to helping release audit's potential and it is something I hear frequently when CAEs describe what they did when they took over an ailing audit function.

Achieving change can be as simple as always looking out for good quality staff to join the audit function even when it is fully staffed. The argument is that without doing this the audit function is often staffed below budget, is stretched to deliver the audit plan and has poor handover disciplines to preserve relationships and know-how.

Actions for Internal Audit to consider:

- Consider how any shortcomings in audit function performance can be linked to shortcomings in staff capability;
- Build a case for the staffing changes that would be needed and the tangible value that should flow from that;
- Consider rolling recruitment so that audit actually meets its headcount targets and has improved knowledge retention.

### Focusing on Strategic Recruits, Selection, Grading

Early on in my tenure as a CAE I was keen to make some staff changes in order to improve the value-add contribution of internal audit. A key area for a pharmaceuticals company is clearly Research & Development (R&D), and so I secured support from the head of R&D to appoint a very experienced manager, Hans Nilsson, for nearly three years. Despite the fact that he was coming close to the end of his career, and was not an experienced auditor, it was clear that he was still keen to make a difference. Hans explains why he wanted to work in the internal audit function:

> "The benefit of working for an internal audit function is that you get the opportunity to work with senior managers across a range of important areas, with a real opportunity to influence change as a result of the profile of internal audit with the board."

The appointment of senior managers into audit has an importance over and above the skills of the individual being appointed, since their appointment is often an important symbol to audit staff – as well as the wider organization – that things need to change and are changing.

I have discussed the appointment of experienced managers close to retirement with some CAEs and we have sometimes described them as "bullet proof": neither inclined to do anything over the top and rash, nor to back down when they know an important issue needs to be addressed.

Such appointments may require audit to rethink the staff grades that may have been set at a time when the focus of audit roles was to primarily look at controls and compliance. If you look at the audit functions that make a step change in their contribution you will often find a reappraisal of the grades of the roles, especially at the CAE and senior management team level. It is worthy of note that many of the high potential non-finance staff that were recruited to internal audit in AstraZeneca were appointed on a secondment basis. They would spend two, three or four years in audit, after which some retired whilst others were given a good role back in the business.

When it comes to the selection of auditors, I would strongly recommend the use of a case study as a selection tool. One way to do this is to create some working papers towards the end of a fictitious audit assignment. The task given to candidates is to identify the key findings and thereafter to present their findings to a manager in the form of a mock closing meeting.

This approach was very successful when I was CAE and I have worked with clients on similar exercises since then. It enables the recruiting audit manager to gain a much deeper sense of the capabilities and development needs of those being interviewed: for example, how clearly can they see what the facts are telling them in terms of overall control environment and business impact?; How well do they manage interviews (and themselves) when under pressure?

I am aware of a number of other audit functions that do a similar thing and I can confidently state that there are points about prospective candidates that can emerge from a well-judged case study that would *never* get picked up in competency questionnaires or interviews.

As a brief aside it is worth noting that for one client, with over two dozen candidates screened using the same case study, *none of them* came up with identical findings! Indeed, many candidates projected previous experiences and preferences into their proposed audit findings, whether or not the evidence in the case study supported this! This reinforces a point made in an earlier chapter about the importance of regular peer reviews to manage the risk of auditor biases in audit assignments.

Actions for Internal Audit to consider:

- Look for high calibre recruits with wider skill sets to join audit on a secondment basis;
- Consider whether current audit staff grading is appropriate;
- Consider a case study process in order to ensure would-be auditors being selected have the "detective gene" of a good auditor and are able to handle themselves effectively when under pressure in a closing meeting.

## Guest Auditors and Guest Advisors

Whilst strategic recruitment is a crucial ingredient to stepping up the value adding contribution of audit, even the largest audit function will only have a few of these roles to fill. Outsourcing and co-sourcing are clearly one solution, but there are other options that should be considered, making the most of the internal capability of the organization. Two key ways to build the capability of an audit function, using resources from within the organization, are through guest auditor or guest advisor arrangements.

Guest auditor arrangements are typically put in place when someone joins the audit function for the duration of an audit assignment, preferably being involved in assignment planning, some or all of the fieldwork, and the closing process. Guest auditors might be highly rated staff (from finance, or risk or another field) that are looking to broaden their experience and networks.

The benefit of a guest auditor arrangement is that the guest gains good experience of an audit assignment and working with another part of the organization, whilst the audit function gets the benefit of an experienced individual with (typically) a different skill base, and – often – the ability to provide fresh insights of real value.

The audit function will typically find that it needs to make an investment in explaining the audit methodology to the guest auditor, as well as coaching the guest through the assignment they are working on. Thus, three or four weeks' effort from the guest auditor might only equate to two or three weeks of equivalent work from a more experienced auditor. However, in addition to getting support for an assignment, the audit function builds wider relations throughout the organization, often finding they become ambassadors for good risk and assurance processes and – in some instances – become interested in joining audit.

A guest advisor is a role that typically requires a more limited time commitment than a guest auditor, but can nonetheless add huge value. Guest advisors can be selected for either specialist technical skills, or for their deep understanding of a process, or even for their understanding of the key stakeholders who need to be influenced, and the sorts of arguments that might be more successful in persuading them.

Guest advisors might be consulted three or four times during an audit assignment, often at the scoping stage, in the middle of fieldwork (as choices are made about areas to pursue and areas to drop), and then as findings are being drafted and action steps negotiated. The time commitment of the guest auditor might only be one, two or three days, but this input can "fast track" audit's work, and make a significant difference to audit's ability to carry out new or more complex assignments.

In the best organizations, the benefits of guest auditors and guest advisors are not just promoted by internal audit but by management, and other functions such as HR, Finance and Purchasing etc.

Actions for Internal Audit to consider:

- Look ahead at audit assignments on the plan and consider whether a guest auditor or guest advisor would help;
- Build a rolling programme for guest advisors and guest auditors, obtaining interest from other functions and publicize successes.

## Outsourcing and Co-Sourcing

In the absence of capability within the audit function, and no suitable guest auditor or guest advisor options, co-sourcing and outsourcing are clearly options that should be utilized. They can provide the competence to enable the internal audit function to work on important risk and value issues. In my experience, a few days' input from a good co-sourced support can save twice as much time (and sometimes more) of research time and effort by a less skilled auditor. Moreover, *co-sourced support often has the confidence to recognize when it has found something of significance, and in addition often has the credibility to persuade the organization that it needs to make changes.*

However, from my own experience, and from discussions with many CAEs, it is easy to be disappointed with the value for money from these arrangements. A few key points are worth highlighting to maximize the value from these arrangements:

- If at all possible, try to avoid seeking outsourced or co-sourced support at the last minute; it usually results in a sub-optimal assignment, since staff with the right technical, interpersonal and team working skills are often hard to find;
- At the beginning of the year, consider sharing the audit plan with a few potential co-source and outsource suppliers and organize a day in which the audit management team is briefed by these potential providers in relation to:
  - Their experience of working in the areas that are in the plan;
  - The sorts of issues they have been able to unearth with other clients;
  - Some of the co-source staff who would be allocated to these assignments.

This process can enable the CAE to clearly identify the co-source provider who is best suited to which assignment and can also be very helpful in gathering insights in relation to the sorts of issues that might need to be closely investigated during the assignment.

- Unless circumstances prevent this, try to deliver important assignments through a co-source arrangement, rather than full outsourcing. Adopting this way of working delivers greater insights into how the co-source team is spending its time and the competence of the co-source team. It should also help to transfer knowledge to the audit staff involved, and also allow for the audit function to input at an early stage in relation to more judgmental areas and appropriate influencing strategies.

Nancy Haig (CAE, global consulting firm) provides another interesting perspective on outsourcing and co-sourcing:

> "My approach to outsourcing is quite different from a number of other CAEs. They may choose to outsource things that are more complicated. I outsource the things that are easy to do, basic compliance and control work (e.g. SOX compliance), because outsource providers can do a decent job and I can get a good value add for that, the fees for such work won't cost me a lot and better still it avoids boring my team. They are generally at the more experienced end of the spectrum, and therefore better able to do more complex work, and would rather do complex work as well. I think my most talented internal audit professionals would probably have quit if I had asked them to continually get involved in performing lots of basic financial compliance work, rather than directing the process."

Actions for Internal Audit to consider:

- Make sure that audit plans explicitly address what could be done if co-sourcing or outsourcing were possible;
- When the plan is approved organize a working session with prospective co-source providers to understand what they might be able to do and to select who will support which assignments;
- Consider the current approach to co-sourcing and outsourcing – regard last-minute requests for co-sourcing support as a sign of waste (Muda), and work to improve the process for obtaining this resource.

## Leveraging Diversity and the Right Amount of Change

An underlying theme from the earlier discussion is the benefit of having a diverse audit function. There can be no one size fits all solution, but an approach that seems to work well in many instances is a "multi-layered, multi-speed" approach to staff rotation:

At a more junior level: Staff who are recruited into the function (often from external audit) who work in audit for two or three years starting with core assurance work and then move into more complex operational audit assignments. They can be a good source of staff for the wider organization and also spread risk and controls thinking across the organization, as well as growing the wider network of the audit function.

More experienced auditors: Staff who have audit experience, as well as perhaps a specific skill area, may be able to provide a degree of continuity in the function. They will stay in the function for longer periods and provide the backbone of the function, understanding risks, processes and the context behind certain decisions, and acting in a coaching role for new staff.

Senior "flagship" appointments: These recruits may have a deep understanding of certain specialist areas, or are recognized and credible leaders with strong networks at a senior level. They may not be professional auditors, but will be able to work well with audit staff, often helping to guide auditors in relation to where to look as well as being able to understand the significance of what the audit function is finding and be persuasive in getting management to pay attention to what has been found.

The correct composition of an audit function requires careful consideration and needs to be viewed alongside its strategy. However, a key message is that the benefits from having a diverse range of staff skills can be considerable. An experienced Health & Safety auditor notes:

> "The audit you get is a function of the experience of that particular auditor and what his interest area is or what he's good at. If you choose another auditor you will often get a completely different type of audit, looking at different things. This applies to both internal staff and when you are dealing with external regulators.

> So if you have a mixed skill set in the audit function you'll end up with much more effective audits because the team can – if well managed – address its biases and blind spots and also propose more robust value adding action plans."

Roger Timewell (former Head of R&D audit, AstraZeneca, now consulting in clinical trial auditing) comments:

> "Having experience outside audit allows an auditor to offer insights that come from being experienced working in organizational processes, and knowing what looks good and what needs work. Note this experience may have nothing at all to do with conventional control or compliance issues, but rather just understanding, for example, how communication channels work in the business, and knowing – from first hand experience – what problems can arise."

Hans Nilsson (Chairman Kanozi Architects AB and former head of R&D audit at AstraZeneca):

> "I enjoyed my time working in audit. It gave me the opportunity to focus on areas that I sensed, from my years of experience, needed improvement, but with the benefit of working with internal auditors who were used to gathering together facts and information, which I could then use to influence key stakeholders to make changes."

In summary, an audit function that is able to build a progressive audit strategy will inevitably need to address key capability gaps and usually this will highlight the need for a more diverse audit function.

Actions for Internal Audit to consider:

- Map out the diversity of the audit function in terms of business skills, audit skills and staff potential;
- Consider the audit strategy and consider how this might be supported by a "multi-track approach" in terms of audit function composition;
- Engage key stakeholders on the benefits from a diverse audit function.

## Promoting Internal Audit

Building an internal audit function with a greater proportion of experienced business managers and talented, high potential staff, who are prepared to work on key issues will inevitably give assignment sponsors and other internal stakeholders a new impression of internal audit. This typically needs to be accompanied by education sessions (before audits and more generally) about the changing role of internal audit and the benefits of having a better risk and control environment generally. Promoting the role of audit within a more strategic context is also likely to attract staff to join as guest auditors or guest advisors or to join on a permanent basis. In particular, audit can also be more explicitly promoted as a career development choice. Stephen Foster (CAE, Cargotec) explains:

> "To me it's about presenting internal audit as something that can give you an excellent set of skills, recognizing it as an environment where you can learn a lot and develop. Of course, what you learn will depend on what you make of your time in audit, but if you play it right, you can really start to gather valuable experience and have influence in areas that you just couldn't do in a pure linear functional environment."

Clearly, organizational cultures can vary and different CAEs have preferred ways of promoting audit, but Phil Gerrard (CAE, Rolls-Royce) provides some simple advice for those who want to give audit a higher profile:

> "Get out there, promote what you do, have confidence in what you do. Don't hide your light under a bushel."

Actions for Internal Audit to consider:

- Communicate the changing nature of internal audit's role, linking it to the wider strategy of the organization, and explain what this means in terms of changing staffing needs;
- Promote the career development opportunities that working in audit can provide.

## Developing a Broad Range of Skills and the Right Auditor Mindset

CAEs who are seeking to build a value adding audit function recognize that whatever the background of staff within the team, there will always be a need to strengthen the team's capability. Jonathan Kidd (CAE, UK Met Office) offers some advice:

> "One of the things I think is really important to focus on is the training and development of the entire audit function. My team have all got defined training plans. They are all very proficient in terms of general audit skills, but we are going beyond that if team members wish to become a specialist in a certain area, where it is going to add value."

Helen Maneuf (CAE, Hertfordshire SIAS) explains her approach concerning the importance of developing capabilities beyond specialist auditing skills:

> "I think auditors really have to work on their people skills. I see them as ambassadors, as 'salesmen' in a way, for both our service and promoting the benefits of good risk and control. Obviously there needs to be substance in what we do, but I think if you can go in there, with a very professional approach, calm, reassuring, helpful but not subservient, nor in any way second class, you can make a very positive impact to an organization. Sometimes I think we don't value our own work and are scared of our role and being challenging.

So that would be my prime recommendation to auditors, is to work really hard on that sort of thing. To really listen. To try and think about how your work fits into the big picture. To be proactive, to be dynamic, to really push the process forward."

Helen's emphasis on not just business acumen, but listening, influencing and broader leadership highlights how CAEs are starting to rethink what it takes to make a truly excellent audit function. In fact, it is worth noting that, prior to being appointed CAE of AstraZeneca, I spent two years as the Director of Global Leadership Development programmes within AstraZeneca, working on leadership development, organizational effectiveness and culture change. This was seen to be positive precursor experience to my work as CAE (and it also explains why I chose my current role coaching and supporting CAEs and working on training and development for audit staff).

Of course, effective development is more than just about attending training and development courses. Action Learning, coaching and mentoring arrangements can also play a powerful role in helping auditors to develop. One senior audit manager shared the following case study concerning coaching:

"I had a very detail orientated auditor that worked for me a few years ago. They analyzed everything, and documented everything down to the end. It gave me comfort that they were following up on all the open questions, which enabled me to sleep a little better at night. But that's not all that I was looking for.

The reason for their approach was partly their past experience, how they had been trained and partly their personality; but I knew it needed to be addressed. With someone like this it's often about providing feedback on a timely basis, but you've got to do it in a way that's appreciative. You've got to let them know that 'Hey, I appreciate the detail that you're getting into, that you're doing a fantastic job'. And in certain type of audits their testing is absolutely a great asset, but that's not something that we can apply across the board. And then it's working with them to explore: 'Do you think we could have stopped that testing earlier'? Or, 'How much more will we get out of doing more testing?' And I might explain that we already know that there's a broader problem in this area, so doing this additional detailed testing, that's not going to get us much further. We already have enough information to conclude this is a major finding. And helping them think that through.

My overall approach is that it's about coaching on the job: talking through work with auditors and reminding them to think about the choices they are making more consciously. That way, when we come to the end of the audit and we go over what was done, and do a lessons learned exercise. Doing this properly can enable help when we're starting the next audit. We can say, okay, remember from the previous audit? In this audit, we're most likely not going to go down into this level of detail. We're going to take it to about here. But letting them know that if they feel that there's a reason to go into more depth, then let's talk about it. Let's talk about why you think it's important - and if we agree it is – we'll do that. But let's have an open dialogue. It helps to shift their mindset step by step by helping them stop working out of habit or from an overly cautious position, and it can result in really positive changes."

Stephen Foster (CAE, Cargotec) offers the following perspective:

"For an audit function to really add value to the business it has to be able to look at things from the perspective of the business.

I personally think it is very beneficial for auditors to spend time working in an operational environment as part of their personal development and I think when we talk about the difference between traditional and modern auditing, I think it's not so much in the processes, it's more in the skill sets and experiences of the people that should be attracted and involved in the audit profession.

Increasingly boards and senior management are recognizing the value of this sort of experience because of the beneficial way it impacts the business and the relevance and added value of the work that is done. It's easy to criticize audit functions that don't have this experience, whereas in reality they have perhaps gone through a process which has been right up to a certain point in time, but not for the current challenges. So businesses need to support them in getting broader experience. At the same time auditors need to really value what they will get from this sort of wider experience, and that's not always the case."

Actions for Internal Audit to consider:

- Take stock of the balance between technical training and other training and development, especially in softer skills;
- Review the quality of on the job coaching to build a culture in which auditors are genuinely thinking about what they are doing;

• Examine secondment opportunities for audit staff into the wider organization so they can gain a deeper appreciation of issues and challenges in other functions.

## Developing the Right Team Culture and Ways of Working

Beyond assembling an audit function comprising a diverse range of talented staff, and working on training and development, it is also worth highlighting the importance of developing the right team spirit and ways of working. As outlined in an earlier chapter, a cornerstone of this is developing processes in which every new assignment is being reviewed for its proposed value add. However, this needs to become part of the internal audit culture. Phil Gerrard (CAE, Rolls-Royce) provides an example of the culture of thoughtful challenge that underpins the ability to deliver value:

"In one of my previous companies, I introduced the concept of Excellence Round Tables. Once you had done your planning, you would present it to a team of your peers, not just those directly involved in the assignment. You would set out the process you were looking at, the key risks identified and the data supporting it. The assignment team would then explain their audit approach and everyone would challenge that and say why are looking at that? Or why aren't you looking at the reward structure, because clearly you've got an issue here, and it's about the drivers of behaviour, so you need to spend more time on that.

So the audit function had a culture of making sure that the assignments that started had at least had their approach validated, challenged and changed by a number of people. They were much more conscious of the bigger picture because they had to support it through internal challenge, helping to give them more confidence about taking those decisions.

It's a means of drawing on the knowledge of the whole team, not just the team on the assignment."

Another key cultural attribute for a progressive audit function concerns how auditors are empowered. John Earley (Partner, Smart Chain International) explains the lean approach to empowerment:

"Empowerment is probably the most overused and over abused word in the English language. Empowerment is not anarchy. A lot of companies that say they're empowered have actually got anarchy. Because they don't put the boundaries around it.

For me, empowerment from a lean perspective is about crystal clarity of what's expected of people. Give them all the tools and training and skills and knowledge to be able to do what they need to do. Define a set of rules that they can work within and say, up to this point you can decide and use your own discretion.

They can learn from that, but you can't go back and say but you shouldn't have done that. You've got to be able to say, maybe it wasn't the best thing to do, but you made the decision and that was the right call. Let's look at how that decision might have been better. So it's a different complete mindset.

So leaders have to lead not manage in a lean environment. That's why you've got to be careful where you put the boundaries. Try and make them as broad as possible, and develop a process centric organization so that the team has end to end visibility about what the whole flow looks like, so they can figure out what the best thing to do is with lower intervention."

Effective team working is also something that can be taken for granted, but at AstraZeneca we used staff surveys (and other discussion groups) as a foundation to understand how we were doing and where we could improve. Over a period of time, we worked on different areas for improvement (including points about my own leadership style) using some of the external coaches I had worked with during my time in leadership development. This is something I now work on with clients, helping to ensure that team discussions flush out all of the important issues and that any solution properly engages all staff views, so that practicalities and blockers are proactively addressed, rather than being ignored, and then emerging later.

Part of the cultural shift that often needs to be made is to create an environment where constructive support and challenge is expected, in which leadership at all levels is expected and in which the function becomes truly comfortable with the 80/20 approach when this seems appropriate.

Actions for Internal Audit to consider:

- What has any staff survey for the internal audit said about the culture of the function, especially in relation to support, challenge, leadership and the 80/20 rule?
- Do staff feel sufficiently engaged on areas for improvement and proposed solutions?

- Implement a programme of ongoing actions to improve ways of working and review progress.

## CONCLUDING REMARKS

In this chapter I have tried to outline how a value adding orientation in internal audit results in a range of important ways in which an audit function must stretch itself in terms of staffing and ways of working. It is not about turning away from traditional audit skills, but blending these with other skills to create a powerful combination of what is needed. If internal audit is a function that needs to be a catalyst for value and productivity, then the analogy is that the audit function needs to have strong chemistry. It is also about letting go of some of the more traditional conventions, while increasing training and development in relation to new ways of working. Norman Marks (GRC thought leader) provides encouragement to developing auditors in new ways:

> "When you hire people you need to train them. Not only do you have to train them to think but you have to break the shackles that bind them. They are actually weighed down and handcuffed and chained to stop them from thinking for themselves, and exercising their own judgment.
>
> We've got to tackle this as an internal audit profession."

This new way of imagining what audit can be also requires a pride and a confidence in the positive role that audit can play as a crucial part of an organization, not just on the side lines. One CAE offers the following insight:

> "Internal audit used to be seen as a second class to the external auditor.
>
> External audit was the professional and intelligent one with the big numbers, the accounts and the press releases, and the internal audit was the poorer cousin.
>
> But that is not true anymore, or at least it shouldn't be."

Thus, the progressive lean way of working is to create a culture in which audit is proud and confident in the value of its crucial role to examine and facilitate the way the organization is operating in order to ensure its short, medium and longer term success.

## SUMMARY OF KEY POINTS FOR INTERNAL AUDIT

- Think about the power of a diverse audit team in terms of the likely impacts on assignment value add and efficiency;
- Consider some strategic recruitment at a senior level, in part for the skills that will be obtained but equally for the symbolic impact it will have;
- Be prepared to look at staff job descriptions and gradings;
- Ensure guest auditor and guest advisor options are used as much as possible;
- Plan ahead to get the most benefit from co-source support and manage closely to deliver value for audit in the short term and build audit capability in the longer term;
- Pay attention to training and development to ensure this includes softer skills and new ways of working;
- Pay attention to the culture within internal audit, so that it does not succumb to too much negativity or perfectionism;
- Promote audit as a leader in cross-functional ways of working, to help shift mindsets that might see audit as something else.

## RECOMMENDATIONS FOR SENIOR MANAGERS AND THE BOARD

- Ask for a summary of the composition of the audit team, analysed by experience inside and outside of internal audit and staff potential;
- Clarify how audit staff grades compare to the key roles that audit must interact with;
- If needed, support the strategic recruitment of one or two key appointments into internal audit, perhaps on a secondment basis;
- Understand what any staff or culture survey says about the internal audit function morale and ways of working;
- Clarify what training and development takes place, both in relation to audit topics but also in relation to softer skills;
- Expect some use of guest auditors, guest advisors and co-source support.

## References and Other Related Material of Interest

Rimanoczy, I. and Turner, E. (2008) *Action Reflection Learning*, Davies-Black

# PART 4
# Final Reflections

# 21
# Further Thoughts about Where and How to Start the Journey Towards Lean Progressive Auditing

As this book draws to a conclusion, I realize that it has not been possible to discuss the specific details of all of the various lean tools and techniques introduced at the outset of the book, nor to share the details of specific best practice methodologies and templates. This has partly been due to the limitations of space and partly because specific methodologies and templates that work for one audit function may not be applicable for another. However, if there is interest in sharing more lean auditing tools, templates and specific assignment methodologies, that is something I would be glad to contribute to in the future.

Nonetheless, I sincerely hope that readers will have found something of value in this book. Perhaps some readers will have received validation that a number of practices they have in place are in line with, or perhaps even ahead of, the good practices suggested herein. Other readers may have identified some areas where there are opportunities to enhance value or improve productivity and may be considering taking action. In recognition of this, it seems appropriate to offer some reflections about where and how to approach the journey to becoming a progressive, lean audit function.

I can recall when I was CAE at AstraZeneca, that a review of our practices against lean principles suggested a number of areas for improvement and I was keen to implement many of them. However, with the counsel of my management team, we adopted a range of pragmatic lean techniques that enabled the function to move forward in a step-by-step manner. In particular, one of the biggest challenges for a hard-pressed audit function is to find the time and resource to make changes. In the AstraZeneca audit context we therefore started with a further streamlining of our audit methodology and our assignment reporting. We also worked to streamline the remediation tracking process, and became much more selective about what we did in terms of follow-up assignments.

I cannot guarantee this approach is suitable for all, but as a starting premise I suggest that thinking through what to stop or what to do less of is a crucial way to unlock time and energy within audit. Having done this, it should be possible to properly engage in other improvement opportunities.

Some of the improvement opportunities identified in this book are more strategic in nature and include the following:

• Improving engagement with key stakeholders on the role of audit and how it can add value;
• Strengthening the link between the audit plan, the delivery of value and management of risk;
• Improving assurance mapping and assurance coordination, so that the work of key compliance and assurance functions, as well as that of management, is properly joined up;
• Continuously reviewing team composition, training and development and ways of working.

However, there are a number of "quick win" areas for audit functions wanting to implement lean ways of working, and these are summarized below:

• Getting the team to consider who is their prime customer;
• Using a Kano approach, working to define the real delighters, satisfiers and dissatisfiers in relation to auditing and modifying ways of working to deliver more delighters and to avoid dissatisfiers;
• Capturing more clearly the rationale for an audit at the planning stage and making sure this is understood as assignments are planned;
• Prioritizing the scope within an assignment based on both risk and value;

- Being clearer about the depth and breadth of assignments and consequently the appropriate resource that should be allocated;
- Managing each assignment as a mini project with milestones for all key steps;
- Improving disciplines for gathering data and documents;
- Encouraging openness from management about known issues or areas of concern;
- Pit stop reviews during assignments to keep auditors focused on value-add and delivery of the assignment to the time and budget allocated;
- Looking at "how big" and "how bad" an issue is to prioritize any findings, and improving work on root cause analysis and the identification of "killer facts";
- Concentrating on strong communication with management throughout the assignment;
- Removing the "to and fro" of written audit recommendations and management responses, with a focus on agreed actions as key;
- Improving the assignment feedback process and post-assignment learning.

My experience is that most audit functions should be able to implement a selection of the quick fix action points within a few months, particularly if auditors are properly engaged and senior managers are sympathetic to making progress. I don't suggest a few months as a macho challenge, but just to make the point that a "let's give it a try", "let's pilot that and see what happens" approach is what the lean mindset is all about. Over-analysis in this context can just lead to paralysis and a continuation of the status quo.

In addition, I do not think that an internal audit function needs to secure an enormous pot of funds from senior management in order to become more lean. At AstraZeneca we made changes without requesting additional funds (we just used our existing resources and existing budget slightly differently) and the same is true for many of the audit functions I have worked with.

Of course "quick wins" have an important place in the lean journey since they can often be energizing for auditors and be seen positively by management. However, in making any quick win improvements, it is important that the CAE should engage senior management and the board or audit committee on what is being done since: i) sometimes their support may be needed and also ii) they are a key customer whose views about adding value must be taken into account.

However, I am personally a believer that actions speak louder than words and therefore my normal advice is to orient the audit function towards lean ways of working without an enormous fanfare. This can be useful where stakeholders are rather uncertain about some of the proposed changes (e.g. shorter reports), but start to see the benefits being realized (e.g. key messages still present and reports issued more quickly).

# 22
# A Brief Look into the Future

Over the course of this book I hope that the reader has gained encouragement that there is a considerable body of progressive, value adding practice in internal audit across many organizations and many countries. I happen to have chosen examples predominantly from the UK and Europe, the US and Australia, where I spend a fair amount of time, but I know I could fill another book with good practices from other countries. Progressive, value adding internal audit really is out there, right now, it's just not evenly distributed across all audit functions or all countries at the moment!

At the time of completing the final manuscript for this book, the IIA have issued a consultation on a new mission for the Internal Auditing profession. In it there is a suggestion that there should be a clearer mission for the profession overall and currently it is proposed this should be to "enhance and protect organizational value" – suggesting lean principles and practices will remain relevant as the profession moves into the future.

For the avoidance of doubt, I am not saying that the future of internal auditing should solely be oriented around lean, but I hope that this book has made a reasonably strong case for taking lean principles seriously when thinking about how we might reimagine internal audit in the future. It is vital that we do not take lean so much to heart that we create a straightjacket for the audit profession. I hope that, throughout this book, the reader is able to see the spirit and philosophy that lean offers, and the practices that have been outlined are intended to be enabling and energizing for audit functions. However, I believe strongly that we should not develop a "fad" like interest in lean, rather we take the best of what it has to offer, alongside other progressive practices, and steadily integrate what works into our normal ways of working, so that we can move the audit profession forward.

Throughout this book the themes of leadership and courage within the auditing profession have recurred. Phil Gerrard (CAE, Rolls-Royce) sums up the lean, progressive mindset:

> "It takes confidence and courage to say no, I'm not doing any more audit work. It takes confidence and experience to say I'm not going to drill down any further. I've got my point. Management have said yes, we agree, we've got an issue, we need to do something about it."

I hope that I have highlighted many of the key lean principles that may be of relevance to auditing. I also hope that I have managed to identify most of the key opportunities to add greater value and drive efficiency. However, I fully recognize that others in the audit profession will be able to build on what I have set out herein. Indeed, one of the most exciting things about writing this book has been the thought that it may act as a catalyst within the internal audit profession to stimulate other ideas and proposals that will help us all move forward.

Speaking personally, I believe there may be a number of areas we need to give greater attention to as an internal audit profession. I know that the IIA standards continue to evolve and I wonder whether they will address some of the key areas highlighted in this book, notably:

- How audit should prioritize and manage multiple stakeholder demands, particularly in relation to getting an appropriate balance between advice and assurance;
- Audit's role in educating key stakeholders and shifting mindsets;
- How audit should navigate between activities that are similar to those carried out in the first and second lines of defence and better factor in, and coordinate, other assurances;
- How to judge a good audit plan;
- How CAEs should approach the task of giving overall assurance opinions, when they have to do this;
- What we mean by "systematic and disciplined" and knowing when to stop testing;
- The importance of development and experience beyond training in core internal audit skills, including the case for multidisciplinary audit functions.

I would also like to see us, as a profession, improve the ways we can help CAEs (and auditors) navigate the many dilemmas they face. It seems to me that some CAEs have become "tamed or captured" by powerful figures in their organization and lack the political savvy and other stakeholder support to stand up for what is right, whilst other CAEs can be a little too brave and end up leaving their role or exiting their organization because they could not take others with them. The way I see it, these compromises and these departures are happening across the world on an ongoing basis, and can easily fall below the radar screen. The best CAEs use formal and informal contacts and networks to help them navigate through sometimes dark and dangerous waters, but in my experience these contacts and networks are not always sufficient.

Consequently, I hope that we can better use techniques such as ethics or practice advisory committees to give CAEs a clearer forum to think through the problems they face. Note my main emphasis is on support for CAEs to navigate through the challenges and dilemmas they face, not disciplinary action (although I appreciate that there is a place for this as well as in any profession).

I appreciate that there are challenges and difficulties with such forums (confidentiality is most commonly cited as a barrier), but – by the same token – I think it is essential we develop better mechanisms to talk about and develop a deeper body of practice about how to navigate our way through the challenges and dilemmas that we face.

In addition, whilst standards and principles go a long way, I am convinced, from my work on Action Learning for auditors, as well as coaching CAEs, that it is through confidential, candid and thoughtful conversations that the best solutions emerge, or at least, the least worst solutions, as is often the case!

I will conclude this book by offering final words of encouragement about the lean auditing journey from Norman Marks (GRC thought leader):

"Becoming lean is a kind of quest, understanding what we are about, which is deliver services that our customers need and will gladly pay for.

Delivering to them with quality and timeliness and efficiency and effectiveness is where you start. Then everything from that flows. Because then you look at everything else and say, why am I doing this? Is there a better way to actually deliver what I need to deliver?

You rethink everything.

Now some things may not get changed, but you may well find that not only do things have to change now, but next month and next year, where you will you'll probably be able to use technology, or other methods to change them yet again.

Lean is basically a continuing process where you are constantly examining what you are doing and saying, is this the best that I can do?"

## References and Other Related Material of Interest

The Institute of Internal Auditors (2014) *Proposed Enhancements to the Institute of Internal Auditors International Professional Practices Framework (IPPF)*. https://na.theiia.org/standards-guidance/Public_Documents/IPPF-Exposure-Draft-English.pdf

# Other Recommended Reading

Argyris, C. (1990) *Overcoming Organizational Defences*. Simon & Schuster.

Ariely, D. (2010) *Predictably Irrational: The Hidden Forces That Shape Our Decisions*. Harper Perennial.

Ariely, D. (2013) *The (Honest) Truth About Dishonesty*. Harper Perennial.

Burgoyne, J., Pedler, M., & Boydell, T. (1994) *Towards the Learning Company*. McGraw-Hill International.

Caldwell, J. (2012) *A Framework for Board Oversight of Enterprise Risk*. Chartered Professional Accountants of Canada.

Chambers, R. (2014) *Lessons Learned on the Audit Trail*. The IIA Research Foundation.

Covey, S. R. (2004) *The 7 Habits of Highly Effective People*. Simon & Schuster Ltd.

Goleman, D. (1985) *Vital Lies, Simple Truths*. Bloomsbury.

Institute of Internal Auditors www.theiia.org/Pages/IIAHome.aspx (has an extensive amount of material too numerous to list in detail).

Kahneman, D. (2011) *Thinking Fast and Slow*. Allen Lane.

Lloyd's of London (2010) *Behaviour: Bear, Bull or Lemming?* http://www
.lloyds.com/~/media/Lloyds/Reports/Emerging_Risk_Reports/Emerging
RiskreportBehaviour_March2010_v2.pdf

Luca, J. de. (1999) *Political Savvy*. Everygreen Business Group.

Maister, D., Green, C. & Galford, R. (2000) *The Trusted Advisor*. Simon &
Schuster.

Marks, N. (2010–2014) *Marks on governance*. https://iaonline.theiia.org/
blogs/marks

Oshry, B. (2007) *SeeingSystems. Unlocking the Mysteries of Organizational
Life*. Berrett-Koehler.

Reason, J. (1990) *Human Error*. Cambridge University Press.

Womack, J. & Jones, D. (1996) *Lean Thinking*. Simon and Schuster, New York.

Womack, J. & Jones, D. (2005) *Lean Solutions*. Simon and Schuster,
New York.

# Appendix – Illustrative Kano Analysis Regarding Internal Audit

## BOARD AND AUDIT COMMITTEE PERSPECTIVES ON VALUE ADD (ILLUSTRATIVE)

### Seen to be value adding:

- Delivering the audit plan within the year;
- Delivering assurance over key concerns or areas of interest for the board/audit committee;
- Providing comfort over core control and compliance areas;
- Providing timely and tailored briefings on the position of the organization in relation to topical issues;
- Offering insights into emerging risks;
- Identifying themes and trends in audit findings;
- Being seen to be influential with senior management.

### Seen not to add value:

- Failing to deliver the audit plan;
- Having a major issue occur in an area that was recently audited (e.g. "Why didn't you spot that issue when you audited that area last year?");
- Appearing un-influential with senior management (and expecting the board to do the running) or appearing in the pocket of management;
- Audit receiving negative feedback in a quality review or from a regulator or from the external auditor;

- Audit "Pushing the nuclear button" on an issue which proves to be relatively minor;
- Indications that management are not remediating audit recommendations;
- The CAE being unable to answer an obvious question when the matter is discussed at the board/audit committee.

## SENIOR MANAGEMENT PERSPECTIVES ON VALUE ADD (ILLUSTRATIVE)

### Seen to be value adding:

- Audit being on hand to do targeted work for some senior managers;
- Audit delivering advisory assignments that are seen to support the achievement of priority objectives;
- Audit producing short, balanced reports on a timely basis;
- Audit working in a joined up way with other functions, including the external auditor, to manage the burden of assurance activities across the organization;
- Audit delivering the audit plan to (or under) budget;
- Audit identifying inefficiencies or cost savings.

### Seen not to add value:

- Audit reports with negative ratings that do not align with senior management's risk appetite;
- Audit report wording that is either inflammatory or that might be unhelpful if disclosed to a regulator or in litigation;
- Anything that comes as a surprise;
- Anything communicated out of chain;
- Audit reports that simply repeat known issues in more detail;
- Audit reports that are issued too late to do anything with.

## LINE MANAGEMENT PERSPECTIVES ON VALUE ADD (ILLUSTRATIVE)

### Seen to be value adding

- Audit showing flexibility concerning the timing of the assignment in relation to other priorities;

- Offering something in the assignment that would be of value to them;
- Keeping management fully on board throughout the process;
- Taking opportunities to suggest that some control activities are wasteful and can be removed to make processes slicker.

## Seen not to add value:

- Auditor coming across as poorly prepared during an assignment;
- Auditors asking follow on questions, or requesting additional information, after interviews or initial requests for information, that appear to be a "second bite at the cherry";
- Anything that suggests audit does not have a firm grip on the key facts;
- Not communicating proposed findings on a timely basis;
- Poor audit ratings, or poor wording which can imply management negligence or incompetence;
- Audit having an emphasis on procedures and paperwork in such a manner that the importance of points made is being lost;
- Being so prescriptive about remediation actions that management do not feel able to move things forward in a way that suits them or reflects other organizational changes.

# Closing Dedication & Thanks

For being there:

My (one and only) brother, Alan Paterson, and Sarah, James, Harry and Aimee. DB, Tante Francoise, Aunt Wilma, Aunt Cathy & Uncle Mick, Ann & Jerry and Linda & Peter.

I haven't forgotten: Mum, Dad, Bernadette, Auntie Jean, Uncle Tom, Little Tom, my grandparents McLaughlan and Paterson and Father Kevin.

For their support over my professional career:

Peter Macrae, John Ward, Hugh Roe, Michael Herlihy, John Cole, John Goddard, Tim Watts, David McGregor, Derek Wood, Jon Symonds, Angela Hyde, Ralph Lewis, Liz Crede (and other colleagues in Sheppard Moscow), Barrie Thorpe, Henry Mintzberg (and all those involved in the IMPM programme), Michael Nolan, John Buchanan, Michele Hooper, Iwan Jenkins, Mannie Sher (and all at the Tavistock Institute) and David Harwood – for being my first client.

Lance Bell (at Visualise that) for the cartoons.

To other good friends and colleagues who have supported me over the years:

Paul Goldsmith, Marco Mai, Tony Crowley, Paul Ennis, David Powell, Jayne Mutter, Paul McNicholas, David Stephenson and Andrew Wright.

Helen Curran, for keeping tabs on everything, LJ, and Jane Stephens, for being a great sounding board, and supporting the idea of doing this book.

Colleagues in the IIA UK, CIPFA UK, MIS and elsewhere – thanks for your support.

To those in my Action Learning groups over the years (you know who you are!) – thank you for your challenge (most of the time) and your support.

For helpful advice:

John Davies, Neil Drummond, Leigh Hodges, Michael McCallion, Pam Lewis Roberts.

And finally to:

Alicia Helman, for all of the interview transcriptions.

Gemma Valler, who sent me that fateful e-mail asking if I would write this book, and all at John Wiley & Sons for giving me this opportunity to write a professional auditing book, but from the heart!

# Index